DEAF LIBERATION THEOLOGY

Following years of theology of deafness based on the premise that Deaf people are simply people who cannot hear, this book breaks new ground. Presenting a new approach to Deaf people, theology and the Church, this book enables Deaf people who see themselves as members of a minority group to formulate their own theology rooted in their own history and culture.

Deconstructing the theology and practice of the Church, Hannah Lewis shows how the Church unconsciously oppresses Deaf people through its view of them as people who cannot hear. Lewis reclaims Deaf perspectives on Church history, examines how an essentially visual Deaf culture can relate to the written text of the Bible and asks 'Can Jesus sign?' This book pulls together all these strands to consider how worship can be truly liberating, truly a place for Deaf people to celebrate who they are before God.

Explorations in Practical, Pastoral and Empirical Theology

Series Editors: Leslie J. Francis, University of Wales, Bangor, UK
and Jeff Astley, Director of the North of England
Institute for Christian Education, UK

Theological reflection on the church's practice is now recognised as a significant element in theological studies in the academy and seminary. Ashgate's new series in practical, pastoral and empirical theology seeks to foster this resurgence of interest and encourage new developments in practical and applied aspects of theology worldwide. This timely series draws together a wide range of disciplinary approaches and empirical studies to embrace contemporary developments including: the expansion of research in empirical theology, psychological theology, ministry studies, public theology, Christian education and faith development; key issues of contemporary society such as health, ethics and the environment; and more traditional areas of concern such as pastoral care and counselling.

Other titles in the series include:

The Bible and Lay People
An Empirical Approach to Ordinary Hermeneutics
Andrew Village
978-0-7546-5801-6

Theological Reflection and Education for Ministry
The Search for Integration in Theology
John E. Paver
978-0-7546-5754-5

Renewing Pastoral Practice
Trinitarian Perspectives on Pastoral Care and Counselling
Neil Pembroke
978-0-7546-5565-7

Engaging with Contemporary Culture
Christianity, Theology and the Concrete Church
Martyn Percy
978-0-7546-3259-7

Deaf Liberation Theology

HANNAH LEWIS
Founder of Deaf Ecumenical Clergy, UK

ASHGATE

Published by
Ashgate Publishing Limited
Gower House
Croft Road
Aldershot
Hants GU11 3HR
England

Ashgate Publishing Company
Suite 420
101 Cherry Street
Burlington, VT 05401-4405
USA

Ashgate website: http://www.ashgate.com

British Library Cataloguing in Publication Data
Lewis, Hannah
   Deaf liberation theology
   1. Deaf – Religious life 2. Church work with the deaf 3. Liberation theology
   I. Title
   230'.0464'0872

Library of Congress Cataloging-in-Publication Data
Lewis, Hannah, 1971–
   Deaf liberation theology / Hannah Lewis.
      p. cm. – (Explorations in practical, pastoral and empirical theology)
   Includes bibliographical references and index.
   ISBN-13: 978-0-7546-5524-4 (hardcover : alk. paper)
   1. Church work with the deaf. 2. Deaf–Religious life. 3. Liberation theology.   I. Title.
BV4463.L49 2007
230.087'2–dc22

2006031846

ISBN 978-0-7546-5524-4

Printed and bound in Great Britain by MPG Books Ltd, Bodmin, Cornwall.

Contents

Acknowledgements

I would like to acknowledge not only those who have helped, in some way, with the development of Deaf Liberation Theology, but also those whose support and encouragement when I was struggling to create a Deaf identity helped me into a position where I could undertake such a task.

So thanks to the Deafened Young People project of the National Deaf Children Society (especially Maggie Wooley, Sara Head and Liz Varlow) who first showed me I could be confidently Deaf and to all members of staff on Iona in summer 1989 who taught me I did not need to accept second best from anyone. Also, thanks to Tom Shakespeare of the Cambridge University Disabled Students Caucus of 1989–92 who first introduced me to the social model of disability in theory and practice and to the members of the Deaf Accord Youth Council whose friendship allowed me to try out my developing skills in sign language and begin to feel part of the Deaf world.

Thanks to Mark Geldard who got me started on the idea of doing a further degree and whose interest in what I had to say led to this choice of topic and Helen Cameron and Robert Beckford whose belief in me kept me going when things got rough.

For support and friendship and mentoring and responding to questions I would like to thank all the members of Deaf Ecumenical Clergy UK and the National Deaf Church Conference. Especially I would like to thank Peter Lees, Don Read, Peter McDonough, Vera Hunt, Sue Dyson, Phil Maddock and Gill Behenna who responded to every query, no matter how silly it seemed. I would also like to thank Don Read, Arnold Rundle and Len Scarff for sending me copies of some of their own notes and booklets on the history of their local Deaf churches.

A lot of my theology and faith has been shaped through an involvement with the Iona Community, dating back nearly 20 years. I have not specifically referred to their work, but the thought and practice of Kathy Galloway and the Wild Goose Resource Group (John Bell, Graham Maule, Mairi Munro and Alison Adam) have been especially inspirational and influential.

I would like to thank my supervisors at Birmingham University, Dr Emmanuel Lartey and Dr Gordon Lynch. Their questions and comments always got me thinking hard. I would also like to thank Dr Paddy Ladd for his constructive comments.

Finally I want to thank my husband, Barry Griffin, without whom this book would not have been finished.

List of Abbreviations

Central Church Committees for Work with d/Deaf People

(CA)CSCDD	(Church Assembly) Committee for the Spiritual Care of the Deaf and Dumb
Succeeded by:	
CECD	Church of England Council for the Deaf
Succeeded by:	
CMDP	Committee for Ministry among Deaf People
Succeeded by:	
CMDDP	Committee for Ministry among Deaf and Disabled People
Also:	
CCMDD	Council of Church Missioners to the Deaf and Dumb
NDCC	National Deaf Church Conference
Succeeded by:	
DAT	Deaf Anglicans Together

Organizations Working with d/Deaf People

BD(D)A	British Deaf (and Dumb) Association
NUD	National Union of the Deaf
FDP	Federation of Deaf People
RAD(D)	Royal Association for the Deaf (and Dumb)
RNID	Royal National Institute for the Deaf

Abbreviations Relating to Sign Language

BSL	British Sign Language (The natural true language of Deaf people developed by Deaf people with its own syntax and grammar). BSL cannot be written down, but an English 'gloss' giving a sense of what has been signed can be produced. This is indicated in the text by the use of *ITALIC CAPITALS*.
SSE	Sign Supported English (An artificial system. Signs from BSL in English grammatical order).

A note on the use of language:

- Deaf (with a capital 'D') refers to culturally Deaf people.
- deaf (with a lowercase 'd') refers to anyone with a significant hearing loss who does not necessarily identify themselves as culturally Deaf. However, when historical quotes and references use 'deaf' to refer to culturally Deaf people, I have not changed it.
- d/Deaf is either used when the status of the person (as Deaf or deaf) is uncertain, or when I want to refer to all d/Deaf people.
- 'Deaf and Dumb' and 'Deaf-Mute' are no longer acceptable ways of referring to d/Deaf people without speech. However, when they are used in historical quotes and references, I have left them as they are.
- 'hearing' refers to those people who use speech and hearing as their primary means of communication.

Introduction

What does the word 'Deaf' mean? Who is Deaf? How can Deaf people be liberated? What does the Christian faith have to say to Deaf people? The answer to these questions depends on the background and experience of an individual. In other words, the answer depends on the context. In most everyday contexts, and within most theological discourse, 'deaf' means simply not hearing. Within this discourse, 'deaf' or deafness has no theological significance; 'Deaf Liberation Theology' is a meaningless concept. Within this discourse we can be deaf to God's word and pray that God will awaken us to God's presence by 'curing the deafness of our ears'.[1] But to me, the words deaf and deafness describe the way I am. Asking God to cure me of my deafness is comparable to asking God to make me a man.

The offence caused by this unreflective use of 'deaf' as a metaphor could be attributed to ignorance on the part of the hearing people concerned. The argument could be that hearing people don't know about d/Deaf[2] people, and that, once educated about d/Deaf people, they would understand that you can have Deaf Liberation theology and that you can cause offence by misusing the word 'deaf'. However d/Deaf people and those who work with them have been trying to educate the church about deafness for about 150 years, to no obvious effect. It would seem that we must turn to alternative theories for the almost total invisibility of d/Deaf people and their concerns within mainstream academic theology and its practical expression within the English Church.

We can argue that this invisibility is due to the fact that the meaning of 'deaf' as 'not hearing' is so embedded in the matrix of meanings and representations and metaphors and assumptions within this particular discourse that it becomes almost impossible to use the word 'deaf' in any other way. If we attempt to do so we are not simply challenging the meaning of the word 'deaf', we are also challenging the whole structure of meanings and representations and metaphors that constitute the discourse. A lack of realization of the nature of the task undertaken is why, despite 150 years of attempting to change the meaning of the word 'd/Deaf' in the English

---

[1] David Adam, *The Rhythm of Life: Celtic Daily Prayer* (London: Triangle, 1996), p. 119.

[2] I have used 'Deaf' to refer to people who would describe themselves in this way, 'deaf' to refer to people and situations that are clearly referring simply to the question of hearing loss and d/Deaf when it is either not clear which I should use or I am referring to all d/Deaf people regardless of how they see themselves.

2

Deaf Liberation Theology

churches, it remains marginal and is considered devoid of theological significance within the dominant academic theological context. To understand and use the word 'd/Deaf' in a very different way, within this context, we need to explore and create alternative theological discourses that are open to the use of the word 'd/Deaf' in a way that we d/Deaf people can identify with.

There have been attempts to theologize on deafness and d/Deaf people over the years. Initially this was with the aim of arousing pity in people's minds, so they would financially support work with deaf people.[3] As work developed, practical manuals were produced focusing on the hows and whys of communicating the Gospel to d/Deaf people and on the perceived pastoral 'problems' of deaf people and their lack of access to the mainstream 'hearing' church.[4] Since the 1980s, more theological work on being Deaf has been done by Deaf people themselves.[5] While these works have used radical new discourses on deafness from sociology and linguistics, they have stopped short of challenging the dominant theological discourse itself.

Having said that, the need for an authentic theology of Deaf people to be a theology of liberation from the domination of imposed discourses has been recognized; Deaf and hearing Christians came together in June 1984 at Claggett in Maryland and produced a statement recognizing both that the church has been part of the oppression of d/Deaf people and that it needs to move to a new position of liberation for both d/Deaf and hearing people.[6] Despite this insight, nothing has yet resulted from this statement in terms of a fully worked out liberation theology for d/Deaf people.[7] Ten years later, one of the participants from Claggett, Mary Weir,

---

[3]   See for example Revd Samuel Smith, *The Deaf and Dumb: their deprivation and its consequences* (London, 1864), Selwyn Oxley, *Work for the deaf: Operations of the Guild of St John of Beverley, for the deaf and hard of hearing* (London, 1925), T. H. Sutcliffe, *The Challenge of Deafness* (Taunton, 1990).

[4]   See for example Daniel Pokorny (ed.), *The Word in Signs and Wonders: a collection of papers delivered at the second International Training Seminar on Christian Ministry Among the Deaf, Washington DC, 1975* (New York, 1977), *The Church Among Deaf People: a report prepared by a working party of the Committee for Ministry Among Deaf People for the General Synod of the Church of England's Advisory Board of Ministry*, Advisory Board of Ministry Paper 14 (London, 1997).

[5]   Notably Peter McDonough, 'Presenting the Word of God in Sign Language' in Peter McDonough (ed.), *Ephphata: Proceedings from the International Catholic Deaf Religious Conference 1996* (Monmouth, 1998) and Robert G. Shrine, *The language and culture of Deaf people: some implications for the Church* (MA dissertation, Open University and St Johns College: Nottingham, 1997).

[6]   Charlotte Baker-Shenk, 'Breaking the Shackles: Liberation Theology and the Deaf Community', incorporating 'The Claggett Statement', *Sojourners*, 14/3 (1985): 31.

[7]   The organization that produced the Claggett Statement (Christians for the Liberation of the Deaf Community) appears to have disbanded; only four follow-up productions are known to exist: two videos about oppression and the oppressor, a policy statement 'No

a d/Deaf Canadian theologian, argues that a theology for the community of d/Deaf (and disabled) people needs to be a theology of liberation,[8] but she goes on to suggest that 'a deaf perspective on theology would put the accent in somewhat different places [to 'Christian tradition']' rather than suggesting a deaf theology of liberation would need to challenge the 'Christian tradition' itself. This phraseology suggests to me that she sees liberation theology for the Deaf as adjusted mainstream theology rather than creating a radically new discourse. Robert G. Shrine, a Deaf theologian and priest, concludes that even within this task of adjusting (rather than challenging and redefining) Christian theology from a d/Deaf perspective, there has been no comparable work or statement in the UK.[9]

It is my argument that we cannot change the marginalization of d/Deaf people and their concerns within the theological discourse unless we also are prepared to challenge and change the dominant theological discourse itself. This book is both an attempt to show the inadequacy of modern western theology from the point of view of Deaf people and also an attempt to see what can be done when we redefine the theological task in Deaf Liberation terms. In other words, by taking issues of biblical hermeneutics, Christology and worship as examples, I am attempting to establish a methodology, sources and norms that can be used by Deaf people to create a comprehensive Deaf Liberation Theology.

Barriers for Deaf Churches' and a brochure called 'It's Time to Listen ... to the Signs and Voice of Deaf People and Hard of Hearing People'.

[8]   Dr Mary Kathryn Weir, 'Made Deaf in God's Image' in International Ecumenical Working Group Conference, *The Place of Deaf people in the Church: the Canterbury 1994 conference papers* (Northampton, 1996), p. 5.

[9]   Shrine, *The language and culture of Deaf people.*

Chapter 1

Framework and Methodology

A Post-modern Framework

The need to redefine the theological task from a particular perspective is not unique to Deaf people; it is one of the defining marks of worldwide Christian theology in the late twentieth and early twenty-first centuries. According to Fernando Segovia, theology is undergoing a process of liberation and decolonization at present as it engages with a new framework for knowledge, variously called post-modernism and post-colonialism.[1]

Aspects of post-modernism that are particularly significant in this process of liberation of theology include the understanding that knowledge is subjective or contextual, constructed and can be used as an instrument of power. The identification of all knowledge, all readings of the text and interpretations of events and behaviour as partial, seen through the lenses of our own contexts and backgrounds, has had huge implications for minority groups, including Deaf people – people who have been told for years that others (white, middle-class, western, academic men) know, better than they do, what is right for them. Such minority groups have been daring to stand up and disagree with the 'experts' and claim that their perception and knowledge of events is more accurate and more relevant for their lives. Initially such so-called 'political' claims and readings of events and texts were dismissed or marginalized by the dominant modernist discourse as 'caricaturing the truth' by being partial and subjective, but in the post-modern world this criticism has no meaning. This concept that all texts are subjective and contextual is why it is an ideal in post-modern texts for all 'authors' to identify where they come from, to place themselves in context so that their particular perspective can be taken into account by potential 'readers'.

The idea that all interpretations of all events, including the 'Christ-event' that is the foundation of Christian theology, are partial and subjective suggests that the claim of any theology to be universal or relevant outside its immediate context is questionable to say the least. All theology is contextual, arising from a specific time and place and having no claim to be authoritative for any other context. Stephen Bevans argues simply 'the time is past when we can speak of one right, unchanging theology, a *theologia perennis*. We can only speak about a theology

---

[1]   Fernando F. Segovia, *Decolonising biblical studies: a view from the margins* (Maryknoll, 2000), p. 10.

that makes sense at a certain place and in a certain time'.[2] In fact, Bevans goes even further, to him theology that is not contextual, that is not reflective of our times, our culture and our current concerns, is 'false theology'.[3] We can learn from others, and others can learn from us, but a theology of others can never be our own, and our theology can never be the theology of others. A theology that is true and relevant for d/Deaf people, however it is understood and expressed, can only be created and developed by d/Deaf people themselves.

What this means for this book is that, wherever possible, I will briefly identify the context of authors I cite whenever it seems to be necessary and cast as wide a net as possible in terms of the different contexts of the theologians whose work I refer to, using the work of theologians from Asia and Africa as well as theologians from the west and feminist, black and disabled theologians as well as the work of more mainstream male theologians. It also means that as a Deaf person writing about Deaf people I will privilege the voice of other Deaf people in this text. Certainly in the second half of the book where I try to construct a Deaf Liberation Theology, I am really not interested in what hearing people, however involved with Deaf people they might be, have said about what Deaf people think and what a theology of Deaf people might look like. This is intended to be a Deaf theology, full of Deaf voices, and if this makes this work more than usually partial and subjective I don't apologize. It is necessary to balance out the hearing-centred discourse that has dominated Deaf life for well over a century.

The main difficulty with perceiving knowledge as partial and subjective is how we assess truth. Burr suggests 'knowledge' is the narratives people construct among themselves to explain what has happened to them and their ancestors which then get retold and internalized in the culture as a self-obvious truth.[4] The insight that 'knowledge' and 'truth' are basically human constructs rather than 'fixed' or 'given' entities opens up the possibility that other interpretations of events can be constructed as new forms of knowledge and truth. This is particularly significant in that it creates space for alternatives to the dominant social and theological representations of Deaf people. These representations, which have governed the way Deaf people are seen and treated in society and in the church, are not the 'natural, common-sense' perspective that they have been portrayed as over the years, but are only one of several possible ways of representing Deaf people. And alternatives have emerged, based not on theory but on the ways Deaf people experience themselves and their relationship with the world. These ways do not make any claims to be true for all d/Deaf people, but do argue that coming from the experience of d/Deaf people themselves they have a perspective that is

---

[2]   Stephen B. Bevans, *Models of contextual theology*, 2nd printing (Maryknoll, 1994), p. 2.
[3]   Ibid., p. 3. (The use of the word 'false' is problematic in post-modern discourse; I will discuss how we might assess things as true or false in a later section.)
[4]   Vivien Burr, *An Introduction to Social Constructionism* (London, 1995), p. 10.

arguably more valid and relevant to d/Deaf life than perspectives produced by hearing people.

One barrier to the use of Deaf experience in the past has been the perception that to be academically valid and taken seriously, knowledge must be written down in a logical format. However, in post-modern times, this criterion has been recognized as a means of power exercised by an educational elite group over minorities. Post-modernism has recognized 'oral' or 'signed' knowledge as a valid form of knowledge production, so I can focus on who is speaking rather than worrying if their productions are defensible. Much of the Deaf writings I have used as sources and for validation are not logical arguments from first principles (a form of knowledge usually restricted to those who can access university courses), but poems and narratives and polemic and accounts of feelings. Sometimes they are written, sometimes accounts of conversations, stories and other forms of 'signed' knowledge. The focus of my reconstructed theology is practical, sometimes emotional but neither abstract nor philosophical; I want to produce theology that directly affects how people feel and act as well as what they believe. The ultimate validation of Deaf Liberation Theology would be if Deaf people found what I say to be a tool in their struggle for liberation; a way of helping them reverse the direction of their lives from restriction and oppression to freedom to enjoy the fullness of life.

The other significant way that power operates in the field of knowledge production is in the construction of history. Often those who are privileged under the dominant discourse have used history as a tool to back up their worldview and perpetuate their power. The counterbalance to this use of history is to focus on the stories of those who have been 'shut out' by conventional history. This approach places its emphasis on the actions of ordinary people rather than on a power holding elite, privileging the point of view of the victimized/oppressed over that of the victimizers/oppressors. It looks for struggles, reversals, popular lore and group memories of hostile encounters as indications of the existence and content of 'reverse discourses' or resistance to the dominant discourse that are present in any context.[5] For my Deaf-centric Deaf church history the idea that the hearing reading is privileged can be demolished, but we do need to ask if we can then privilege the Deaf reading as more 'correct' or whether we have to present two incompatible points of view, accepting that we may never know the 'truth' of what happened and leaving it up to the individual to decide which view they prefer to use? This is one option, but I prefer to argue that one view is 'for' Deaf liberation, 'for' enhancing the life of Deaf people and the other is 'against'; and as far as I am concerned, the Deaf-centric reading is more affirming, more empowering and therefore preferable to the hearing reading. The other important use of Deaf-centric history is in its potential to inspire and encourage Deaf people in their lives by showing that the way things are at the moment is not the only way they have to be.

---

[5]   Pauline Marie Rosenau, *Post-modernism and the social sciences: insights, inroads, and intrusions* (Princeton, 1992), p. 67.

Deaf Liberation Theology has to be linked to these alternative Deaf discourses of the past so that it is rooted deep within authentic, life-giving Deaf history and culture.

My Context

This is an appropriate point to include a brief description of my own particular context. I am a 30-something Deaf middle-class woman priest in the Church of England. I was born with hearing in one ear (which finally disappeared when I was aged 9½) so I learnt to speak, read and lip-read English fairly easily. Living in a borough where deaf children were actively discouraged from learning to sign, I was educated in a mainstream hearing school, where I effectively taught myself through reading textbooks, and I did not have many opportunities for contact with other d/Deaf people. The only bright spot in the profound social isolation that resulted from this policy was my local church where my father was the vicar. Despite a distinct lack of access to worship and participation in the structures of the church, I found there an acceptance, affirmation and encouragement of myself as a person that I experienced nowhere else.

My parents were involved in the local National Deaf Children Society's group, and through them I was invited to participate in the Deafened Young People's Project (or DYPPIE's), my first real encounter with sign language, Deaf adults and the idea that I might have an identity as a Deaf person that did not make me a substandard hearing person. In the years since this event, I have 'acquired' sign language from other Deaf people and been involved on the fringes of the Deaf world and with the Deaf church as and when my educational and professional development would let me. This involvement with the Deaf world and the Deaf church has varied according to what else was going on in my life. For example, when I was at university and a member of 'Deaf Accord' youth council, I was meeting with other Deaf young people two or three times a term for 'business' followed by social events. After leaving university, while going through the training process for the ordained ministry and developing a relationship with my (hearing) husband, I had much less contact with other Deaf people. This has changed since being ordained. I meet up with other Deaf churchfolk on a monthly basis, meet Deaf friends for meals and chats, take services in my local Deaf church, attend local Deaf clubs and residential conferences with the National Deaf Church Conference and Deaf Ecumenical Clergy UK.

Alongside this growth of a positive Deaf identity through contact with the Deaf world came a development of my understanding of what the Christian faith should be (and so rarely was) like. This development was almost entirely through my involvement with the hearing church; the Deaf church as I encountered it from time to time in my teens and my early twenties seemed just as boring and irrelevant as the hearing church, despite being much more accessible. My experiences of the Church of England as a child as described above were enough to suggest to me that no matter how boring and irrelevant the church seemed, no matter how inaccessible its acts of worship and Bible study groups were, this was not the way the Christian faith was intended to be. This perception was reinforced through my involvement with the Iona Community.[6] As a teenager on holiday on Iona, I discovered that worship could be imaginative, relevant and fun; as a volunteer working at Iona Abbey one summer holiday, I realized that inclusiveness was a primary Christian value and as an associate member of the Community since 1989 I am committed to finding 'new ways to touch the hearts of all' in my life and my work. Part of the motivation behind seeking ordination was a conviction that if I could get a foot in the door of the power structures of the church then I could make a difference in the way that the Christian faith was encountered by other people who felt excluded by the church the way it was.

My experiences also left me convinced that the only way people could encounter Christianity in any meaningful way was as the person that God intended them to be. As I studied theology, first as an undergraduate and then as a postgraduate, I read abstract, philosophical tracts, written by white, hearing, academic men that asked and answered questions that had no meaning for me. At first I thought I was failing to understand what I was reading, that I just didn't know enough to make sense of these writings. I could relate to the urgency of their search for meaning and their quest for God, but I could not share their conviction that if I knew exactly who Jesus Christ was, in metaphysical terms, or which bits of the Bible were 'factual' and which were not, then I would find God. It was not until I encountered Liberation Theology that I realized it wasn't that I could not understand what these theologians were saying, it was that the questions they were asking were not my questions. It was not my failings and inadequacies that made it hard for me to understand these men, it was the fact that they were coming from a completely different context to me.

I experienced liberation in my life through my encounter with the Deaf community, and liberation in my faith in my encounter with Liberation Theology. These encounters led to a desire to explore what relevance theologies of liberation might have for other d/Deaf people; was it just me that found it helpful or did it have insights that might help make sense of God for my d/Deaf brothers and sisters? This was the inspiration behind this book; the basic question 'Can there be a Deaf Liberation Theology?'

---

[6]   'An ecumenical (that is without denominational affiliation) Christian community that is committed to seeking new ways of living the Gospel in today's world … committed to 'rebuilding the common life' through working for social and political change, striving for the renewal of the Church with an ecumenical emphasis, and exploring new, more inclusive approaches to worship' (quoted from *Coracle* magazine, August 2002, p. 2).

A Post-modern, Post-colonial Theological Method

So what is Liberation Theology? Where did it come from and how might it relate to Deaf experience of the world? Segovia argues that any theology done within a post-modern framework of knowledge and truth as subjective, constructed and contextual is liberated and decolonized. No longer bound to a particular, abstract, philosophical worldview or constrained by western thought forms, resources and history, Christian theology becomes wide open to a variety of influences and is enabled to engage with a huge range of human questions in a way that has not been experienced before. While this liberation may be perceived by some as a threat to 'theology as we know it', Guy Collins argues that this is a vital opportunity for a theology that has increasingly become purely self-referential and which often ignores the deep problems of our world.[7] The significance and task of theology is under debate; as far as Collins is concerned, the theological story is the continuing story of God's involvement with humanity and therefore it is impossible for it not to engage with everything that has happened and is happening in our world. As he argues, 'if we profess a faith that is about liberating truth, then it is almost impossible to see how fundamental questions [of the world] can be avoided'.[8] He also quotes David Tracy in arguing, 'all refusals to face action, praxis, politics and history are fatal not only to theology but to the proclamation and the manifestation of the event of Jesus Christ that empowers theology'.[9] In other words, engaging with this process of liberation and decolonization is necessary not only to keep theology credible as a subject, but also to keep theology true to its basic calling to proclaim the good news of Jesus Christ in the world.

The Purpose of Theology: Formulating a Theological Method

If we are arguing that the traditional method and understanding of theology is tied to its particular context of the modern, western academy and that this context does not include the questions of others – women, black people, people from the 'third world', disabled people or Deaf people – then what we are arguing is that we need to redefine a theological method that is appropriate to our own context as Deaf people in twenty-first century England. To do this we first need to examine the demands our specific contexts make of the theological task, or, in other words, ask what is the purpose of theology in our own context.

As will become clear, a basic distinction in this work is between theologies that are life-giving or life-enhancing and those that are restrictive or destructive of life. Thus Bevan's 'false theology' referred to earlier is theology that is destructive of life. Things that are life-giving are part of a process of liberation; those that restrict

---

[7]   Guy Collins, 'Questioning Theology: Affirming Culture', *Theology*, CIV/820 (2001): 263.

[8]   Ibid., p. 265.

[9]   Ibid., p. 269 quoting David Tracy, *Analogical imagination* (London, 1981), p. 393.

or destroy life are part of a process of oppression. So the aim of theology, I would argue, is to contribute to the process of liberation through its exploration of the continuing involvement of God in human life. Theology needs to recognize that all knowledge is intimately involved in power relations and actions, so 'neutrality' or some kind of middle path is not possible; if a theology is not contributing to the process of liberation it is very likely to be contributing to oppression. Many different theologians from non white-male-western contexts have criticized traditional theology for being actively oppressive in different ways. I argue that Deaf people have been equally oppressed by 'traditional' theology and that we too need a theology that is not only contextual (in that it speaks to and of our own specific context) but is also a theology of liberation; a theology that is not only relevant, but which is actively working against all that restricts life and for that which is life-giving. All liberation theology[10] is contextual theology (as all liberation theology speaks about a very specific context of oppression) but not all contextual theology has liberation (in terms of resistance to oppression and the production of social change) as its primary purpose.

The failure to recognize the basic distinction between liberation and contextualization I would suggest grows out of a fundamental misunderstanding of what liberation theology is. Clodovis Boff, in describing the characteristics of the epistemology of Liberation Theology, says that it is much more than 'one theology among others',[11] it is not a module to be studied and applied, but a way of life to be learnt and practised; in the words of Boff it is a 'new theological spirit' expressed in passionate, concrete and prophetic language. Liberation Theology, in this understanding, does not necessarily oppose or substitute for other ways of doing theology, but it does critically engage with all other theologies from a particular point of view. For Boff, and other Latin American Liberation Theologians, this particular point of view is the overwhelming need of the poor of Latin America for justice and bread, for material liberation from the oppressive structures that make and keep them poor. All theology, or God-talk, done in this context has to be about developing the meaning of the Gospel as historically liberating for the poor of Latin America; if this aim is forgotten or subdued under others, theology can easily be manipulated as a tool for alienation and injustice. It is this understanding of Liberation Theology as a methodology and a way of life that contributes many fundamental insights to help us shape a new, liberating theological discourse in the completely different context of Deaf people in twenty-first century England. As Boff himself argues, as long as there are social inequalities, there is a need for social emancipation and therefore liberation theology.

---

[10]   When Liberation Theology is capitalized it is referring to the specifically Latin American version; when it is in lower case, it is referring to all theologies of liberation.

[11]   Clodovis Boff, 'Methodology of the Theology of Liberation', translated by Robert Burr in Jon Sobrino and Ignacio Ellacuría (eds), *Systematic Theology: perspectives from Liberation Theology* (London, 1996), p. 3.

Liberation Theology, as a way of life, is not something that can be done in abstract from a privileged place in an academy; it requires a practical rather than a theoretical relationship with the practice of liberation and implies a 'living contact with the struggle of the poor'.[12] Without this practical engagement in the struggle, words like 'the poor', 'oppression' and 'new society' are simply dictionary definitions. Liberation theologians (which includes anyone, trained or not, trying to 'think the faith in the face of oppression')[13] therefore need to be actively engaged in the struggle for liberation, and to be doing their theology to be used as a tool for the struggle, not as an intellectual exercise in itself. This is why Liberation Theology calls for an 'option for the poor', a statement of faith that God is on the side of all who are poor and oppressed against their oppressors. This is not (as it is sometimes understood) a way of saying that poor people deserve God more than others, but because in the post-modern world of subjectivity if you are not committed to the struggle for liberation, you are against it. I assess other people's writings not only by what they say, but also by how far they practise what they preach (as far as I can know it). I also apply this criterion to my own theology; to do this with integrity I need to be committed to and actively participating in the wider struggle for Deaf liberation; participating in local actions for the recognition of BSL and using my position in the church and my intellectual skills to encourage Deaf people to develop confidence in their own skills as leaders and in creating theology in BSL. The purpose of a liberation theology then, in the light of all I have written above, is its commitment to social change, not as a political aim in itself, but as part of the wider liberation involved in the kingdom of God. Bevans argues that this commitment to social change in the light of Christian principles leads not only to social transformation, but a 'deeper and more challenging knowledge of God as such'.[14] This is where 'Liberation Theology' as a Latin American phenomenon meets other 'theologies of liberation'. Feminist theology, for example, is equally committed to social change as the ultimate aim of its theology.[15] Feminist theology not only challenges the discourse of patriarchy, it also attempts to create a new theology that will change the lives of the women (and men) who engage with it. This commitment to social change is why I feel that other theologies of liberation give us a methodology for challenging the discourse of 'deaf' in traditional western theology. First we need to deconstruct that discourse and show how the way Deaf people have been constructed in the church is actively oppressive, and then we need to reconstruct theology from the perspective of our engagement in the struggle for Deaf liberation.

---

[12]   Boff, 'Methodology of the Theology of Liberation', p. 6.

[13]   Ibid., p. 9.

[14]   Bevans, *Models of contextual theology*, p. 66.

[15]   See for example Pamela Dickey Young, *Feminist theology/Christian theology: in search of method* (Minneapolis, 1990).

Theological Method: Sources

This process of deconstruction and reconstruction is one way of describing the methodology of theologies of liberation in general, and Deaf Liberation Theology in particular, but a more specific discussion of sources and norms is required. One of the most crucial differences between theologies of liberation and other ways of doing theology is in the point they start from and the sources they refer to. Theologies of liberation begin with people trying to make sense of the good news of Jesus Christ in their world, not as an exercise in making the Gospel relevant, but as an imperative way of addressing an almost unbearable situation. Gustavo Gutiérrez, one of the founders of Liberation Theology, expresses this concern clearly when he says his theology begins with the question 'how is it possible to tell the poor, who are forced to live in conditions that embody a denial of love, that God loves them?'[16] So Deaf Liberation Theology begins from the point of Deaf people identifying themselves as oppressed, and looking for liberation and Deaf Christians involved in this struggle demanding a faith that helps rather than hinders them. Mary Weir, a theologian from Canada who is d/Deaf, argues that Deaf people need theology to help them in their struggle for liberation: 'theology needs to be at the centre of any liberation impulse, for people need its impetus and powerful motivational undergirding as well as its reminder that every social movement, every thrust for deeper fulfilment must find its centre and meaning in the presence and purpose of God'.[17]

Beginning with the concrete concerns of the oppressed not only demands active involvement in the struggle for liberation as described in the previous section, it also requires a whole new range of sources to be utilized by theologians. Boff, for example, highlights the need for understanding the roots of oppression in socio-economic terms before we can construct a meaningful theology.[18] Deaf people need first to understand our social, political and cultural context and the historical forces acting on this context. If we do not understand this context as fully as possible, then we face the danger that our theology will be superficial, and will not achieve its purpose of real social transformation in the lives of Deaf people.

In addition to the urgent needs of the oppressed and the social analysis of context, the experience of the people themselves is considered to be a new and valid source of theology in the theologies of liberation. This raises methodological questions along the lines of what is 'experience' and how can it be defined so that it is of practical use. This question is particularly important within the post-modern framework, where there is no such thing as 'universal', 'raw' or 'uninterpreted' experience; all 'experience' is specific to a particular context and interpreted in the

---

[16] Gustavo Gutiérrez, *A theology of liberation: history, politics and salvation*, rev. edn with new introduction by the author, translated by Inda Caridad (London, 1988), p. xxxiv.

[17] Weir, 'Made Deaf in God's Image' in International Ecumenical Working Group Conference, *The Place of Deaf people in the Church* (Northampton, 1996), p. 5.

[18] Boff, 'Methodology of the Theology of Liberation', p. 11.

process of reflection and retelling. Despite the post-modern arguments for the uniqueness of individual experience, most theologians who use experience as a source do argue, for pragmatic reasons, that certain experiences are common to particular groups, and therefore that a specific 'community' experience can be identified without ironing out the very real differences that exist within communities. For Deaf Liberation Theology 'Deaf experience' as a source is the narrative of Deaf people of what has happened to them at home, in school, at work, at church and within the internal life of the Deaf community itself. This narrative is found in written form in Deaf edited magazines and sermons as well as the 'oral' or 'signed' tradition that is ineradicably part of Deaf culture. This experience is used to identify the urgent questions arising from the context, and to read and interpret 'texts' from the Bible, from other disciplines, from church tradition, from liberation theology, always looking for what resonates with my experience as a Deaf person and the experience of the Deaf community as told and written.

Theologies of liberation also use the more traditional sources of theology, the Bible and 'Christian tradition'. Liberation Theology in fact, within its largely Roman Catholic context takes for granted that these are significant elements of their theology, and therefore they do not always speak about their use, which is perhaps why they so often are criticized for ignoring them. However, Boff does argue that liberation theology insists on the 'givenness of faith', that the people themselves are 'at once oppressed and religious'[19] so that the 'experience' of the people is always reflected on and retold in the light of 'the faith' as taught by the Roman Catholic Church. This dialectical relationship between 'experience' and 'faith' is why many Liberation Theologians argue their theology starts from 'praxis' rather than experience. Bevans suggests that 'praxis' is often misunderstood to mean simply 'practice' when it is a specific technical term that refers both to 'reflected-upon action and acted-upon reflection',[20] where action can be said to refer to the experience of living under and resisting oppression and reflection to the lenses of faith through which it is interpreted. This process of reflecting on action and acting on reflection means that even if the theology starts in dialogue with 'traditional' Roman Catholic theology and readings of the Bible it quickly moves away from this in the course of reading the Bible from the starting point of the poor. Boff identifies certain traits that are characteristic of Liberation Theology readings of the Bible and Christian tradition; these include prioritizing the application of texts over the explanation of their meaning, seeking the transforming energy of biblical texts in interpretations that will lead to change in individuals and in society, accentuating the social context of the message (without reductionism) and incorporating popular readings of the Bible by the people themselves.[21] In terms of relating to the Christian tradition, Liberation Theology in Boff's eyes seeks to maintain a 'bond of basic continuity' with the 'living faith

---

[19]   Ibid., p. 2.
[20]   Bevans, *Models of contextual theology*, p. 65.
[21]   Boff, 'Methodology of the Theology of Liberation', p. 17.

tradition of the Christian people' and 'interrogates the past in an effort to learn from it and to be enriched by it'.[22] This relationship with past tradition is not uncritical. Liberation Theology seeks to highlight the limits as well as the contribution of theologies of the past, and to rehabilitate 'forgotten, fertile theological threads' such as the social teachings from the patristic theology of the second to the ninth centuries, and the accounts of the extreme lives of many saints and prophets who have often been condemned as heretics.

Unlike Liberation Theology (and possibly Black Theology), which have been criticized for their naïveté in reading the Bible and relating to Christian tradition,[23] feminist (and womanist)[24] theologians have a far more troubled relationship with these 'traditional' sources of theology, and many of the difficulties of this relationship seem to be shared by Nancy Eiesland, so far the only disabled liberation theologian. The topic of feminist, womanist and disabled relationship to and use of the Bible will be addressed in more detail in Chapter 6, but at this point it is appropriate to say that there is a strong argument for rejecting the use of Christian tradition or the Bible as irredeemably patriarchal and anti-disabled in these theologies. Young addresses this discussion, and concludes that most feminist theologies do seem to use the Bible and the Christian past as sources that provide 'themes, clues and catalysts' to some extent.[25] She concludes that for theology that is identifiably Christian, it is required to engage with two 'givens': the received Christian witness (including tradition and the Bible) and the specific context in a dialectical relationship. If a theology ignores the first it is not Christian, if it ignores the second it is meaningless for its intended audience.[26] Feminist theology, like Liberation Theology, does, however, broaden what is meant by 'Christian tradition' to include previously omitted, ignored or condemned texts, including writings previously labelled as marginal or heretical as well as the continually ignored witness of women throughout history. I too am aiming to widen the understanding of 'Christian tradition' as I attempt to identify an authentic Deaf Christian tradition to use as a source.

Underlying all the sources used in theologies of liberation – the concrete concerns of the oppressed, socio-political-cultural analysis, 'experience', the Bible and 'Christian tradition' – is one vital presupposition. This is the assumption that not only is all human knowledge related to a specific context, but so is all self-revelation of God. In other words, all revelation takes place within a particular historical context and material situation and human relationships and this revelation is an ongoing event. This understanding is why theologians of liberation, including Deaf Liberation theologians, feel free to add to traditional texts as

---

[22] Ibid., p. 18.

[23] See Bevans, *Models of contextual theology*, p. 71 for example.

[24] Womanist refers to black women who are exploring the multiple oppressions that arise from being both female and black.

[25] Young, *Feminist theology/Christian theology*, p. 71.

[26] Ibid., p. 58.

sources because they believe that God's revelation of God's-self and God's plan
for the world is not restricted to the Bible or to the 'official church', but continues
to be revealed in the questions of the oppressed, in secular theories, in the
experience of individuals and communities and in the previously unknown and
unrecognized aspects of 'Christian tradition'.

Theological Method: Norms

The other significant part of a theological method is the norms by which 'any given
theological sources or formulations are judged to be adequate or inadequate for
theology in general or for the type of theology being done'.[27] It is in looking at the
norms of a theology that its place in the spectrum of theological thought becomes
clear; traditional theology, for example, whatever it uses for sources, refers to
norms from Scripture, the *magisterium*[28] of the church or human reason in some
combination or other as having the final say on any theological source or
formulation.[29] However, theologies of liberation see these traditional norms as
insufficient at best and irrelevant at worst, so what norms can we refer to? The
overwhelming norm in use seems to be the concept of 'liberation'. In an earlier
paragraph I have defined 'liberation' very broadly as referring to a process that is
life-giving, a process that moves a person or a community away from everything
that restricts or destroys life towards that which enhances or creates life. Social
liberation from a Deaf perspective means liberation from hearing norms and the
'pressure to become copies of hearing people'[30] and also liberation from the
oppression caused by lack of access to education, media, information, employment,
religion and so on. For me, social liberation as a Deaf person means above all the
freedom to develop as a 'first-class Deaf person' rather than constantly playing
'catch-up' as a 'second-class hearing person' in today's world.

   This is in accord with 'liberation' as defined by the American theologian
Walter Wink who understands it as liberation from whatever deprives human
beings of the opportunity to realize as fully as possible their own God-given
potential.[31] He does however have one caveat to this criterion, and that is that true
human liberation can never be achieved at the expense of suppressing the God-
given potential of another human being. He agrees that, for liberation and social

---

[27]   Ibid., p. 19.

[28]   *Magisterium* is a technical term from the Roman Catholic Church referring to the
college of the Pope, cardinals and bishops who are the final source of authority in that
denomination. They and only they can decide if something is true for that church or not. It
can also be used in a more general sense of referring to a group of privileged people who
judge all theology according to their own criteria.

[29]   See for example Young, *Feminist theology/Christian theology*, p. 20.

[30]   Shrine, *The language and culture of deaf people*, p. 7.

[31]   Walter Wink, *Engaging the powers: discernment and resistance in a world of
domination* (Minncapolis: 1992), p. 74.

transformation, the status quo needs to be challenged, the 'mighty need to be brought low' but he argues that the oppressors need to be liberated as much as the oppressed.[32] This is not about making 'liberation' so general that it means nothing, but recognizes that for the oppressors to be liberated in personal terms they may, in fact, require a drop in income and social status and a radical rethink of their values in life. Liberation in theological terms is not purely about the material needs of humanity (although this dimension must never be forgotten) but also about spiritual, mental and emotional needs as well. Those experiencing 'spiritual poverty' in so much of the wealthy west need liberation as much as the materially poor people of the world. Gustavo Gutiérrez understands liberation as not only from the oppression that forces people to live in conditions contrary to God's will for their lives; it is also liberation of the mind (or the emotions, or the psyche) from internal oppression in the face of any kind of servitude.[33] Whichever kind of liberation is considered most important depends on the context; Boff says that in Latin America the people have faith but no bread so liberation from poverty is the most urgent question, but in another context where bread is plentiful other questions such as liberation from a basic lack of self-esteem, or lack of education or employment may be more urgent. The important thing is that decision over which liberation is most urgent and which is therefore used as the start point and norm of theology is not a decision of 'theological truth' but a question of purely methodological and pastoral convenience. The 'first' question addressed in order of execution is not necessarily 'first' in terms of importance in theological terms.[34]

The decision between different forms of liberation for Boff is not so much a decision between physical/material liberation and mental/emotional/spiritual liberation as a decision between the former and what he calls 'soteriological' liberation. This is the liberation from sin and death through Jesus Christ historically taught by the Christian church, usually referred to as 'salvation' or 'being saved'. Gutiérrez also includes this understanding of liberation as liberation from sin in his discussion of the different 'levels' involved. For him, this level is the only final and complete liberation from social oppression and reconciliation with God and humanity.[35] This is an understanding shared by Boff: he argues that [the Christian] faith cannot be exhausted by the social and political dimension, that, even in situations of the most dire oppression and poverty, it includes a personal dimension of individual conversion and an eschatological dimension of salvation and resurrection as well 'precisely because the poor are not only poor, but men and women called to eternal communion with God'.[36] It is this soteriological dimension to their understanding of liberation that provides Liberation Theology with its rebuttal to criticisms that it is merely justifying a particular political viewpoint;

---

[32]   Ibid., p. 97.
[33]   Gutiérrez, *Theology of liberation*, p. xxxviii.
[34]   Boff, 'Methodology of the Theology of Liberation', p. 4.
[35]   Gutiérrez, *Theology of liberation*, p. xxxviii.
[36]   Boff, 'Methodology of the Theology of Liberation', p. 4.

secular theories such as Marxism are simply tools to be used in the service of a full and comprehensive liberation of the oppressed in that particular context and are subjected to the critical judgement of the poor and their context and not the other way round.

In the end a critical and dialectical balance between 'social' and 'soteriological' liberation, or between 'Christian tradition' and 'experience', appears to be the most commonly used and effective norm in liberation theology.

Framework and Methodology

In conclusion to this chapter then, having surveyed the ground of theology and Deaf people, I have outlined an epistemological framework and methodology that I will use. This framework prioritizes the voice of Deaf people when it comes to speaking about their own lives; uncovering silenced Deaf voices, and freeing bound Deaf hands is an important focus for this work.

After examining the sociology of Deaf people and the history of the Deaf church I turn in the second half of this book to construction of a new Deaf Liberation Theology. I look at how Deaf people might read and use the Bible, one of the primary sources in Christian theology. I look at Jesus Christ and what he might mean for Deaf people today. While these two chapters have practical applications within the church, especially for preaching and teaching, I turn to an immediately identifiable practical subject and the issue of worship and Deaf people. All three chapters draw on a variety of sources: the Bible, Christian tradition, both mainstream and Deaf, Deaf experience and questions, and other theologies of liberation. The formulations that result are tested according to whether they contribute to the liberation of Deaf people in the sense of the threefold liberation of physical, mental and soteriological as defined by Gutiérrez. These three parts of the reconstruction are not comprehensive and nor are they meant to be so. There is much left to be done to come up with a comprehensive Deaf Liberation Theology – in fact, I believe it is a never-ending task as the context is always changing. This book, I hope, will be the catalyst for this task.

Chapter 2

DEAF-WORLD: Being Deaf in the Twenty-First Century

What is it like to 'hear' a hand?
You have to be deaf to understand.
What is it like to be a small child,
In a school, in a room void of sound –
With a teacher who talks and talks and talks;
And then when she does come around to you,
She expects you to know what she's said?
You have to be deaf to understand.

...

What is it like to be curious,
To thirst for knowledge you can call your own,
With an inner desire that's set on fire –
And you ask a brother, sister, or friend
Who looks in answer and says, 'Never Mind'?
You have to be deaf to understand.

What it is like in a corner to stand,
Though there's nothing you've done really wrong,
Other than try to make use of your hands
To a silent peer to communicate
A thought that comes to your mind all at once?
You have to be deaf to understand.

What is it like to be shouted at
When one thinks that will help you to hear;
Or misunderstand the words of a friend
Who is trying to make a joke clear,
And you don't get the point because he's failed?
You have to be deaf to understand.

...

What is it like to comprehend
Some nimble fingers that paint the scene,
And make you smile and feel serene,

With the 'spoken word' of the moving hand
That makes you part of the word at large?
You have to be deaf to understand.[1]

The extract is from a poem called 'You Have to be Deaf to Understand', written by
a Deaf man from Gallaudet University in America. During the course of the poem,
Madsen describes experiences that will be recognized by many if not most Deaf
people as describing an important part of their lives. Despite the requirement that
'you have to be deaf to understand' I will endeavour, in this chapter, to describe
some aspects of life as Deaf people experience it today and attempt some
theoretical analysis of this experience with the use of models to describe the
dominant and alternative constructions of what it means to be Deaf. For some
readers, familiar with Deaf studies, this chapter might be skipped; but the appeal
for taking on board the social model of disability as well as the cultural model of
being Deaf is important in Deaf Liberation Theology. The fact that a relationship
between the two models does exist is why we can usefully read and engage with
the work of disabled liberation theologians such as Nancy Eiesland and John Hull.

Power differences between people mean that some models have more impact
on people's lives than others; so, of the three models described below, the medical
model dominates the way many d/Deaf people experience the world because it is
the one held by the medical establishment (who first diagnose children as deaf and
guide their parents as to the best way of dealing with it) and by most of the
educational establishment (who determine the language in which d/Deaf children
are educated). Deaf clubs may use a different model, but, while they can offer Deaf
people a great deal in the way of opportunities to meet other Deaf people, and also
support and confidence-building activities, they have no establishment power to
change the way Deaf people experience the world. I believe that models that
d/Deaf people primarily experience as negative are taken to be invalid as a basis
for doing theology. On the other hand, models that positively affect d/Deaf people
are, in themselves, a foundation for liberation or transformation and as such have
theological value.

A Brief History of the *DEAF-WORLD*

How can one describe the community's life in dry statistics and data? But, come to that,
how can one describe it in words? Perhaps the life, bustle and laughter when deaf people
get together and have the chance to use their language in full flow is best left to the
imagination. Notable scenes in deaf culture include the standing joke of the club
committee trying to push people out at closing time, and crowds standing around in the
street signing for a good hour afterwards. Or of people of all ages staying up half the

---

[1]   Willard J. Madsen (1971), in George Taylor and Juliet Bishop (eds), *Being deaf: the
experience of deafness* (London: 1991), p. xii.

night together, telling jokes and stories, signing songs or poems or playing sign language-based games. Or of a regional rally, where a town centre is taken over by sign language for a weekend, and people from all over the country greet old schoolfriends across the street on their morning promenade.[2]

The strain of their feelings vanish in the deaf community they felt at home with their language … they feel normal people … The average deaf community is so closely-knit that is usually very difficult for deaf persons to draw line when they wish to plan for a private occasion … A deaf twosome are very lucky if they can limit attendance of their wedding 150 to 200. The two some arrange a big hall for these big numbers also have two separate parties on the same day, e.g. during the day the families and close friends attended then in the evening all their deaf friends attended.[3]

Deaf people are found in history since records began. The writers of the Old Testament, for example, are fully aware of the existence of deaf people in the ancient Near East,[4] and the New Testament records Jesus' healing of a deaf man.[5] References to deaf and/or 'mute' people using sign language as an alternative means of communication are found in many classical Greek and Roman authors, including Plato,[6] as well as in the New Testament[7] and in ancient Jewish sources.[8] Deaf individuals continue to appear in historical records, for example in the context of French and Spanish monastic communities in the seventeenth and eighteenth centuries,[9] and in seventeenth-century England.[10] While there is

---

[2]   Paddy Ladd, 'The Modern Deaf Community' in Susan Gregory and Gillian M. Hartley (eds), *Constructing Deafness*, 2nd edn (London, 1994), p. 35.

[3]   A deaf man, 'Growing up in the deaf community' in J. G. Kyle and B. Woll, *Sign Language: the study of deaf people and their language* (Cambridge: 1985), p. 265.

[4]   For example Isaiah 35:5, 'The ears of the deaf shall be unstopped'.

[5]   Mark 7:31–7.

[6]   Plato, *Cratylus*, 422e. See Simon Timothy Horne, *Injury and Blessing: a challenge to current readings of biblical discourses concerning impairment* (PhD thesis, Birmingham University, 1999), p. 233 for a full list of references in the Bible and classical texts to deaf people and their use of sign language or gestures in communication.

[7]   When Zechariah is rendered mute in Luke 1:20–23 he uses gestures to communicate.

[8]   Paddy Ladd, *Understanding Deaf Culture: In search of Deafhood* (Clevedon, 2003), p. 93 gives examples from the Torah and Mishnah.

[9]   See for example B. Truffaut, 'Etienne de Fay and the History of the Deaf' in Renate Fischer and Harlan Lane (eds), *Looking Back: a reader on the history of Deaf communities and their sign languages* (Hamburg, 1993), p. 14.

[10]   Peter W. Jackson, 'John Dyott 1606–1664' in Peter W. Jackson and Raymond Lee (eds), *Deaf Lives: Deaf people in history* (Feltham, 2001), p. 55 (John Dyott was a born Deaf man who was considered a hero in the skirmish between Parliamentary and Royalist forces in Lichfield during the Civil War) and Robert Latham and William Matthews (eds), *The Diary of Samuel Pepys*, volume VII (London: Harper Collins, 1995), p. 363. The entry for 9 November 1666 refers to a dumb boy who communicated with Pepys and his colleague by use of signs.

evidence that Deaf people tended to marry each other,[11] and otherwise form a distinct social group,[12] the first evidence for the emergence of the modern Deaf self-understanding can be found in early nineteenth-century France and its rapid spread into the USA and the UK throughout that century.

Perhaps the defining characteristic of this modern Deaf self-understanding is simply as people who use a different language from the world around them. When they are together, using their language, there is no communication barrier; the lack of hearing is not an issue. The sign concept of *DEAF-WORLD* or *DEAF-WAY*,[13] suggests that Deaf people do, to a certain extent, understand themselves as members of a separate culture.[14] This took its sharpest form in the movement for a Deaf Nation Utopia in the USA that began in 1831 and came closest to realization in 1856 when John James Fournoy proposed an elaborate scheme for political independence and state sovereignty for Deaf people on an unpopulated piece of land in the USA.[15] In France the first autonomous national organization for Deaf people, *Societe Centrale des Sourds-Muets*, was established by Berthier in 1834. This organization met every year on the birthday of the abbé de l'Epée (the founder of the first French school for d/Deaf people) for a grand banquet and celebration of sign.[16] Bernard Mottez argues that these banquets were much more than convivial insular gatherings of Deaf people; in speeches and contemporary accounts by the Deaf people themselves they were perceived as the birth and focus of a 'deaf-mute nation'.[17] In the UK an all-Deaf committee was arguing in 1860 for the erection of a separate church for the deaf and dumb on the grounds that they 'were as much entitled to a special and perfectly constituted service in their own language as

---

[11]   Many of the discussions of Deaf people in Jewish law for example refer to the debate over whether gestures were adequate for a marriage to be legal.

[12]   Pierre Desloges, 'A Deaf person's observation about an elementary course of education for the Deaf' in Harlan Lane (ed.), *The deaf experience: classics in language and education*, translated by Philip Franklin (Massachusetts, 1984), p. 43.

[13]   *DEAF-WORLD* is contrasted with the *HEARING-WORLD*, and refers to any situation where a Deaf person can expect to be one of many Deaf people and therefore can relax in the knowledge that communication will not be a struggle. In effect, the *DEAF-WORLD* consists of the Deaf clubs and schools and churches and any gathering of Deaf people in a pub or for a meeting. *DEAF-WAY* is a comprehensive term that refers to the ways of behaving and thinking that are common in the visual *DEAF-WORLD*, for example, flashing lights or stamping on the floor to gain attention rather than shouting or clapping as would be used by hearing people.

[14]   Paddy Ladd, *In search of Deafhood: towards an understanding of British Deaf culture* (PhD thesis, Bristol University, 1998), p. 85.

[15]   Jonathan Rée, *I see a voice: a philosophical history of language, deafness and the senses* (London, 1999), p. 200.

[16]   Ibid., p. 204. See also Ladd, *In search of Deafhood*, p. 105.

[17]   Bernard Mottez, 'The Deaf Mute Banquets and the Birth of the Deaf Movement' in Fischer and Lane (eds), *Looking Back*, p. 145. 'Deaf-mute' was the accepted term at the time.

foreigners are, who, living in London, attend services specially provided to meet their conditions'.[18]

This Deaf self-construction as a separate linguistic group came under threat in the late nineteenth century as scientists and legislators attempted to categorize and control anyone who was not perceived as 'normal' by the majority society. Alexander Graham Bell, for example, presented a paper to the National Academy of Sciences in 1884 entitled *Memoir upon the formation of a deaf variety of the human race*[19] in which he expressed his concern that the intermarriage of Deaf people was resulting in the birth of more Deaf people and the consequent weakening of the human race. His solution was to advocate a greater 'integration' of Deaf people by teaching them to communicate via aural/oral means, to eradicate the language of signs that he considered separated Deaf people from hearing, and therefore prevent Deaf people from marrying each other and having children. This fear of a 'Deaf race' led to Deaf women being forcibly sterilized both in the USA and the UK within living memory. Murray Holmes writes in 1979 of at least three cases he knows of where a 'travesty of genetic counselling' (one vicariously through a hearing sister) led to the sterilization of the Deaf women concerned.[20] He also writes of clinics that profess to offer a diagnosis of deafness before birth, with the explicit option of abortion if the test is positive. All this medical control is despite the fact that only one in ten children born to d/Deaf parents are d/Deaf themselves.

Bell was not the only person who felt intimidated by a strong, separate Deaf social grouping in an age when difference was increasingly seen as a political threat. Teachers of the Deaf met in Milan in 1880 for an 'International Congress for education and welfare of the deaf'. Despite the fact that the majority of schools for Deaf children at this time (over 200 worldwide) used the 'manual method' (teaching using sign or manual language) and there were many Deaf teachers and other Deaf professionals and tradesmen successfully educated by this method, the delegates at the congress were mostly hearing teachers from schools using the 'German' or oral methods of teaching. They passed a resolution:

> Considering the incontestable superiority of speech over signs in restoring the deaf-mute to society and in giving him the more perfect knowledge of the language, the Congress declares that the oral method ought to be preferred to that of signs for the education of the deaf and dumb … and considering that a great number of the deaf and dumb are not

---

[18] Association in Aid of the Deaf and Dumb, *Appendix to Annual Report*, 1860, p. 24, in Clifford Kenneth Lysons, *Voluntary Welfare Societies for Adult Deaf Persons in England, 1840–1963* (MA thesis, Liverpool University, 1965), p. 42.

[19] Alexander Graham Bell, *Memoir upon the formation of a deaf variety of the human race* (Washington DC, 1884).

[20] A. M. Holmes, 'Bicultural Adaptation and Survival: Integration or Disintegration' in Raymond Lee (ed.), *Writings from deaf liberation: a selection of NUD papers 1976–1986* (Feltham, 1992), p. 103.

receiving the benefit of instruction recommends that the governments should take the necessary steps that all deaf and dumb may be educated.[21]

This resolution was promulgated throughout the western world, wherever schools for the Deaf existed, by the delegates at the conference and was implemented to varying degrees. In the UK, a royal commission met in 1889 to look into the situation of the blind and the deaf and dumb in the UK. Despite vigorous arguments by two hearing missioners[22] in favour of manualism,[23] and written submissions from such prominent and articulate Deaf people as Francis Maginn (who was not invited to give evidence),[24] the commission effectively ruled in favour of oralism as the most desirable method for teaching Deaf people.[25] In 1893 an Act of Parliament made the education of Deaf children compulsory between the ages of seven and sixteen; to obtain state financial assistance, schools had to organize speech lessons for all pupils judged capable of learning to speak, and as far as possible give primacy to the oral method in the classroom. This meant that the only pupils taught in sign were those Deaf who 'from a low mental condition or other mutilating causes, are unable to learn to speak sufficiently well to benefit by ordinary oral instruction'.[26]

The downgrading of sign in education had a drastic effect on the *DEAF-WORLD*. Sign language was pushed underground in schools as ex-pupils remember being punished for being seen to sign and signing to each other in secrecy in the dormitory at night.[27] The dominance of oralism in schools resulted in most Deaf people leaving school with an inadequate education. Once out of school,

---

[21]   Quoted in Andreas Markides, 'The Teaching of Speech: Historical Developments' in Gregory and Hartley (eds), *Constructing Deafness*, p. 116.

[22]   'Missioners' refers to the leaders of the missions to the adult deaf and dumb (usually the main social centre for all adult deaf people) found throughout the UK. At this point in time, the missioner could be lay or ordained, deaf or hearing and was not necessarily a member of the Church of England.

[23]   Manualism refers to the method of teaching Deaf children through manual or sign language.

[24]   Brian Grant, 'Francis Maginn (1861–1918)' in Fischer and Lane (eds), *Looking Back*, p. 101.

[25]   See Harlan Lane, *When the mind hears: a history of the deaf* (London, 1988), p. 366 and M. G. McLoughlin, *A history of the education of the deaf in England* (Gosport, 1987), p. 45. The actual recommendation was that all children should be taught by the oral method for their first year, and thereafter only those who cannot benefit from the oral method should be taught using the combined (both speech and signs) or the manual method.

[26]   Abraham Farrar, *Arnold's Education of the Deaf* (London, 1901). (A revised edition of Thomas Arnold's book originally published in 1888 and the main text for all proponents of the oralist method.) Quoted in McLoughlin, *A history of the education of the deaf in England*, p. 24.

[27]   David Wright, *Deafness, an autobiography*, 2nd edn (London, 1993) or any other autobiographical account that covers experience at a residential school for the deaf.

adults were not 'banned' from signing, but were often ashamed of it, and their decreasing literacy meant the 'pencil-and-paper' method of communicating with those who did not know sign was no longer a realistic option. In addition, as the manually educated generation of *STRONG-DEAF* grew older and died, there were no educated, literate, articulate Deaf people to continue the fight for the *DEAF-WORLD*. The construction of Deaf people as incapable and in need of expert aid dominated every aspect of Deaf life and became a self-fulfilling prophecy.

Despite the impact of removing sign language from education and the forces of 'audism'[28] the *DEAF-WORLD* construction never entirely disappeared. It may not have been articulated to the same degree as before, but traces of Deaf people rebelling against the dominance of the hearing world can be glimpsed throughout history. For example, Arthur Dimmock, the first Deaf historian of modern times, mentions groups of Deaf people being 'barred' from the missions in the late nineteenth and early twentieth centuries for being seen in public houses.[29] In other words, some Deaf people were creating a space to meet and socialize together outside of the hearing-controlled environment of the missions. It is, of course, possible that these Deaf people simply fell out with the missioners or other people at the missions or that they objected to the 'religious morality' that dominated at these places. However, it seems to me that neither the 'personality clash' argument nor the 'religious morality' argument is sufficient explanation for groups of Deaf people regularly meeting in a place where they were very much the minority, very much open to verbal and physical abuse for their use of sign language rather than the cosy world of the Deaf mission. These pub groups disappear (from the records at least) for a generation, but resurface in the 1960s. In the meantime, as Paddy Ladd argues, there was still resistance to the dominant perception of Deaf people to be found. This resistance was not expressed in obvious ways, but covertly, in myriad small ways by Deaf people determined to live their lives their way described by Ladd as '1001 victories'.[30]

During the 1970s, this covert resistance began to give way to a more overt fight. One of the groups of Deaf people meeting in pubs formalized themselves as the National Union of the Deaf, the NUD, to campaign against what they saw as the oppression of their community and the denial of their language and heritage.[31] This was the beginning of the resurgence of Deaf pride throughout the UK.[32] Ladd identifies a number of other factors, including the development of the welfare state

---

[28]   A term created by Tom Humphries, *Communicating across cultures (Deaf/Hearing) and language learning* (PhD dissertation, Union Graduate School, Cincinnati, OH, 1977) to describe the educators and others who colonized Deaf people.

[29]   A. F. Dimmock, *Cruel Legacy* (Edinburgh, 1993), p. 51.

[30]   Ladd, *In search of Deafhood*, p. 183.

[31]   'NUD 1976' (the inaugural pamphlet of the NUD, published in November 1975), in Lee (ed.), *Writings from deaf liberation*. See also Ladd, *In search of Deafhood*, pp. 194, 197, 208 where he describes this process as one of the founder members of the NUD.

[32]   Ladd, *In search of Deafhood*, pp. 35–7.

in the 1960s and 1970s that lessened the power of the missioners over Deaf people, and the making of TV programmes such as *See Hear* (one of the results of campaigning by the NUD). *See Hear* brought prestige to the Deaf community, rendered Deaf people and their language more visible, boosted Deaf people's confidence and pride and drastically increased the number of lay people wanting to learn sign language (and thus the number of possible interpreters not locked into the omnipotent missioner model and with a professional code of conduct of interpreting what is said/signed rather than speaking for the Deaf person). Another significant factor in the resurgence of Deaf pride was the rediscovery of Deaf history (as opposed to the history of the education of deaf people) with the publication of Harlan Lane's *When the mind hears: a history of the deaf* in 1984 which led to the academic recognition of Deaf Studies as a subject in its own right.

The final factor identified by Ladd and many others as being significant in the resurgence of Deaf pride was the recognition of sign languages as true languages with their own grammatical structure rather than as an elaborated system of mime or gesture, parasitic on spoken languages. This was first demonstrated for American Sign Language (ASL) by linguist William Stokoe in 1960,[33] and for BSL by Mary Brennan and others in 1980.[34] This recognition strongly critiqued the medical model, which, at best, sees sign as a method of teaching English derived from spoken language and at worst as 'monkey gestures used by a group of sub-humans who did not even have a language'.[35] It also confirmed for Deaf communities across the world that they were right in having pride in their language; in having, over the years, used it as a focus for the development of their self-understanding and self-esteem.

Deaf experience over the years can thus be summarized as a mixture of positive experiences of community life and a distinctive language, mixed in with a daily experience of oppression focused on educational methods and the impact of welfare workers or missioners in the Deaf missions or Deaf clubs. To analyse this experience, it is helpful to recognize that there are at least two fundamentally different constructions of what it means to be Deaf in existence; one is centred on the idea that Deaf people are hearing people who cannot hear, which is known as the medical model and described in the next section. The other one grows from the Deaf self-experience described above that Deaf people are simply people who use a different language and have their own distinctive ways of behaving. This Deaf self-experience has been formalized as the 'cultural model' in recent years. The academic expression of the 'cultural model' was in part in response to the 'social model' of disability, which was formulated by disabled people as an alternative to

---

[33]   William Stokoe, *Sign Language Structure*, Studies in Linguistics Occasional Papers, 8 (1960).

[34]   Brennan, M., Colville, M. and Lawson, L., *Words in hand: a structural analysis of the signs of British Sign Language* (Edinburgh, 1980).

[35]   Paddy Ladd, 'The modern Deaf community' in Gregory and Hartley (eds), *Constructing Deafness*, p. 37.

the 'medical model'. I will briefly describe and critique both alternative models and attempt to examine how they can be used in the formulation of a Deaf Liberation Theology.

The Medical Model

Michael Oliver was the first person to articulate the medical or individual model as a way of looking at issues affecting the lives of people with a disability in 1983.[36] He based this model on the analysis by disabled people into the question of just why they were so disadvantaged in society. The Open University Issues in Deafness course was the first to use it specifically to provide a framework for understanding the experience of deaf people in the late 1980s and early 1990s.[37] The medical model constructs deaf people as individuals who cannot hear and whose needs can be determined by the measurement of their individual hearing loss in decibels (dB), itself an arbitrarily constructed standard of measurement.[38] It assumes that hearing is normal, that deafness is a deviation from the norm, a problem afflicting the individual, which must therefore be corrected by a medical approach of working on that individual.

In its basic form, the perception of deaf people simply as deviant hearing people is a model that can be seen in writings by hearing educators and missioners working with Deaf people from the beginning of Deaf education in France with the abbé de l'Epée in 1760 and the beginnings of mission work with Deaf adults in the UK in the 1820s. Uneducated and Deaf people were likened to 'savages', or even animals in their behaviour.[39] In the twentieth century comparisons with animals and savages recede, and articles begin to focus on the tragedy of being deaf. For example, Tom Sutcliffe writing in 1990: 'Do people ever think as they sit in the Albert Hall and listen to the massed choirs pouring forth their volume of beautiful sound, do they ever consider the tragedy of the totally deaf person being cut off from the slightest sound of it all?'[40] Deafness is seen as an individual tragedy, it reduces people to the status of 'dumb' animals, and there is no 'cure'.

This model not only determines the parameters of who is Deaf, it also attempts to define what the needs of Deaf people are. For example, the Church of England report *The Church Among Deaf People* argues that to 'grasp the implications of deafness, it is first necessary to recognize the function of hearing and its place in

---

[36] See Michael Oliver, *Understanding Disability: from theory to practice* (London, 1996), p. 30.

[37] See Gregory and Hartley (eds), *Constructing Deafness*, p. 2.

[38] Gregory and Hartley (ed.), *Constructing Deafness*, p. 2 and also the extract 'Assessment of Impaired Hearing' by William Noble in the same book, pp. 87–95.

[39] Abbé Sicard. Quoted in Harlan Lane (ed.), *The deaf experience*, p. 87.

[40] Sutcliffe, *The Challenge of Deafness* (Taunton, 1990), p. 44.

human life and communication'.[41] This approach starts with hearing sounds as an essential part of what it means to be a human being and therefore anyone not hearing, that is who is d/Deaf, is lacking something. Not hearing is a problem that has to be solved before the d/Deaf person can live a 'normal' life. If a person cannot be made to hear by using hearing aids, or by the operation of a cochlear implant[42] then it is considered that their life and their experience will always be somewhat less full and less than normal compared to a hearing person.

The medical model has dominated every aspect of the lives of d/Deaf people for most of their history. In education it has meant that the focus for the last 100 years has been on teaching d/Deaf children to speak and lip-read and be 'integrated', with sign language only being used, if at all, as a means of teaching speech and lip-reading. In technology it has resulted in a focus on the development of 'cures' and hearing aids and cochlear implants at the expense of devices to enable d/Deaf people to use communications technology that is such an essential part of the modern world. In psychology and medicine it has meant that d/Deaf people are seen as deviant because incurable. There is evidence of many cases where d/Deaf people have been misdiagnosed as 'learning disabled' or schizophrenic and they have been portrayed as essentially isolated, aggressive and impulsive.[43] In social work terms it has resulted in the assessment of d/Deaf people in terms of how 'normal' their lives are compared to 'normal' [hearing] people and the conclusion that d/Deaf people are necessarily dependent on the services of a 'trained deaf specialist'. Finally, in the church it has meant d/Deaf people have been excluded from positions of leadership and responsibility and treated like children, incapable of fully engaging with the word of God. A few individuals succeed in transcending these imposed limits, but this only throws into sharper relief the lack of opportunity available to others. In other words, the medical model disempowers d/Deaf people by placing the focus on the inability of d/Deaf people to hear and making hearing a necessary factor in both what it means to be human and what is required to make any decisions about your own life and those of others.

The cumulative effect of these experiences has been the internalizing of the medical model by many d/Deaf people. What this means is that many d/Deaf people believe society's assessment of their capabilities and expectations of life and label themselves 'thick'. They believe that their way of communicating (sign) is inferior to speech and lip-reading (so, for example, many deaf people will not use full BSL in front of hearing people, even those hearing who can sign). They believe that the 'experts' – teachers, audiologists and chaplains – know better than

[41] *The Church Among Deaf People* (London, 1997), p. 4.
[42] An operation to insert electrodes in the ear which directly stimulate the auditory nerve with the sounds from an external 'speech processor'.
[43] Harlan Lane, *The mask of benevolence: disabling the deaf community* (New York, 1993), p. 54.

they do what they need. Many Deaf 'readers'[44] and assistant chaplains do nothing without first checking with the senior (hearing) chaplain that it is OK. Basically, Deaf people experience themselves as deservedly second-class citizens. One Deaf man was wearing a 'James Bond, 007' tie. When I admired it he said, only half jokingly, '*THIS – 007 – WRONG. I'M DEAF – BETTER 003½*'. Like many d/Deaf people, he had internalized the medical model to the extent he felt he was only half a person compared to hearing people. The internalizing of the medical model and the lack of power also mean d/Deaf people find it hard to realize that they can do anything to change their situation in terms of education, further training or simple resistance. This impact of the medical model in itself would be sufficient grounds for its criticism on the theological grounds that all are equal in the eyes of God[45] and that Jesus came to call all people to life in abundance[46] (that is Jesus came to call all people to experience life to the fullest limit of their God-given potential) and this model fulfils neither criterion. It is simply neither liberating nor transforming in its effects on people's lives. However, it can also be critiqued on other grounds as well. In practical terms it is simply ridiculous. It points to the situation of being hearing and tells d/Deaf people 'that is what you have to aim for', an aim that is clearly impossible. Even the best lip-reader will never follow a spoken conversation as effortlessly as a hearing person. Mairian Corker likens this aim to climbing a precipice; every time you get near the top, the top moves higher.[47] Deaf children in schools are set up to 'fail'; they are expected to learn to speak and lip-read by understanding teachers who speak to them and then learn to read, write and add up through this very imperfectly understood medium. It is comparable to expecting children from Bengali-speaking homes to learn other scholastic subjects from English-speaking teachers without having first being taught any English. Even then they have a first language, which a young d/Deaf child does not.

The power of the medical model has always been its appeal to apparent 'common sense'. It seems self-evident that someone who lacks one of the 'five senses' should be limited in what they can do and need help from those with everything in full working order, that it is 'normal' to communicate via hearing and speaking and that this is the natural order of things. However, the ideas of 'common sense' and 'normal' and 'natural' have been strongly challenged in the post-modern world. It may be 'normal' for a hearing person to communicate with someone via aural/oral means. But it is equally normal for me to need to look at a person when they speak to me; I have done it all my life. It may be normal for a hearing person to pick up the phone and speak into it and listen to the answer. It is

---

[44] Lay people who have had some theological training in things such as preaching and leading worship.

[45] Galatians 3:28.

[46] John 10:10.

[47] Corker, *Counselling: the deaf challenge* (London, 1995), p. xii.

equally normal for me to type my message into the 'minicom'[48] and read the answer off the screen in front of me; it is the only way I have ever used the phone for a conversation. Finally, the idea of the 'natural order of things' has been challenged by the emergence of multiple, alternative constructions of what it means to be d/Deaf put forward by d/Deaf people themselves that deny the assumption that 'this is the only way things can be'.

Alternative Models: the Social Model

This model was formulated by Oliver, among others, in the 1980s as a deliberate alternative to the medical model, and used as a basis for political campaigning. It looks at how disabled people (which includes d/Deaf people in the eyes of the world) are constructed in society (that is the medical model) and suggests an alternative construction based on a distinction between the physical impairment of a person and the social structures that disable them, or prevent them from full participation in society. Thus disabled people are constructed as an oppressed group in society.[49] In the late 1970s and early 1980s, at about the same time as the NUD was formed, disabled people began to organize themselves into groups campaigning for full participation in society. One of these groups, the Union of the Physically Impaired Against Segregation (UPIAS), produced in 1976 a document entitled *Fundamental Principles of Disability,* stating the basic principles of the social model. This document has been the foundation for all subsequent articulations of this model. Unlike the medical model, which says an individual has problems participating in society because they are disabled in the sense of being functionally limited compared to 'normal' people, this model argues that the barriers to full participation are 'society's failure to provide appropriate services and adequately ensure the needs of disabled people are fully taken into account in its social organization'.[50] What this means is it is not that wheelchair users are unable to use public transport; it is public transport that is inaccessible to wheelchair users. It is not that blind people are unable to read; it is that the information has been presented in visual rather than audio or tactile form. It is not that d/Deaf people cannot hear the platform announcements at railway stations; it is that the information is only offered in an inaccessible way.

Disabled people received this articulation of the social model of disability with enthusiasm because it made immediate connections to their own experiences. For many in fact, it was not only a useful political concept; it was also experienced as a

---

[48] '... a telecommunications device, which enables text to be sent down the telephone line in exactly the same way as speech to another minicom user ...' (definition from Mairian Corker, *Deaf and Disabled or Deafness Disabled?* (Buckingham, 1998), p. 147).

[49] Oliver, *Understanding Disability*, p. 22.

[50] Ibid., p. 32.

transformation of consciousness or a liberation of self. As Oliver quotes from David Hevey:

> I had learnt to live with my private fear and to feel that I was the only one involved in this fight. I had internalized my oppression. I cannot explain how significantly all this was turned around when I came into contact with the notion of the social model of disabilities rather than the medical model which I had hitherto lived with.[51]

Hevey describes this experience as 'an almost evangelical conversion' and as a 'flash on the road to Damascus' and narrates how it completely changed his discomfort with his disability, his sense of it as a private cross to bear and his festering hatred of himself. The social model is an alternative construct, powerful in creating a positive sense of identity and increasing the self-esteem of all disabled people.

Alternative Models: The Cultural Model

The cultural or cultural-linguistic model was formulated partly as a response to perceived inadequacies of the social model for Deaf people and their lives, and also out of the recognition of sign languages as true languages and the political and conceptual focus this gave to those fighting for Deaf Liberation. Deaf people began to construct themselves as a linguistic minority, directly comparable with other linguistic minorities in the UK.[52] The NUD argued that they have a right to describe themselves as Deaf with a capital 'D' to distinguish themselves from people who simply have a hearing loss. This is suggesting that Deaf is a proper noun, similar to Jewish or Muslim or Black or Aborigine.[53] The construction of Deaf people as a linguistic minority has been the foundation for recent campaigning by the Federation of Deaf People (FDP) and the British Deaf Association (BDA) for formal recognition of BSL by the government as an official minority language in the UK – a campaign that was partially successful in that in February 2003 the British government did indeed recognize BSL as a true language and committed itself to working out what this meant in practice. The campaign continues for a full recognition of BSL that recognizes the need for adequate provision of education for Deaf children in residential schools and therefore for the survival of the culture itself.

---

[51] Ibid., p. 41.

[52] George Taylor, 'Deaf People, Ethnic Minorities and Social Policy' in Gregory and Hartley (eds), *Constructing Deafness*, p. 243.

[53] Lee (ed.), *Writings from deaf liberation*, p. ix. More recently Ladd has suggested that 'Deafhood' might be a suitable replacement for 'deafness' in distinguishing between cultural and audiological understandings of what it means to be d/Deaf. Ladd, *In search of Deafhood*, p. 44.

Ladd uses Gramsci's definition of culture as an organization of the inner self of a person, which aids that person to understand their own history, value, function in life, rights and obligations. He concludes that the concept of Deaf culture is not only a self-construction of Deaf people, but can also be validated in a wider, academic sense. Deaf culture is 'a socially complex community with its own beliefs, norms and values which can be traced through historical time'.[54] Deaf culture can most easily be understood as a minority culture; or in other words, a culture that exists within a bipolar and oppositional framework and has to deal with issues of resistance and compliance to the majority culture.

Understanding Deaf Experience: Colonialism

This disempowering of Deaf people through the destruction of the Deaf self-construction can be compared with the colonization experienced by most non-European continents under the empire building policies of the European nations from the sixteenth century onwards. Colonization can be defined as a process of physical subjugation, imposition of an alien language, culture and mores and the regulation of education on behalf of colonial goals.[55] Harlan Lane compares the experience of Deaf people with that of the people of Burundi when that country was taken over by Belgium. Burundi had an elaborate and efficient system of government in place, but the Belgians chose to represent it as a medieval, feudal system and the people of Burundi were perceived as children in need of guidance and control. The Belgians established schools to teach the Burundians to speak French so they could have native tax collectors who could communicate with the wider government. Similarly, Deaf people can be argued to have had a society with its own structures and values that was ignored by hearing people who saw them as people in need of guidance, control and 'civilization' and who needed to be taught the language of the dominant majority to be able to function. I would contend that this argument slightly over-idealizes what the *DEAF-WORLD* was like in any country; the relationship between Deaf people and the society around them is more complex than the relationship between a self-sufficient society and its conquerors. Nonetheless, colonialism is a valuable parallel to use in a discussion of this construction of what it means to be Deaf.

The Cultural Model in Action: BSL and Community

One of the questions raised by the cultural model is the question 'who is Deaf?' or, in other words, who is culturally Deaf, who 'belongs' to the Deaf community? This question is actually a recent one, created by the dominance of the medical model and the structures of colonialism, since historically it was quite clear who was Deaf and who was not. Before the development of hearing aids and the making of

---

[54]   Ladd, *In search of Deafhood*, p. 216.
[55]   Lane, *The mask of benevolence*, p. 31.

educational decisions according to arbitrary audiological categories, all d/Deaf children spent at least part of their education at residential schools for the d/Deaf. This was probably the single most important factor in the formation of a Deaf 'community' or group of Deaf people who constructed themselves as culturally different.[56] Even during the heyday of oralism in schools, these Deaf children still learnt to communicate in sign and to identify with each other rather than seeing themselves as isolated in a hearing world. When they left school, they would often marry another Deaf person[57] and continue to socialize with Deaf people in the Deaf club or Deaf mission and develop their sign and sense of themselves as part of a different group. For example, today there are many elderly members of Deaf clubs, who with the advent of hearing aids became defined as 'hard of hearing' (by the medical establishment) and are able to hear and understand sounds quite well. However, as children, before the development of electronic hearing aids, they were educated at a Deaf school and so their first language is still sign language, their social life still centred on the Deaf club and they identify more strongly with Deaf people than they do with other 'hard of hearing' elderly people; 'audiologically they are not deaf; socially they are'.[58]

Attempts to define who is 'Deaf' have led to controversy over the exact role of sign language (ASL in the USA and BSL in the UK) in defining who is part of the Deaf community. At one extreme Lillian Lawson has argued that only native[59] signers are truly members of the Deaf community; all others are on the fringe.[60] A broader understanding includes the use of sign language as only one factor (although a very significant one) in what it means to be Deaf. Other factors include the possession of an audiological impairment (and the shared experience of navigating the hearing world), participation in Deaf community activities and an identification with the Deaf world which results, for example, in Deaf people relating to each other across the usual barriers of religion, class and nationality.[61]

While I would not argue with the primacy of BSL in the definition of the Deaf community or with the fact that those of us who learn sign as adults will never have the mastery of the language or the instinctive understanding of Deaf culture of those who learnt it as small children, I do not find too narrow a definition of who is a member of the 'Deaf community' to be helpful. As more and more young

---

[56] Ladd, *In search of Deafhood*, p. 30.

[57] J. Schein, in *At home among strangers* (Washington DC: Gallaudet University Press, 1989), states that in the USA 90 per cent of Deaf people who get married, marry another Deaf person. The UK seems to show a similar pattern.

[58] Paul C. Higgins, *Outsiders in a hearing world: a sociology of deafness* (Beverly Hills and London, 1980), p. 44.

[59] Deaf children of Deaf parents and those who learnt to sign very young at residential school.

[60] Lillian Lawson, 'The role of sign in the structure of the Deaf Community' in Gregory and Hartley (eds), *Constructing Deafness*, p. 32.

[61] For example Higgins, *Outsiders in a Hearing World*, p. 38, Kyle and Woll, *Sign Language: deaf people and their language*, p. 8.

deaf people are educated in mainstream schools and learn to sign as an adult, becoming effectively bilingual, the understanding of who is 'Deaf' will need to have the resilience of flexibility if it is not to become an outdated concept as the old, monolingual Deaf community dies.

In addition to its focus around BSL, another key feature of Deaf culture, as identified by Ladd, is its collectivity. He suggests that the sign concepts of *WE*, *DEAF* and *ALL* are inextricably linked to each other, and also that the consistent focus of Deaf activism on education in BSL (and the consequent survival of Deaf culture in the future) rather than better jobs or TV programmes for themselves supports the theory that Deaf culture is a collective, rather than individualistic culture.[62] This collectivity, in a society where the family unit and the individual are usually considered as primary relates to the fact that for many Deaf people, the Deaf community is more significant for their personal and social development than their family. Ladd's research has showed that Deaf primary relationships are described by his Deaf interviewees as akin to or even replacing the birth family relationship.[63] In a Bible study at a National Deaf Church Conference (NDCC) in 2000, when asked if they ever got 'homesick', most of the Deaf people there responded that they never got homesick, but they did get 'schoolsick' in the holidays when away from the Deaf community of the residential schools. The collectivity of the Deaf community is not just an abstract theory; along with BSL it is vital in creating an alternative identity for Deaf people that helps them to survive in a hostile world.

A Model Under Threat? The Future of the Deaf Community

The resurgence of Deaf pride in Deaf culture is under threat. Most d/Deaf young people now are educated in mainstream schools, usually with barely adequate support. They are not taught sign language or encouraged to have any contact with the Deaf community. Often they are operated on and fitted with cochlear implants without their consent. This may give them some sense of hearing and assist in learning speech, but it further increases the focus on making the individual child fit in with society rather than teaching the child that a supportive, positive, alternative perception of the world exists. There is a threat that in future the Deaf community (or at least the genetic *DEAF-OF-DEAF* core which is essential to its survival) may be totally eradicated through genetic engineering.[64] The location of socialization into the Deaf community for many has now moved much later in life. For many deaf young people, going to a university, such as Wolverhampton, which has a large d/Deaf student community, is one way of learning about alternatives to the individual medical model. For others, seeing sign language on TV and desiring to learn it and going along to the Deaf club once they reach some level of

---

[62]   Ladd, *In search of Deafhood*, p. 442.

[63]   Ibid., p. 298.

[64]   Ladd, *Understanding Deaf Culture*, p. 456.

independence is another way in. However, this is a rather ad hoc method of learning about alternative constructions, and it means many deaf young people slip through the net. It also means that many more deaf people are going through their teenage and identity formation years isolated from people with similar experiences, convinced they are permanently second best, always trying to catch up and be like their hearing contemporaries.

The focus on mainstream education, and the consequent closing of Deaf residential schools has created whole generations of young d/Deaf people who are not fully, culturally Deaf in the above sense, having joined the community as young adults and who also grew up less isolated from the hearing world due to improved access to television programmes and other aspects of the hearing world.[65] However, new forms of Deaf community are emerging as technology changes, and which show features in common with traditional Deaf community contexts as well as significant differences. One example of this new form of Deaf community is on the internet with the formation of the 'e-group' Deaf-UK and its subsidiaries.[66] This group consists of over 1,000 members, and while hearing people are welcome to join, is very definitely 'Deaf space'. In other words, it is considered a safe space in which d/Deaf people can unload their frustrations and feelings about the hearing world without any patronizing comeback. It is also a forum for information sharing and dissemination, and debate about the many issues that affect Deaf people and their lives. In this way it takes the Deaf club culture, where Deaf people meet to share information as well as to socialize, out into a wider context. One thing that I find interesting about it is that although the Deaf people on it have access to the internet, and therefore the information available on it, for many Deaf people, their first port of call for information and questions about various issues, not just Deaf related ones, is Deaf-UK.[67] This suggests to me that some traditional Deaf cultural values, for example, collectivity are manifested on the internet; finding out information is not just about access and finding someone who is bilingual to translate the information provided, but also about trust and a high value placed on personal experience. Even in today's information-accessible

---

[65] This is quite a significant improvement from the point of view of Deaf teenagers in oral situations given the importance of TV in the majority culture. I grew up before subtitles became common and so I was very isolated from the hearing world as well as being separated from the Deaf world, an isolation which is less profound for d/Deaf young people in the majority culture today.

[66] An 'e-group' is a system whereby one email sent to the group is forwarded, automatically, to all the group members, thus providing an easily accessible forum for discussion. Deaf-UK can be found on <http://groups.yahoo.com/group/deaf-uk/> or for information about it and links to it on <http://www.deaf-uk.org.uk/>.

[67] For example message no. 18778 posted on 24 April 2003 is a request for advice and information about the SARS virus in Canada. Follow-up messages directed the enquirer to the Foreign Office website, the Department of Health minicom line and other sources of information, but all the information found out by anyone was brought back to Deaf-UK and shared with everyone.

world Deaf people are more likely to trust and value information obtained from other Deaf people and discussed with other Deaf people.[68] Deaf-UK is also introducing d/Deaf young people, educated in mainstream schools, to the idea of Deaf culture and Deaf history and traditions. It may not be able to replace Deaf residential schools as the core of Deaf culture, but it certainly is doing a good job in helping Deaf culture to survive until such a time as we can achieve our dream of bilingual, bicultural upbringing for all d/Deaf children.

Another interesting feature about Deaf-UK in particular, and the culture of Deaf young people in general, is the features it shows in common with the hearing world, such as the use of English (although some contributions are in 'BSL English', that is English words in BSL order). As I said above, Deaf young people have a far greater access to aspects of the hearing world than even ten years ago; this is creating a generation of Deaf people more open to and influenced by hearing culture and mores. Ladd welcomes this creation of multiple identities, but fears that without a strong tradition of their own, minority, history and culture, such multiple identities will simply be assimilated into the majority culture.[69] This situation is comparable to that of many young Asian and black people living in the UK today. They too are trying to put together their histories, traditions and cultures with western values in the world around them, and their parents fear that this means the end of their traditional way of life. Paul Gilroy suggests that the identities and culture of people caught up in a 'diaspora',[70] instead of being understood as 'pure cultures' contaminated by new influences, should rather be seen, in their own right, as complex, compound formations. This is a concept that needs far more exploration in the Deaf world; it is too soon to assess how far the culture of Deaf young people is a Creole rather than an assimilated culture, but it does suggest that the present reality of young Deaf people educated in mainstream schools does not necessarily mean the end of Deaf culture. Like all cultures, Deaf culture will change and the challenge to the cultural model is to include sufficient elasticity in its formulation so as to be able to incorporate such changes in its framework.

Assessment: The Debate Between the Social and the Cultural Models

The social and the cultural models challenge the medical model by creating valid and valuable alternative identity for Deaf people and a way for them to understand

---

[68] This was brought home to me recently in a personal way. Having become pregnant, people keep telling me to make friends with other pregnant mums for mutual support and information; however my instinctive preference, even as a fully bilingual Deaf woman, is to make contact with other Deaf mums via the Deaf parenting project, available through the internet.

[69] Ladd, *Understanding Deaf Culture*, p. 446.

[70] Understood as a movement away from the origins – either geographically as for Asian and black people, or culturally as for Deaf people.

their experience in more positive terms and thus release the possibility of transformation and liberation of self.

The social model alone has been judged inadequate to describe and analyse the experience of Deaf people, the Deaf community and their needs from society. Its fundamental focus on full integration and access as the definition of liberation does continue to oppress Deaf people who need a fully functioning Deaf community and language to experience full liberation. However, I would suggest that this model contains insights that are helpful to d/Deaf people struggling for liberation, and that, from the point of view of liberation theology and its relationship with secular tools, it is more useful to keep it in mind as a balance to and critique of the cultural model than to reject it out of hand.

As far as the cultural model goes, I would go as far as to say that learning to see self as part of a wider Deaf community, as in the cultural model, rather than as an individual with a medical problem, can be described as an experience of liberation and 'healing'. It has been of incalculable value over the years in providing for Deaf people a basis for a sense of self-esteem, a positive Deaf identity[71] and a focus of resistance against the oppressive worldview of the medical model.[72] However it is open to criticism on several grounds from a Christian, liberation theology perspective. Firstly, there is the issue that not all deaf people identify with this model, which raises a question from a liberation perspective what is the effect on deaf people who are not 'in'? How are they to experience personal liberation? This model can be assessed as being rather exclusive in its definition and focus on Deaf rather than all d/Deaf people. And given the emphasis of Deaf culture on BSL from childhood as being a major qualifier of who is 'in', what is the impact on deaf young people trying to join the community as a way of trying to find a liberating identity? If they 'choose' to be 'Deaf', despite very imperfect sign language and are then rejected or marginalized by the community of choice, they can be left with even greater feelings of negativity and low self-esteem and may never return to the Deaf community to improve their sign.[73] This is why I feel that a Deaf Liberation Theology can usefully engage with the social model in addition to the cultural model as being more immediately accessible to some deaf people.

One of the potential dangers of the cultural model alone is that it is perfectly possible for a society to accept sign language as a true language and the idea of Deaf culture and continue to oppress Deaf people. This is one of the reasons for the survival of Deaf culture over the last 120 years; when necessary, Deaf people could withdraw from the majority culture so they did not risk a challenge that may have threatened the existence of their culture. The Deaf church is a clear example of an organization that accepts sign language and Deaf culture and continues to oppress d/Deaf people in different ways. This relationship between the *DEAF-WORLD* and

---

[71] David Brien, 'Is there a Deaf Culture', (first presented 1981) in Gregory and Hartley (eds), *Constructing Deafness*, p. 50.

[72] Ladd, *In search of Deafhood*, p. 39.

[73] Corker, *Deaf and Disabled or Deafness Disabled?*, p. 30.

the hearing world can be compared to 1960s USA, when 'white liberals' enthusiastically supported civil rights for black people, but only as long as it did not mean they had to make any changes in the way they lived their lives. When Martin Luther King Jr began talking about poverty and the need for economic equality, which might entail white Americans losing their economically privileged status, they backed off from their support.[74] In a similar way, 'hearing liberals' can all too often affirm Deaf culture and sign language until it begins to encroach too closely on their own lives and they are asked to change or to give up something and then proceed to argue for the need to educate individuals about d/Deaf people to encourage change in the future.

Ladd suggests that this a weakness of Deaf culture, rather than the cultural model in itself. In his argument, it is impossible to fully understand and accept the cultural model, with its emphasis on reforming education and rejection of hearing control and continue to oppress Deaf people through the medical model.[75] While accepting this point, I would argue that Deaf Liberation Theology still needs the individualism of the social model to balance the focus of the cultural model on sustaining a strong Deaf community as its main objective. As I argued in Chapter 1, liberation theology is not, ultimately, about creating a utopia, whether Deaf or hearing; it is about working towards an ultimate kingdom of God in which all people, individually and collectively, are liberated to reach their full potential in whatever way that might be.

I described the cultural and social models as being complementary; neither one is sufficient alone for d/Deaf people in liberation terms but together they work towards the realization of the kingdom of God. Both models link our fight to change society with the fight of women and black people and poor people and all others fighting to eliminate the structures and power relationships that lead to oppression. The specific issues we face may be different, but the effects of internalized oppression on individuals and communities are the same. The cultural model, historically and experientially, is so fundamental to alternative constructions of what it means to be Deaf that it is not possible to operate without reference to it, and it is balanced by the individualism and differing political focus of the social model. From the point of view of theology, models are not ends in themselves, but tools to be used in the struggle for liberation at every level. Deaf Liberation Theology is not *about* d/Deaf people, however they are constructed; it is *for* all d/Deaf people, all people whose primary way of relating to the world is visual and who experience oppression and are seeking liberation and the ultimate reality of the kingdom of God.

---

[74] James H. Cone, *Martin & Malcolm & America: a dream or a nightmare* (London: Fount, 1993), p. 232.
[75] Ladd, personal communication.

Chapter 3

DEAF-CHURCH:
A History of Deaf People and the Church

The sign language term *DEAF-CHURCH* refers to between 100 and 125 congregations, in every area of the UK, where the main language in which worship is conducted is BSL or SSE[1] and the majority of the congregation would identify themselves as Deaf. Nowadays most of these congregations are attached to the Church of England in some form or another, usually by being under the care of a full- or part-time diocesan[2] chaplain. The Roman Catholic Church also has congregations of sign language using Deaf people who meet separately from English-speaking hearing congregations. Outside of this framework there are interpreted or 'integrated'[3] services in various denominations and Deaf house-groups or Christian fellowships meeting in a variety of areas. It is difficult to assess the significance of these groups in the construction of the *DEAF-WORLD* because, by their nature, they tend to be episodic (meeting for as long as the group holds together) and do not have much in the way of historical records. While I am hopeful that Deaf Liberation Theology will be of relevance for all people who identify themselves as Deaf and Christian, this chapter will focus on the established[4] *DEAF-CHURCH* as having played a significant role in the construction of the *DEAF-WORLD* and what it means to be Deaf in the UK.

Within these parameters, the congregations that make up the *DEAF-CHURCH* are very varied. Some of these congregations meet in purpose-built churches or chapels, usually attached to the *DEAF-CLUB*, or a multi-purpose room within the club; others meet in Anglican churches at a different time to the English-speaking congregation. Some congregations meet weekly, others fortnightly and others monthly or even less frequently. Worship might be on a Sunday afternoon or on a

---

[1]   Sign Supported English; this is a hybrid form of sign language that uses the signs from British Sign Language in the English word order. The problems related to the use of SSE will be discussed elsewhere.

[2]   The diocese is the basic administrative unit of the Church of England. It is an area the size of a county, or sometimes larger, with at least one bishop, based at a cathedral, who oversees all the activities of the individual churches and clergy in the area.

[3]   Mixed d/Deaf and hearing congregations with a service usually in English with a sign language interpreter providing a translation into BSL.

[4]   The state churches in each country of the UK, for example, the Church of England (which is Anglican) and the Church of Scotland (which is Presbyterian).

midweek evening. There are varying types of services, some with Communion and some without. In some dioceses, chaplains conduct all the services, in others, lay ministers and readers[5] take all or part of a service. Some congregations meet simply for worship and fellowship, others provide discipleship opportunities such as Bible-study groups or other activities in between services. The chaplain, with the help of readers and lay ministers, will act as 'pastor' to the d/Deaf people in their congregation, visiting them when they are sick or in other times of need and is usually the link with the hearing church via the diocesan structures. Some dioceses have a council or committee for ministry among Deaf people which co-ordinates the activity of the *DEAF-CHURCH* in that area, while in others, the chaplain works alone. At a national level, there has existed since 1927 a formal link with the nationwide structures of the Church of England through what is now called the Committee for Ministry among Deaf and Disabled People or CMDDP. There also exists an organization called Deaf Anglicans Together (prior to 2005 this was known as the National Deaf Church Conference), a Deaf-controlled group which provides regular national gatherings for fellowship, worship and learning.

The Origins of the *DEAF-CHURCH*: A Traditional Account

Nowhere in the history of the Deaf church is the influence of the two major models (medical and cultural) of what it means to be Deaf, more clearly seen than in descriptions of how the *DEAF-CHURCH* originated. *The Church Among Deaf People* has a number of paragraphs locating the origins of the present-day congregations in the missionary and philanthropic activities of nineteenth-century Victorians. For example, it states 'deaf community groups ... were largely based around ... "Missions" ... originating in the early nineteenth-century church activity, trying to take the Gospel to those who could not hear it'.[6] This report briefly details the origins of two area organizations, the 'Leicester and County Mission for the Deaf' in the 1890s and what is now the Royal Association for the Deaf (RAD) in 1841. It mentions that Deaf school-leavers came together to maintain the faith they had learnt in their residential schools, but does not name any of them and gives the impression that these groups did not develop until 'wealthy hearing people' and 'a hearing clergyman named Revd Samuel Smith' became involved. The report goes on to say:

> similar stories can be told about many towns in this county. The Victorian outreach to
> the poor and deprived in society was touched by the obvious needs and deprivation of

---

[5]   Readers are licensed by the bishop of the diocese to preach and lead worship. Other lay ministers may or may not be so licensed, and are usually more informally trained, if at all. The two terms are often used interchangeably.

[6]   *The Church Among Deaf People* (London, 1997), p. 8.

deaf people, and the newly educated Deaf school-leavers wanted to express themselves in faith and life with other deaf people.[7]

This view of the origins of the *DEAF-CHURCH* as being largely due to the initiative of hearing people is often found within the Deaf churches themselves. Many Deaf people believe, rightly or wrongly, that their own church was started by hearing people or a hearing person.

These assumptions about the origins of the *DEAF-CHURCH* reflect a 'medical' view of the origins as held by many hearing chaplains and internalized by the Deaf people in the church. By this, I mean that Deaf people are presented in this understanding of the origins of the Deaf church as passive recipients of the philanthropy of hearing people and as semi-savage individuals who could not be followers of Christ until they had been taught or, in other words, 'saved' by hearing people and their 'civilization' or way of seeing the world.

It is undeniable that this is how some of the hearing people involved in the early days of the *DEAF-CHURCH* saw themselves. For example, Revd Samuel Smith, who was appointed missioner to RAD in 1855 and became its first chaplain in 1861, refers to the uneducated deaf and dumb as savages, atheists and heathens. Even once they have attended school, learnt language [that is English] and had some scriptural teaching they are still not 'advanced' enough to attend church and read religious books themselves. It is absolutely necessary that special provision be made (presumably by hearing people) for their religious instruction and worship.[8] In 1916, the Convocation of Canterbury (the forerunner of the General Synod)[9] appointed a committee to enquire into current provisions for the spiritual care of deaf mutes and suggest further developments needed. Their first report calls on evidence from missioners, bishops and the Council of Church Missioners to the Deaf and Dumb to briefly survey the story so far.[10] This report, alone of all the discussions of origins, locates the first mission in Leeds in 1839 with a non-denominational Sunday service held by James Cook, previously a teacher of the deaf. Other mentions of the Leeds mission places its origin in 1854 with either

---

[7]   Ibid., p. 12.

[8]   Smith, *The Deaf and Dumb: Their deprivation and its consequences* (London, 1864).

[9]   The Church of England is divided, for administrative and oversight purposes, into two provinces: Canterbury (constituting of the dioceses in the south and the Midlands) and York (which consists of all the northern dioceses). Until the formation of the General Assembly in *c.* 1918 there was no committee covering the whole of England.

[10]   Committee for the Spiritual Care of Deaf Mutes, *The Spiritual Care of Deaf Mutes*, Report presented to the Convocation of Canterbury, lower house, 499 (1916).

Revd Edward Jackson[11] or James Cook[12] and a later consolidation by James Herriot. This report does acknowledge the involvement of 'the deaf themselves' in starting missions in various areas, but names only one of them (Davis who began the Stoke-on-Trent mission in 1868) and appears to favour the idea that most missions were initiated by teachers (with the implication that they were hearing) from schools for the deaf. This also suggests that the Deaf themselves were passive recipients of the charity of hearing people who took pity on their isolation from 'ordinary spiritual ministrations'.[13] This view is also presented in the 1917 report to the Convocation of York: 'mission work among the adult deaf and dumb ... some owe origin to headmasters of institutes [schools], others to the efforts of individuals who were keenly interested in work among the deaf and dumb'.[14]

George Firth explains statements such as this by reference to the context of the time when 'the preaching of the Gospel was the prime duty of an organization for the Deaf on the principle that religion is good for women, children and the unfortunate'.[15] His view of the origins of the *DEAF-CHURCH* seems to be firmly in the medical model: 'the majority [of Deaf people] owe a real debt of gratitude to these people [those who have had the welfare of Deaf people at heart] who have worked day and night for the sake of deaf people'.[16] Interestingly enough, this introduction to his collection of biographies about notable characters in the *DEAF-CHURCH* suggests that all those actively involved in its formation were hearing; yet the actual text of the biographies includes those of many active Deaf missioners. However, partly due to the sources he uses (letters from and interviews with elderly people, Deaf and hearing, involved with the *DEAF-CHURCH*) he does not really cover the earliest period in the life of the *DEAF-CHURCH* and so he seems to assume the Deaf missioners were all educated in the missions started by hearing people and then were able to minister to other Deaf. Kenneth Lysons, a social worker exploring the development of welfare services for deaf people up to the 1960s, presents a similar view on the origin of the missions to the deaf and dumb. He sees the development of mission work as involving both the congregating of Deaf persons drawn together by a desire to meet with others in like conditions and the intervention of an individual motivated by a mixture of compassion, evangelistic zeal and/or charitable concern, who endeavoured to

---

[11]   Committee for the Spiritual Care of Deaf Mutes, *The Spiritual Care of the Deaf and Dumb*, Report presented to the Convocation of York, 313 (1917), Peter W. Jackson, *Britain's Deaf Heritage* (Edinburgh, 1990), p. 73.

[12]   Clifford Kenneth Lysons, *Voluntary Welfare Societies for Adult Deaf Persons in England, 1840–1963* (Liverpool, 1965), p. 57, Peter W. Jackson and Raymond Lee (eds), *Deaf Lives: Deaf people in history* (Feltham, 2001), p. 97.

[13]   Committee for the Spiritual Care of Deaf Mutes, *Spiritual Care of Deaf Mutes*.

[14]   Committee for the Spiritual Care of Deaf Mutes, *Spiritual Care of the Deaf and Dumb*.

[15]   George C. Firth, *Chosen Vessels* (Exeter, 1988), p. 138.

[16]   Ibid., p. 4.

obtain premises for religious/social purposes.[17] Like Firth and others, Lysons appears to be suggesting that Deaf people needed the involvement of philanthropic hearing people to get the missions off the ground.

The Origins of the *DEAF-CHURCH*: An Alternative Perspective

The history of Deaf people by Deaf people (the cultural model view of history) however has a different theory for the origin of the missions. Dimmock, for example, writes that the missions were founded by the Deaf themselves in the mid-nineteenth century by 'Deaf individuals possessing superior education and financial means'.[18] Peter Jackson, in *Britain's Deaf Heritage* and *Deaf Lives*, shares this perspective. Although there are earlier records of prayer meetings open to adults at Deaf schools,[19] the first adult Deaf congregation met in Edinburgh on 13 June 1830.[20] This gathering arose out of a group of Deaf people deciding they needed a meeting place for prayers and social contact. Four Deaf men, Matthew Robert Burns, Alexander Blackwood, Joseph Turner[21] and Walter Geikie,[22] are all credited as the co-founders of this group in a small room in Lady Stairs Close.[23]

The success of this congregation in Edinburgh appears to have been a factor in the formation of the first of the English missions in London, now known as RAD.[24] A group of unnamed Deaf graduates of the Bermondsey School met together in 1840 or 1841 and founded the Adult Institute for the Deaf and Dumb (AIDD). This was a residential institution for deaf men (women were not admitted until 1845) that had the dual purpose of providing employment/training as required and also 'to adopt suitable measures by which the deaf and dumb may have the benefit of religious instruction and be brought to a sound knowledge of the gospels'.[25] A man named George Crouch (the hearing father of five deaf children) was involved in the formation of this institute, and also a 'young man from Edinburgh who had attended services there conducted by Mr Blackwood'.[26] Selwyn Oxley, in an historical pageant written in 1928, names this 'young man from Edinburgh' as Matthew Robert Burns,[27] but this is unlikely. According to Jackson and Lee, Burns did not move south from Scotland until 1841 when he was appointed headmaster

---

[17]   Lysons, *Voluntary Welfare Societies*, p. 31.
[18]   Dimmock, *Cruel Legacy*, p. 51.
[19]   Jackson, *Britain's Deaf Heritage*, p. 69.
[20]   Jackson and Lee (eds), *Deaf Lives*, p. 33.
[21]   The first Deaf teacher in Scotland.
[22]   Deaf artist and member of the Scottish Academy.
[23]   Jackson and Lee (eds), *Deaf Lives*, pp. 23, 33 and 72.
[24]   Royal Association for the Deaf.
[25]   Lysons, *Voluntary Welfare Societies*, p. 32.
[26]   Ibid., p. 32.
[27]   Selwyn Oxley, *A pageant entitled 'The deaf of other days': in twelve episodes* (London, 1928).

of the newly formed Bristol Institution for the Deaf and Dumb.[28] However, Burns was certainly working for the AIDD, after leaving Bristol, for a year from 1844. After this Burns was appointed assistant secretary and biblical instructor to a mission based in Shaftsbury Hall and run by a hearing minister, Robert Simson or Simpson, from the Scottish Hospital.[29] Initially, Burns did not get much opportunity to preach, but in 1849 he was made honorary secretary and paid instructor and became well known as a preacher and a founder (along with other Deaf men including John Jennings) of the Society for the Propagation of the Gospel among the Deaf and Dumb.

One possible reason for Burns's separation from the AIDD is hinted at by George Firth. He suggests that Burns was strongly evangelical and disapproved of the use of the Church of England Book of Common Prayer by the AIDD. Evangelicals were a major cross-denominational religious movement in the mid-nineteenth century: 'throughout the mid-Victorian age, the evangelical movement was the strongest religious force in British life'.[30] Evangelicalism was a way of faith for people who wanted to think about God for themselves, people who no longer wished to accept the 'state religion' as given, but who passionately believed in spreading the benefits of Jesus Christ to as many people as possible. It was an empowering faith in its focus on the responsibility of an individual to actively read the Bible for themselves (rather than simply listen to whatever was read in church) and on Christianity as an individual response to the Gospel (rather than simply going along with the rules of church membership). It is a movement that can be likened to the Civil Rights movement of the 1960s in its energy and creativity, a time when new ideas abounded and people from all strata of society had the option to decide between maintaining the status quo and thinking for themselves. It is hardly surprising, in the religious ferment of the times, that an educated, articulate man such as Burns was passionately interested in issues of faith and wanted to share it with his Deaf brothers and sisters in their own form of communication.[31]

For reasons unrecorded, but quite possibly economic, the Society for the Propagation of the Gospel among the Deaf and Dumb reunited with the AIDD in 1864. By this time, the AIDD had shut down its residential facilities, reformed itself as primarily religious in its purposes (although with a brief to provide 'advice and friendly aid' to any deaf person in need), renamed itself the Association in Aid of Deaf and Dumb (AADD), begun to raise funds to build its own church building and appointed a hearing man, an ex-teacher of the deaf, Samuel Smith, first as

---

[28]   Jackson and Lee (eds), *Deaf Lives*, p. 34.

[29]   Jackson and Lee (eds), *Deaf Lives*; p. 34, Lysons, *Voluntary Welfare Societies*, p. 38.

[30]   Owen Chadwick, *The Victorian Church*. Part 1 (London, 1966), p. 4.

[31]   It is worth noting that Lysons also records the Deaf church as being inspired by the evangelical revival; however, in line with his general medical view, he attributes the evangelical fervour and philosophical ideals purely to hearing clergy involved with the Deaf church. Lysons, *Voluntary Welfare Societies*, p. 180.

missionary and then chaplain in 1861 after his ordination by the Bishop of London.[32]

Burns retired in 1866 having had a great deal of influence on the earliest stages of the *DEAF-CHURCH* in both Scotland and England. His preaching and encouragement seems to have inspired at least three other Deaf men, John Jennings, Edward Rowland and James Herriot, to undertake mission work among their Deaf brothers and sisters in south London,[33] south Wales[34] and Manchester.

James Herriot is another giant character in the early days of the *DEAF-CHURCH*. Seventeen years younger than Burns, he and his wife Isabella were among the first members of the Edinburgh Deaf and Dumb congregation in 1830. A tailor by trade, he moved to Salford, near Manchester, in 1843 to try to improve the prospects of his firm, which had been badly affected by the recession. Half of his employees were Deaf and his shop soon became a focus for the adult Deaf in the area. This led Herriot, also from a Scottish nonconformist background and possibly inspired by the same evangelical fervour that so affected Burns, in 1846 to approach a local Presbyterian minister and ask for the use of a room in his church for the newly formed Manchester and Salford Adult Deaf and Dumb Benevolent Association with Herriot as preacher. After two years at the Presbyterian church internal politics meant the fast-growing society had to leave the premises. Herriot approached the Bishop of Manchester to help provide a meeting place, but he was unable to help due to the non-denominational nature of the society so Herriot renovated a room in his own business as a chapel for services to continue for three years until he raised enough funds to rent separate rooms in Manchester city centre.[35] Herriot was so successful in raising funds that the local school (the Manchester Institution for the Deaf and Dumb), also reliant on local subscribers, felt threatened and founded a rival, Church of England organization[36] for graduates of the school with the aim of trying to put Herriot out of business. Herriot's Manchester and Salford Adult Deaf and Dumb Benevolent Association had an all-Deaf management committee whereas the school's association (which became the Manchester Adult Deaf and Dumb Institute) was run by a hearing committee.[37] An all-Deaf management committee was almost unheard of at that time, but Herriot was a fervent believer in the self-help potential of Deaf people; from his point of

---

[32]   Ibid., p. 40.

[33]   Jennings, despite his own poverty, worked among poor Deaf people for a long time, eventually founding the South London Mission to the Deaf and Dumb in 1882. Jackson and Lee (eds), *Deaf Lives*, p. 106.

[34]   Edward Rowland, after being invited to preach by Burns, felt called to missionary work among the Deaf and dumb moved to south Wales and initiated the Glamorgan Mission to the Deaf and Dumb in Cardiff in 1869. Jackson and Lee (eds), *Deaf Lives*, p. 158.

[35]   Jackson and Lee (eds), *Deaf Lives*, p. 96.

[36]   Originally known as the Manchester Society for Promoting the Spiritual and Temporal Welfare of Adult Deaf and Dumb. Lysons, *Voluntary Welfare Societies*, p. 47.

[37]   Jackson and Lee (eds), *Deaf Lives*, p. 97 and Lysons *Voluntary Welfare Societies*, p. 49.

view, Deaf organizations were for mutual benevolence, for Deaf people to raise money to help each other with employment, welfare and religion.[38]

Herriot's ideal of the Deaf organizations as non-denominational mutual benevolence societies (where every member contributed something and received something) can be compared with the initial ideals of missionary societies in Africa and Asia. David Bosch speaks of the motif of love in early evangelicalism, when all people were seen as brothers and sisters, because all were children of God and objects of the love of Christ.[39] Wolffe identifies the ideal of sharing of possessions as practised in the early Jerusalem Church as being a feature of early evangelicalism as advocated, for example, by John Wesley.[40] These ideals proved too impractical to implement, but the link between religious revival and social and cultural transformation continued into the early nineteenth century and was very possibly the inspiration for Herriot's ideal of the equality of Deaf and hearing people and the need for mutual benevolence. Herriot was influential in the consequent origin and consolidation of benevolent societies and missions in most of the northern industrial cities (except the rest of the Manchester societies such as Bolton and Oldham, which went to the rival Manchester Institution for people to conduct services, possibly because their members were graduates of the school and had been discouraged from approaching Herriot by the headteacher Andrew Patterson and his colleague William Stainer).[41] Liverpool Deaf and Dumb Benevolent Society was established by a Deaf man, George Healey in 1864, with help from Herriot. A teacher, James Cook, had started services at Leeds but Herriot consolidated the gathering of Deaf people into a society. He was also involved in the early days of the Halifax, Huddersfield and Bradford societies throughout the 1860s and 1870s.[42]

The influence of what can be called the Edinburgh evangelical movement in the *DEAF-WORLD* was strong, but there were other Deaf men, seemingly unconnected with this group who founded missions to spread the news of the Gospel among their Deaf contemporaries. William A. Griffiths campaigned for seven years in Birmingham to find a suitable venue for services for Deaf people. He studied late into the night to improve his English so he could write letters to local newspapers. Eventually, in 1867 his persistence paid off and he found a room in a local Baptist church for prayer meetings and services for the Birmingham

---

[38]   Jackson and Lee (eds), *Deaf Lives*, p. 97.

[39]   David J. Bosch, *Transforming Mission: paradigm shifts in the theology of mission* (Maryknoll, NY, 1993), p. 288.

[40]   John Wolffe (ed.), *Evangelical faith and public zeal: evangelicals and society in Britain 1780–1980* (London, 1995), p. 8.

[41]   Lysons, *Voluntary Welfare Societies*, pp. 57 and 59. See also Len Scarff, *A brief history of the Bolton Deaf Church and the involvement of Church of England priests and others, in religious services to deaf people in the Bolton Deaf Society area.* Personal communication.

[42]   Lysons, *Voluntary Welfare Societies*, p. 54; Jackson and Lee (eds), *Deaf Lives*, p. 97.

Deaf.[43] In 1870 or 1872 Birmingham Town Mission, hearing of his work, established a special branch for the Deaf and appointed Griffiths as full-time missioner on a salary much smaller than he was already receiving as a brass-chaser.[44] Griffiths continued working with Deaf people in Birmingham until his retirement in 1917, overseeing the change from being a branch of Birmingham Town Mission to an independent society for the adult deaf and dumb in 1906. On his retirement, after 50 years of service, a memorial to him was erected in the chapel of the Deaf club. When new premises were erected in 1986, the memorial was moved into the new chapel. Nowadays, none of the members of the Birmingham Deaf church know anything about Griffiths other than his name.

Stoke-on-Trent Deaf church is another that owes its origin to a Deaf man who gave up a trade to preach the Gospel to his Deaf brothers and sisters. Charles Davis was a cobbler with his own shop; like Herriot, he employed several Deaf men and his shop developed into a meeting place for local adult Deaf. Davis is said to have been active in 'seeking out his "afflicted brethren", teaching them signs and finger spelling and leading them in prayer to a knowledge of Christ'.[45] In 1868, with the support of local notables he started what became the North Staffordshire Mission in Stoke-on-Trent with himself as a full-time missioner.[46] We do not know if either Griffiths or Davis were regarded as evangelicals, but Davis is reported to have 'preached and expounded on a chapter [of the Bible] rather than the prayer book',[47] which certainly suggests that he is influenced by the non-denominational evangelicals and Birmingham Town Mission is likely to have been evangelical in its inspiration.

Thus, by the time of the great turning point of the Milan Conference in 1880, there were approximately 16 adult missions to the deaf and dumb in England and Wales and five more in Scotland. Of the 16 missions in England and Wales, the 'Edinburgh evangelical group' appears to have directly influenced nine, with two more founded by Deaf men with demonstrable evangelical inspiration. Three missions were founded by a school (the Manchester Institute) with at least one of those from the initiative of a group of Deaf people and only two, Winchester and Nottingham, from the philanthropic/missionary impulses of Church of England clergy.[48] Both Manchester Adult Institute for the Deaf and Dumb and Winchester Diocesan Mission had Deaf men officially recognized by the Church of England as

---

43   Jackson and Lee (eds), *Deaf Lives*, p. 83.

44   Ibid. See also Lysons, *Voluntary Welfare Societies*, p. 57 who locates the initiative with Birmingham Town Mission rather than Griffiths.

45   North Staffordshire Deaf and Dumb Society, *The glass wall: a century of progress 1868–1968* (Stoke-on-Trent, 1968), p. 4.

46   Lysons, *Voluntary Welfare Societies*, p. 57 (although Davis is only mentioned here as a 'deaf and dumb shoemaker'); Firth, *Chosen Vessels*, p. 28; Jackson, *Britain's Deaf Heritage*, p. 103; North Staffordshire Deaf and Dumb Society, *The glass wall*, p. 4.

47   Firth, *Chosen Vessels*, p. 28.

48   Lysons, *Voluntary Welfare Societies*, p. 64.

leaders of worship.[49] This suggests that it is not so much a patronizing view of the 'Victorian outreach to the poor and deprived', in which Deaf people are passive recipients of hearing benevolence that we need to look to for the origins of the *DEAF-CHURCH*, but to the great evangelical revival of the early nineteenth century inspiring Deaf men to act for themselves. It is not hearing philanthropists and evangelists we need to honour as our founders, but such renowned Deaf preachers and missioners as Matthew Robert Burns, John Jennings, Edward Rowland, James Herriot, George Healey, Charles Davis and William Griffiths. The early *DEAF-CHURCH* of the mid-nineteenth century was largely non-denominational and a place where religious minded Deaf men were responsible for their own worship of God and preaching the Gospel to other Deaf people. It was an environment where two Deaf men were heading for ordination in the 1880s and an all-Deaf management committee flourished. It was a place where Deaf people could meet together, use their language, relax in their culture; the origin not only of the *DEAF-CHURCH* but also of the adult community of the *DEAF-WORLD* itself. It was a place where some attempts were made to fight for the right of Deaf people to training and employment. It is possible to argue that by the standards of the day, these early missions were basically counter-cultural and 'nonconformist'; more interested in working to bring in the kingdom of God among Deaf people than in making them conform to the norms of society. In fact, I would go further and argue that the pre-Milan Deaf church foreshadows Deaf Liberation Theology in its bringing together of the preaching of the Gospel with such political actions as establishing an all-Deaf management committee and Deaf lay preachers and working with trades unions to reform injustices against Deaf people in the workplace. In its early stages it can be compared with the American Black churches which undermined the white rhetoric of slavery by teaching that all people, black and white, were equal before God. In a similar way, the early *DEAF-CHURCH* taught both implicitly and explicitly that Deaf people were equal to hearing people before God.

We do need to be careful not to fall into the trap of romanticising the nineteenth-century *DEAF-CHURCH*. It had many of the weaknesses of its time, in particular the relegation of women to the status of second-class citizens and it only covered a relatively small part of the country. However, I would argue that in the first 'generation' of each mission of that time it was certainly a church with the potential to be liberating and transformational. From a Deaf point of view, the question must be 'What went wrong?' How did we end up with the largely hearing controlled church of today, a church where Bob Shrine can identify a move from Deaf people being objects of mission to sharing in ministry in the last ten years as

---

[49]   Saul Magson and others in Manchester. See Jackson and Lee (eds), *Deaf Lives*, p. 125. Richard Pearce in Winchester. See Jackson and Lee (eds), *Deaf Lives*, p. 147; Jackson, *Britain's Deaf Heritage*, p. 146 and Lysons, *Voluntary Welfare Societies*, p. 64.

being something new[50] and Deaf church members speak of their 'up-front' participation in the worship of the church as readers and preachers as a recent innovation. What happened to the strong, confident Deaf leaders of the past?

DEAF-CHURCH to Deaf Church 1880–1970

The development of the *DEAF-CHURCH* after 1880 can be divided into the 'era of the missioners' which will be discussed in this section and the 'era of the chaplains' to be considered in the next.[51] The main differences between the two eras (and between the 'era of the missioners' and the early *DEAF-CHURCH*) are the focus of the work undertaken by the mission and the sources of funding. The 'era of the missioners' was an era of voluntary/state-funded organizations, focused on welfare work, with the optional provision of religious services. The welfare side of the work developed into modern day social work among d/Deaf people and split off, with the associated funding, from the Deaf church in the 1970s and 1980s. So we find the Deaf church in the 'era of the chaplains' a largely church-funded organization, focusing on the provision of religious services to d/Deaf people.

The 'era of the missioners' began with an explosion in the number of Deaf churches across the country. Forty-five missions are listed in a handbook produced in 1913. Of the 29 or so started since 1880, seven seem to have been started as branches of existing missions before becoming independent, ten as Church of England diocesan missions (most of which seem to have been established as a result of agitation and encouragement by the newly formed British Deaf and Dumb Association or BDDA),[52] one by an individual[53] and only two, Plymouth and Bristol, by groups of Deaf people. The new mission at Bristol was primarily founded for the purpose of providing worship and preaching for Deaf people in their language, but the Plymouth mission, founded only 12 years later, seems to

---

[50]   Robert G. Shrine, *The Church's mission among deaf people: reflections on principles and practice* (dissertation submitted for the Diploma of the Committee for Ministry Among Deaf People, August 2000), p. 24.

[51]   Shrine, *The Church's mission among deaf people*, p. 15.

[52]   Lysons, *Voluntary Welfare Societies*, p. 69, British Deaf and Dumb Association, *Official programme of the seventh biennial congress of the Deaf* (1901) reports grants going to newly established diocesan missions and the need to encourage dioceses to provide missions in areas (largely rural) that were not already covered. British Deaf and Dumb Association, *Sixth biennial report* (London, 1903) records the initiation of the Chester Diocesan Mission.

[53]   Miss Jane Besmeres who, in 1886, started what became The Church Mission to the Deaf and Dumb in South Staffordshire and Shropshire after 'having had experience in educating a deaf and dumb boy'. This mission became the present-day Wolverhampton, Walsall, West Bromwich and Burton-on-Trent Deaf churches. 'The Story of the Mission' in Church Mission to the Deaf and Dumb in Walsall, Wednesbury and Mid-Staffordshire, *Annual Report*, 73 (1960).

have been more concerned with the provision of welfare services.[54] The remaining nine new missions, notably including all three in Lancashire, are unknown in their origin, although Firth tells us that James Muir, a Deaf man, was missioner in Blackburn from 1884 and initiated services in many places in that county.[55] These statistics appear to suggest that dating from around 1880–90, the origin of missions can be located more in the Victorian conviction that religion was good for the poor and deprived and less in the desire of Deaf people to evangelize their own people.

This shift in purpose and motivation and dynamic of the missions at the end of the nineteenth and beginning of the twentieth century was not confined to missions to and of the Deaf, but was part of a wider social shift. This social shift was triggered by the rise in industrialization and prosperity of Britain and the associated shift in the relationship between employers and employees (and also between Britain and all its colonies), who changed from being human resources to being cogs in an economic wheel. Bosch argues that however 'nonconformist' (in its wider sense) first generation missions (to Africa and Asia) were, the second and subsequent generations seemed more convinced that the kingdom of God could be equated with western civilization in general and with the British Empire in particular. Chadwick provides a wider perspective on this change when he suggests that the political and economic dominance of the British Empire engendered a Church of England so confident that this prosperity meant God was on their side that they had no doubts that their civilization – their political, economic and cultural structures – were God-given and it was their duty to share them with all of the world in addition to enforcing them in their own country.[56] These dynamics, combined with the vote for oralism at the Milan Conference, contributed to the movement of the *DEAF-CHURCH* as a Deaf owned and controlled organization to the Deaf church or church for the deaf.

There were three important and related factors in this movement, which had profound implications for the *DEAF-WORLD* in addition to the *DEAF-CHURCH*. These were the funding of the missions (and hence the important question of who held the purse strings), the growth of hearing missioners as 'gatekeepers' between the *DEAF-WORLD* and the rest of the hearing world and the change from mostly non-denominational to mostly Church of England missions.

The missions at the end of the nineteenth century may have had Deaf missioners, but like all charitable organizations of that time, they were controlled by a management committee or trustees whose qualifications for the job came from the fact they were born into a certain class in society. Dimmock identifies this shift to 'charitable organizations' with the start of paternalism, 'the curse of the deaf

[54] Bristol was founded in 1884 (Lysons, *Voluntary Welfare Societies*, p. 57) and Plymouth in 1896 (Arnold Rundle and Paul Northam, *The Plymouth Deaf Clubs from 1897 to 1997* (printed booklet, Plymouth, 1997).
[55] Firth, *Chosen Vessels*, p. 51.
[56] Chadwick, *The Victorian Church*, p. 1.

community'.[57] What he means by this was that management committees were made up of upper- and middle-class hearing people such as local vicars or magistrates who often had little real knowledge about Deaf people, but nonetheless made decisions which had a profound impact on their lives. For example, the chair of Bolton Deaf Society from its inception in 1869 until 1950 was the vicar from either Bolton Parish Church or one of the other churches in the area.[58] The Plymouth Deaf and Dumb mission was initially presided over by a local magistrate and a doctor.[59] Management committees were the ones who 'held the purse strings' of the missions; they decided on issues of policy, on issues of how the mission should be run and appointed missioners to carry out their wishes. Deaf people were portrayed merely as passive recipients of the benefits of the missions. Annual reports of the societies compiled by the management committee indicate the perception of Deaf people held by these committees and their motivation for the work. Such reports speak of missioners 'who leave no stone unturned to better the condition of these afflicted people' and missions that were 'inestimable help and comfort to the afflicted people whom it sought to benefit'.[60] Annual reports from the 1930s continue this theme that the missions existed to help the unfortunate and helpless deaf and dumb. A report from Walsall in 1935 depicts the hearing missioner as solving problems (with housing and employment) within a week that Deaf people had been unable to deal with over a long period of time.[61] The provision of spiritual services and worship accessible to Deaf people was still part of the aims of the missions, but now it was more to impart 'moral fibre' and consolation in their affliction than sharing the Gospel.[62] The prayer of the Guild of St John of Beverley, established in 1886 by hearing missioners and revitalized by Selwyn Oxley in the 1920s, seems to sum up the place of the Christian Gospel in the work of the missions:

O God and Father of our Lord Jesus Christ, Who went about doing good, Who unsealed the ears of the deaf and made the dumb to speak, teach Thy people, after his example, to pity and succour all they suffering children. Send Thy Holy Spirit to bless and prosper our endeavours; may they be the means of making thy saving grace known to our

---

[57] Dimmock, *Cruel Legacy*, p. 25.

[58] Len Scarff, *A history of the Bolton Deaf Society provision of religious services from 1869.* Personal communication.

[59] Rundle and Northam, *The Plymouth Deaf Clubs from 1897 to 1997*, p. 3.

[60] 'Bolton Deaf and Dumb Society annual report' and 'Bristol Christian Mission to the Deaf and Dumb annual report', *British Deaf Times*, 11/19 (1905): 166.

[61] Church Mission to the Deaf and Dumb in Walsall, Wednesbury and Mid-Staffordshire, *Annual Report*, 49, 1935.

[62] For example a questionnaire distributed by RAD to all missions in 1901 asks the respondents to make judgements about the moral condition of their deaf; the programme of the seventh BDDA congress in 1901 speaks of the need to render the victims of this incurable malady [of being deaf] the only effectual consolation in their affliction, which is to point them to the 'better land'.

afflicted brothers and sisters, to their everlasting welfare and the Thine honour and glory, through Jesus Christ our Lord. Amen.[63]

This dependence on management committees was brought about by the fact that until the 1950s most of the missions had no source of income for their work other than annual subscriptions. No state assistance could be given to the missions, and neither could any grants be made by the Ecclesiastical Commissioners of the Church of England[64] due to the work being classified as extra-parochial, although a few of the individual dioceses made small grants for the work in their area.[65] The ability of the Deaf themselves to subscribe to their own societies seems to have been decreasing over this period, so the societies were relying more and more on hearing outsiders for their income. Increased industrialization had led to increasing unemployment among Deaf people; their traditional crafts skills were being undermined by the increasing use of machinery and the fear that Deaf people would have more accidents than hearing people.[66] The decline in literacy that followed on the promulgation of the oral method of education also contributed to the increasing unemployment; previously Deaf people had communicated directly with their employers with paper and pencil, now they had to rely more and more on missioners who could hear and speak to act as go-betweens. This increasing unemployment not only meant the ability of Deaf people to contribute to their own societies (and thus to have some active involvement in the missions) was diminished, it also resulted in a greater need for and dependence on the welfare and employment services of the missions.

The National Assistance Act of 1948, which gave local authorities the responsibility of caring for d/Deaf people in their area, often resulted in the missions being appointed agencies for the work. The funding that resulted from this was regarded as so much 'manna from heaven' according to Donald Read, but resulted in the work of the missions as becoming more and more about welfare and less about spiritual matters and missioners changing to welfare workers who saw the church work side of the missions as a burden.[67]

It was not only the perceived need for financial support that reinforced the dependence of Deaf people on the missions; it was also the need for interpreting services of the missioners. Acting as a specialist go-between or 'gatekeeper'

---

[63]   In Oxley, *The deaf of other days*. This prayer may also be found in a lightly updated version in Church Mission to the Deaf and Dumb in Walsall, Wednesbury and Mid-Staffordshire *Annual Reports* from 1961 onwards. This suggests it was regularly used in many Deaf churches.

[64]   The central funding body and landowners of the Church of England.

[65]   National Bureau for Promoting the General Welfare of the Deaf and Dumb, *The Deaf Handbook*, 2nd edn (London, 1924), p. 49.

[66]   National Bureau for Promoting the General Welfare of the Deaf and Dumb, *The Deaf Handbook* (London, 1913); Firth, *Chosen Vessels*, p. 84 quoting F. W. G. Gilby, chaplain of RAD in the 1860s.

[67]   Donald Read, *Some facts on North-East Deaf Churches* (2000). Personal communication.

between Deaf people and the rest of the hearing world became an increasingly large part of the missioners' work.[68] They were the link between their employers (the hearing management committee, who would rarely know sign) and the Deaf users of the missions and welfare services. This meant the management committees tended to prefer hearing missioners; as Lysons points out 'committees have a natural preference for a person with normal hearing', because then there are no communication difficulties.[69] There were still Deaf missioners around; some, such as Leslie Edwards, David Fyfe and George Annand Mackenzie, were considerable achievers with very strong and determined characters, but they were very few.[70] Being able to hear began to be considered an essential requirement for the work of the missioner. Deaf people had begun to internalize their domination by hearing 'colonists' and believe what was thought of them: that they were not capable of running their own affairs.

Alongside the changes in funding and the role of the missioner during this period of the Deaf churches was what can only be described as a takeover of the missions to the deaf and dumb by the Church of England. Read describes a dispute in 1953 with the missioner of the South Durham and North Yorkshire mission over his attempts to change the mission from ecumenical (or non-denominational) to Church of England.[71] This must have been one of the last missions to change over, although the records of the Plymouth mission in 1964 report the refusal of the committee to the proposal that the mission should become Anglican even if the provision of worship was mostly Anglican in nature.[72] The attempts of the Church of England to control the missions began in 1905 with the formation of the Council of Church Missioners to the Deaf and Dumb (CCMDD), which was only open to Anglican clergy and licensed lay readers.[73] In 1916, in response to the persuasions of the Revd J. Mansfield Owen (whose cousin was Deaf) the Convocations of Canterbury and York began to take notice of the needs of Deaf Mutes. They commended the conditions laid down by the London diocese in 1854 for the diocesan recognition (and therefore support and occasional funding) of RAD; this was that the Book of Common Prayer was accepted as the basis for instruction and the missioner should be a 'churchman'.[74] This report recognized that the many undenominational missions were 'doing excellent work' and that the Church of England 'did not wish to supplant them' but in case of their decline 'the Church

---

[68]　Ladd, *In search of Deafhood*, p. 148.

[69]　Lysons, *Voluntary Welfare Societies*, p. 123.

[70]　Jackson, *Britain's Deaf Heritage*, p. 216.

[71]　Read, *Some facts on North-East Deaf Churches*.

[72]　Rundle and Northam, *Plymouth Deaf Clubs from 1897 to 1997*, p. 20.

[73]　'The proposed Council of Church Missioners to the Deaf' in *British Deaf Times*, II/22 (1905): 22.

[74]　Committee for the Spiritual Care of Deaf Mutes, *Spiritual Care of Deaf Mutes*. 'Churchman' means Church of England as opposed to 'Chapel', which referred to any other Protestant denomination.

should recognize its duty to step into the gap'. In other words, it was desirable that the Church of England should take control of the missions; as Chadwick says, this was the time when the Church of England woke up to the fact it was no longer the only denomination in the country and realized that it had to compete with others to capture the hearts and minds of the people.[75] In a later report, we are told that the Church of England feared the work among the Deaf would be largely secularized (and therefore an important contact with the Deaf would be lost) by the work of the newly formed National Institute of the Deaf (NID, the forerunner of the RNID), which was not qualified to make spiritual provision, 'which is the greatest need' if the Church did not 'act with energy now'.[76] The Committee for the Spiritual Care of Deaf Mutes recommended that a central advisory council be established to co-ordinate the work of the missions and the training of the missioners.[77] This council was established in 1923 and was instrumental in developing the qualification that became the diploma of the Deaf Welfare Examination Board (DWEB).[78] Initially, this qualification (which led to work as a missioner) was only open to Anglicans, and excluded most Deaf people who by this time had insufficient English for such training courses. By the time the Church gave into pressure from the Ministry of Health in 1952 to open it to all who worked with Deaf people, regardless of their denomination, the Deaf church was well and truly run by Anglican missioners, who had succeeded in changing most of the undenominational missions to Anglican.

Ladd argues that one of the results of the Church of England takeover meant the end of the involvement of (Deaf) lay preachers and the rise of (hearing) chaplains.[79] This was certainly a factor in the continuing disempowerment of Deaf people; an article on the 'deaf of Bonnie Scotland' in the *British Deaf Times* of 1904 points out that Deaf lay preachers can 'occupy the pulpit' of the 'free' Church of Scotland chapel for the deaf in Edinburgh, unlike the few purpose built churches in England where 'the deaf preacher is shut out unless he is ordained'.[80] Deaf lay preachers and readers did continue to exist in quite considerable numbers in even the Church of England missions for many years; however their role as time went on seems to have diminished into one of 'watering down criticism or ill feeling against the missioner'[81] rather than being church leaders as such. Read, who attended various churches in the Northumbria Deaf Mission during the 1950s,

---

[75]   Chadwick, *The Victorian Church*, p. 4.

[76]   Central Advisory Council for the Spiritual Care of the Deaf and Dumb, *Annual Report* (1926).

[77]   Committee for the Spiritual Care of Deaf Mutes, *Spiritual Care of Deaf Mutes*, 1916.

[78]   Lysons, *Voluntary Welfare Societies*, p. 140.

[79]   Ladd, *In search of Deafhood*, p. 34.

[80]   'The Deaf of Bonnie Scotland: The modern Athens' in *British Deaf Times*, I/8 (1904): 145–7.

[81]   Dimmock, *Cruel Legacy*, p. 51.

provides a personal example of this disempowering of Deaf readers and lay preachers. He, along with five others, was encouraged by the missioner to help with services and preach. However, they were all discouraged by him from becoming licensed lay readers (or, in other words, recognized by the diocesan bishop and the wider hearing church as lay ministers) as being unnecessary if they were only going to work with the Deaf church.[82] Other implications of the Church of England takeover of the missions did not really become clear until the subsequent 'era of the chaplains'.

The Church Among Deaf People argues that another contribution the church made to Deaf people was the provision of services in sign language, which helped keep sign alive and at a high level at a time when it was banned in schools.[83] This claim is debatable; without doubt, sign was in use in the missions and their services and some missioners were prominent in the campaign against the banning of sign in schools,[84] but this did not mean that sign was regarded as anything but inferior to speech and lip-reading. Sign was kept alive and at a high level by Deaf adults themselves; if it had not been used at the missions, it is doubtful that Deaf people would have attended as regularly as they did. In fact, as Dimmock records, where Deaf people had a choice over which church to attend, they would go to the one where the vicar had the best sign language.[85]

In summary then, the period from 1880 to the 1970s saw a change from a *DEAF-CHURCH* to a Deaf church where the (usually hearing) missioner did everything for the Deaf that attended and the focus shifted from a church where Deaf people could meet and worship in their own language to a place where the Deaf came to obtain welfare assistance. Non-denominational missions disappeared, taken over by the Church of England control of the training of missioners. The strong, individual gospel preached in the early *DEAF-CHURCH* was replaced by a 'gospel of consolation' mediated through the hearing missioners. The underpaid missioners worked very hard and their commitment to the welfare of 'their deaf' has never been doubted. However, these good intentions were not enough to prevent the missioners and the missions contributing to the disempowerment of Deaf people during this period. As described in the previous chapter, the continuation of a *DEAF-WAY* during this time relied on those who rebelled against the control of the missioners in 1,001 small ways. In conversations with some of the older, still practising and believing Deaf men and women, who have been involved in the Deaf church since the 1950s I suspect that much the same kind of covert resistance can be found in the 'Sunday services' context. This resistance, in addition to the traditions quietly passed down from the previous, pre-Milan age,

---

[82] Read, *Some facts on North-East Deaf Churches*.

[83] *Church Among Deaf People*, p. 13.

[84] Revd William Sleight and Revd J. Mansfield Owen are on record as the only two members of the Royal Commission of 1890 who disagreed with the ruling in favour of the oral method of education. Lysons, *Voluntary Welfare Societies*.

[85] Dimmock, *Cruel Legacy*, p. 51 and personal correspondence.

can give us the 'seeds' of a Deaf Liberation Theology, and will be discussed further in the second part of this thesis on the reconstruction of a *DEAF-CHURCH* and a *DEAF-THEOLOGY*.

The Church Among Deaf People: 1970–Present

The separation of the welfare and spiritual functions of the missions that took place in the late 1960s and early 1970s may have been good news for the Deaf community as a whole, as one of the factors in the resurgence of Deaf pride, but it was not good news for the Deaf church. Read describes how, in the late 1960s, the local authorities started to set up their own welfare departments for the deaf, changed missioners to social workers and stopped the grants to the missions. Some missions tried to go back to raising their own income, but this did not work. The public thought the missions would simply duplicate the services provided by the local authorities and overlooked the fact that the local authorities did not look after the spiritual welfare of Deaf people. Throughout the 1970s the missions or Deaf clubs closed one by one without any warning and without any consultation with the Deaf people. The first they knew about it would be in the notices one Sunday, when the missioner informed them that the next Sunday's service would be the last.[86] In some cases, such as Bolton, the Deaf clubs remained open, and the missioner/welfare worker stayed on and, as a practising Christian, continued taking the services and signing for visiting clergy until they retired.[87] In other cases, such as Northumbria, there were sufficient active Deaf and interested clergy in the area to maintain the services in some form or another, often in local parish churches, in effect starting 'new' Deaf churches in areas that had previously been served by missions.[88] In yet other situations, such as Walsall, the missions closed, and no provision was made for the continuation of worship so services simply stopped.[89] In some areas, such as Plymouth, they already had a chaplain, who continued as before.[90]

The net result of the removal of local authority support from the missions and the demise of the missioners was that the dioceses slowly took over responsibility for the provision of worship for Deaf people across the country. In some cases, as in Lichfield, the diocesan Bishop realized that the services had stopped and appointed a chaplain to remedy the situation.[91] In other situations, the Church of England Council for the Deaf (CECD, the successor to the Central Advisory

---

[86]   Read, *Some facts on North-East Deaf Churches*.

[87]   Scarff, *A history of the Bolton Deaf Society provision of religious services from 1869*.

[88]   Read, *Some facts on North-East Deaf Churches*.

[89]   Peter Lees, personal communication.

[90]   Rundle and Northam, *Plymouth Deaf Clubs from 1897 to 1997*, p. 24.

[91]   Peter Lees, personal communication.

Council and forerunner of the Committee for Ministry among Deaf People) had to campaign for the provision of chaplains. A survey by the NDCC in the early 1980s edited by Brian Murray, the Organizing Secretary of the CECD, shows a Deaf church still in transition from one era to the next. Thirteen dioceses are still served by local voluntary organizations with a principal officer carrying the responsibility of chaplain and finding it difficult to find time for anything other than social work. Thirteen dioceses employ full- or part-time chaplains, three of whom are seconded to teams of social workers. Fifteen dioceses have honorary chaplains and Deaf lay ministers, sometimes with social workers acting as interpreters for honorary chaplains. In some of these dioceses, the Deaf lay workers provide pastoral care, in others the only provision is for worship. Finally, in one diocese, Lichfield, the spiritual care of Deaf people is through a council with representatives from the local voluntary societies and the diocese with joint funding and the chaplains' stipend provided by the diocese.[92]

Shrine has labelled this period the 'era of the chaplains': a time when work was funded by dioceses and the role of the Deaf church changed from general welfare work among Deaf people to an organization that exists 'to encourage and strengthen the participation of Deaf people in the life and witness of the Church'.[93] In other words, what is now referred to as the church among deaf people exists to promote access to the services and structures of the hearing church by d/Deaf people and to promote increased 'deaf awareness' throughout the hearing church. As one person has put it the 'Deaf church' is now more part of the 'church' and therefore is more affected by issues of the wider church. One of the results in this increased focus on the relationship with the 'church' has been an increase in the clericalism of the Deaf church. What this means is that the ordained clergy increasingly dominated the life of the Deaf church, and Deaf clergy were few and far between until the mid-1990s The adequacy of provision for Deaf people in any diocese is judged by whether there is a chaplain among deaf people, and if they are full-time, part-time or honorary. The number of Deaf lay ministers and readers is not taken into account.[94] This clericalism mirrors that found in the wider Church of England as Holy Communion, which can only be taken by clergy, became the main weekly service in almost every parish in England. In the Deaf churches, a similar trend can be noted. Len Scarff records how the evening prayer service (which can be conducted by any licensed lay person) was dropped and Holy Communion or

---

[92]   Brian Murray on behalf of the National Deaf Church Council, *Spiritual and Pastoral Care for the Deaf*, draft report for presenting to the Archbishop of Canterbury (*c*. 1984).

[93]   *The Church Among Deaf People*, p. 14.

[94]   Murray, *Spiritual and Pastoral Care for the Deaf*, classifies Deaf churches according to the provision for ministers. Possessing qualified, full-time chaplains comes first, followed by a combination of unqualified full-time chaplains, part-time and honorary chaplains. Lay ministers are only included in this classification scheme if they are full-time qualified social workers.

Eucharist left as the only service provided for Deaf people.[95] The report *The Church Among Deaf People* records that all services are Eucharistic at 70 per cent of places where the Church of England regularly holds services for Deaf people.[96] By the standards of the hearing Church of England, this is accepted, even desirable; but no one seems to have questioned its desirability from the point of view of Deaf people.

The focus on the provision of chaplains has also meant that the Deaf church has been very negatively affected by the financial and staffing problems of the Church of England in recent years. Whenever a chaplain among Deaf people moves or retires much special pleading for the 'special needs' of the Deaf people is required to justify the appointment of a new chaplain, even if one can be found.

Another development in the Church of England since the 1960s that has been paralleled in the Deaf church has been the issue of congregational participation in worship. The increase in opportunities for lay Deaf people to participate in the worship is the biggest change identified by Deaf members of the church. In some churches Deaf people now do the Bible readings and lead the intercessions. In many churches, hymns to be signed by all were introduced. In some churches the whole congregation is encouraged to sign together the responses and set prayers of the Communion service. Without a doubt, the Deaf members of the churches experience this move as positive, but it is possible to question, as in the hearing church, just how much the rhetoric of congregational participation hides the fact that nothing fundamental in the distribution of power has really changed.

One final trend over the last 20 to 30 years, again echoing the hearing church, has been the decline of churchgoing. There is not sufficient space to go into the reasons for this here, but basically religion is now an option for the few who are interested rather than compulsory for all. Those who attend Deaf churches today are, by and large, those who genuinely believe in the Christian faith. Like most clergy, chaplains complain that their congregations are small, elderly and resistant to change.[97] The Deaf church, like the church as a whole, is seen by the wider [Deaf] community as an irrelevant anachronism with young people growing up in ignorance of the Christian faith. However, in the *DEAF-WORLD* of today, there is another reason for lack of interest in religion and that is the fact that the church among deaf people is perceived as one of the last outposts of hearing colonialism. Younger Deaf people give the continuing use of SSE in services as a reason for not attending church.[98] The continuing dominance of hearing leaders, no matter how well meaning, is something that Deaf adults do not need to accept in any other sphere of their lives and so they will not accept it in the church.

---

[95]   Scarff, *A history of the Bolton Deaf Society provision of religious services from 1869*.

[96]   *The Church Among Deaf People*, p. 17.

[97]   Shrine, *The language and culture of Deaf people*, p. 4.

[98]   *The Church Among Deaf People*, p. 19.

For the first 20 or so years of the church among deaf people in the 'era of the chaplains', it seems to have gone the opposite way from the rest of the adult *DEAF-WORLD*. Instead of being part of the resurgence in Deaf culture or *DEAF-WAY* and Deaf pride it became one of the last bastions of SSE and colonialism and covert resistance on the part of Deaf people. Instead of joining in the Deaf historians' search for *STRONG-DEAF* role models of the nineteenth century, it perpetuated the illusion that the Deaf church owes its origins to hearing Victorian philanthropists. Instead of using the considerable resources of the Gospels in the service of social justice and being a part of the fight for the recognition of BSL and full civil rights for Deaf people, it has often preached a spiritualized gospel that, in my experience, has led many members of the Deaf church to reject the Federation of Deaf People (FDP) as 'too political'. The church among deaf people has, like many organizations, appointed Deaf representatives at all levels of management, and encouraged Deaf leadership, but this has not necessarily resulted in any real shift of power. This period has seen the smallest number of Deaf people in a leadership position in the Deaf church than ever before. The most important issues at present in the church among deaf people are how to translate the new services of the Church of England into sign[99] and how to get more Deaf people on to the General Synod.[100] In general, the present-day church among Deaf people does seem more concerned with giving Deaf people access to the hearing church than empowering them to find a liberating God.

Into the Twenty-First Century

The early *DEAF-CHURCH* (and its covert continuation within the Deaf church) is comparable to the Black church in the USA in its origins among Deaf people reading the Bible for themselves and in its ability to sustain Deaf people in their self-belief as children of God; but unlike the Black church, it did not provide the powerhouse and personnel for the fight for equal rights. In this, the Deaf church is more similar to the Latin American Roman Catholic Church, in that its membership consists of a people so disempowered by their colonization that it took a 'top down' movement from Vatican II and the conference of Latin American bishops at Medellín to kick start the process by which people could experience the Christian church as an agent of liberation rather than as an agent of oppression.

It is this 'top down' movement that we see today, as Deaf people are trained and ordained in both the Church of England and the Roman Catholic Church and relate their faith to their experiences of oppression and liberation. These Deaf people include almost the full spectrum of those who belong to the Deaf

---

[99]   See for example Chaplains conference papers, 2001.
[100]   Ibid. See also *Signs*, the magazine of the NDCC.

community, from *DEAF-OF-DEAF*[101] through to those who were born Deaf (or deafened in very early childhood) from hearing families and educated in Deaf schools, and those who come from Deaf families but were born hearing and became Deaf in later life, to those of the modern generation of Deaf people born Deaf or deafened in childhood and educated in mainstream schools.[102] In other words, this new generation of Deaf clergy includes both those who have BSL as their first language, and those whose first language (although not always preferred language) is English,[103] and also those who grew up in a Deaf community through Deaf schools and Deaf clubs, and those whose involvement with the Deaf community dates from adulthood. However, when these Deaf clergy began to relate their faith to their experiences of oppression and liberation, they met subaltern Deaf people who have silently carried on the *STRONG-DEAF* traditions of the Church, resisting oppression in 1,001 small ways. Their stories provide a major start point for a reconstructed Deaf Liberation Theology, but before then, before we can progress toward an alternative vision of resurgent, truly *DEAF-CHURCH*, we need to explore the theological and sociological foundations that both construct and underpin the place of Deaf people in the church today.

---

[101] That is born Deaf with Deaf parents, and often from several generations of Deaf people.

[102] Of the 16 Deaf clergy in the UK at the moment, one (6 per cent) (Roman Catholic) is *DEAF-OF-DEAF*, a further seven (44 per cent) (two Roman Catholic and five Church of England) were educated in Deaf schools, three (19 per cent) were educated as deaf children in mainstream schools. The remaining five (32 per cent) are all deafened. One deafened Roman Catholic is Korean, and his educational experience is unknown, one was born hearing in a Deaf family and the remaining three Deaf clergy were deafened as adults, but have become fluent in sign language and identify with the Deaf community.

[103] 'Preferred language' is a concept for those Deaf people who have English as their first language, for whatever reason, but will always choose BSL above English when they have a choice.

Chapter 4

Deaf People Constructed in Theology

Examination of the present-day 'church among deaf people' suggests that despite the growing influence of the cultural model on the way Deaf people interact with the hearing world, it still has had a very limited and superficial influence on the Deaf church. In this chapter I suggest that one reason for this superficial engagement is that the theological constructions of what it means to be Deaf which underpin the relationship between the church and Deaf people are intimately tied to the medical model. Before we can fully engage with the liberating cultural and social models, we need to name and deconstruct these theological constructions as oppressive of Deaf people.

Deaf people, historically, have tended to be classed with disabled people; therefore, I will need to discuss the theological construction of d/Deaf people as part of the construction of a wider group of people with disabilities. There is no single dominant view of disability in the Bible and no single construction of disability in the Christian church; that being so what I aim to do is to sketch out a number of the most common ways of constructing disability in general and deafness in particular, and show how these constructions are linked to the medical model and experienced as oppressive in terms of d/Deaf people's lives and identities. The constructions were first elucidated by Nancy Eiesland, in her book *The Disabled God*, perhaps the first work of liberation theology in the lives of disabled or Deaf people.

Morally Impure

The first way of constructing disability within the Bible is within a framework of sin and punishment. This is based on the ancient concept that goodness and evil were rewarded appropriately by material happenings. For example, when Job is struck with his misfortunes, his friends think he must have sinned to be so struck down.[1] Although the Book of Job does appear to demolish this particular view (we are specifically told that Job was a good man and that his afflictions were not intended by God as a punishment) this seems to have been the pervasive mentality throughout ancient times. Brett Webb-Mitchell mentions that the ancient Babylonians and Egyptians are shown to have called on 'shamans' to exorcize the

---

[1]   'Who that was innocent ever perished?', Job 4:7.

evil spirits in sick or disabled people. It appears that these spirits only possessed those who 'deserved' it and therefore either those with disabilities or their parents had sinned and were being punished.[2]

The link between physical organs, or illness and moral default, is strongly apparent in the New Testament as well as the Old. Jesus appears to have found it necessary to have to forgive people their sins at the same time as physically healing them on several occasions.[3] John Hull, a blind theologian, points out that Jesus himself appears to make the connection between sin and disability explicit in these passages: for example in John 5:14 where he warns the lame man healed at the pool of Bethesda 'Do not sin any more, so that nothing worse happens to you'.[4] While Jesus does, in another passage,[5] refute the idea that disability must have been caused by the sin of the individual or their parents, that he needs to do this does suggest that his 'audience' were making such a connection and that Jesus himself appears to be profoundly ambivalent about the connection between sin and disability.

Simon Horne, however, argues that sin is only one of many perceived causes of disability (or impairment)[6] in ancient times,[7] and that disability and disabled people are generally accepted as part of life in the ancient world with the impairment being caused, ultimately, by God's will, but not necessarily as a punishment. He quotes Exodus 4:11[8] and argues from other ancient texts that this view of impairment as being given by God for many reasons was widespread in the ancient world.[9] Sin was occasionally, explicitly, identified or suggested as a cause for various impairments[10] but this association between sin and impairment was profoundly ambivalent. Many ancient writers were hesitant in applying the general

---

[2]   Brett Webb-Mitchell, *Unexpected guests at God's banquet: welcoming people with disabilities into the Church* (New York, 1994), p. 51.

[3]   See for example the story of the paralysed man in Luke 5:18–26 and the blind man in John 5:14.

[4]   John M. Hull, *In the beginning there was darkness: a blind person's conversation with the Bible* (London, 2001), p. 49.

[5]   John 9:2–3, '"Who sinned, this man or his parents that he was born blind?" Jesus answered "neither this man nor his parents sinned; he was born blind so that God's works might be revealed in him"'.

[6]   Horne is explicitly using the social model of disability and therefore refers to 'impairments' rather than 'disabilities' because he is focusing on the individual 'difference' from the majority rather than the social consequences.

[7]   Simon Timothy Horne, *Injury and Blessing: a challenge to current readings of biblical discourses concerning impairment* (PhD thesis, University of Birmingham, 1999), p. 95.

[8]   'Who gives speech to mortals? Who makes them mute or deaf, seeing or blind? Is it not I, the Lord?'

[9]   Horne, *Injury and Blessing*, p. 153.

[10]   Ibid., p. 172.

principles to the experience of individuals,[11] and were much more likely to focus on the health of the soul as being indicative of spiritual health than the health of the body.[12] Impaired individuals were more than capable of having 'whole' souls, and this was far more important than having a 'whole' body. He suggests that the perception of ancient texts as being almost unvaryingly negative is, in itself, a result of the medical model uncritically appropriating a selected number of texts, and ignoring the many which refer to disability as a natural part of life in the ancient world.[13]

Horne's theory is supported by the fact that it is not until the domination of science and its associated desire to categorize and explain everything in the nineteenth century that the perceived link between sin and disability appears again in history. Mendelism, or the theory of heredity, gave it a scientific foundation at that time by apparently 'proving' that deafness was 'caused' by deaf people marrying each other and having children and therefore deaf people could be blamed for 'propagating their own kind'. Dr Scott, the headmaster of Exeter School for the Deaf, wrote in 1870 that he believed 'deafness is hereditary, caused by bad conditions, consanguinity and the sin of the parents'.[14] Despite the fact that only one in ten deaf babies are born to d/Deaf parents, this conviction led to a firm belief that it was possible to reduce, if not eradicate, deafness if d/Deaf people would stop marrying each other and having children. The perceived link between sin and disability may still be encountered in modern society: Stewart Govig has unearthed a quotation from an official in the US Department of Education in the 1970s: '[There is] no injustice in the universe ... a persons external circumstances fit their internal spiritual development ... those handicapped people who seek to have others bear their burdens and eliminate challenges are seeking to avoid the central issue of their lives'.[15] John Hull describes how he was asked by a taxi driver 'what did you do that God made you blind?' as an example of a widespread conviction of some kind of necessary connection between sin and disability.[16] Arthur Dimmock, the Deaf historian, refers to a significant practical impact of this construction when he tells the stories of Deaf women who were forcibly sterilized to prevent them having children.[17] Some d/Deaf people have internalized this attitude to the extent that all Deaf clergy and readers have been asked, from time to

---

[11] Ibid., p. 179.

[12] Ibid., p. 329.

[13] Ibid., p. 147.

[14] W. R. Scott, *The Deaf and Dumb and their education and social position*, 2nd edn (London, 1870), p. 32. Quoted in McLoughlin, *A history of the education of the deaf in England* (Gosport, 1987), p. 190.

[15] Stewart D. Govig, *Strong at the broken places: persons with disabilities and the Church* (Louiseville, KY, 1989), p. 21.

[16] Hull, *In the beginning there was darkness*, p. 51.

[17] Dimmock, *Cruel Legacy* (Edinburgh, 1993), p. 47.

time, '*WHY GOD MAKE ME DEAF?*'[18] Jay Croft, a Deaf priest in the USA, says that the first reaction of hearing parents of deaf children is to blame themselves for having done something wrong, to feel that God is punishing them for their sins by giving them a handicapped child.[19] Even more recently in the USA, when a Deaf lesbian couple chose a Deaf man to be a sperm donor in the hopes they would have a Deaf child, the language of the reaction in the media revealed attitudes towards a link between deafness and supposed morality that Deaf people thought had disappeared. The Deaf woman and her partner are accused of placing a burden on their son,[20] of being selfish by intentionally placing their son at a disadvantage,[21] of being guilty of child abuse,[22] of denying the human rights of the child,[23] of being 'cruel and unusual parents'[24] and so on. Given that there is little difference between choosing a Deaf man as a sperm donor and (for heterosexual Deaf women) choosing to marry a Deaf man in the hopes of having a Deaf family, these articles and letters, and many other similar ones, suggest that Deaf people are still, at some level, held culpable for the existence of deafness.

Another way in which the link between sin and disability emerges in a particular way is in the construction of Deaf people as 'naturally less moral' than hearing people. The abbé Sicard, successor to the abbé de l'Epée as head of the School for the Deaf in Paris, writes at the beginning of the nineteenth century that the uneducated deaf person has the morality of a child 'referring everything to himself, acting on natural needs with violent impulsiveness, unmoderated by any rational consideration, to satisfy all appetites, no matter what',[25] and is therefore a beast that needs pacifying and a savage that needs humanizing. This construction of Deaf people as basically immoral is despite the witness of such prominent contemporary Deaf men as Pierre Desloges and Ferdinand Berthier that the uneducated Deaf people in cities and towns such as Paris were in regular contact with each other, communicated in their own French Sign Language (LSF)[26] and were generally, with the exception of the sense of hearing, the same as other uneducated people.[27] Calling uneducated Deaf people beasts and savages in their

---

[18]   In the sense of 'What have I done that God made me deaf?'

[19]   Croft, 'The Lord Loves Justice' in Pokorny (ed.), *The Word in Signs and Wonders* (New York, 1977), p. 258.

[20]   Ken Connor, president of Family Research Council quoted in Cybercast News Service, 2 April 2002.

[21]   Ibid.

[22]   'Robert M', Cybercast News Service, 3 April 2002.

[23]   'David', Rainbow Network, 12 April 2002.

[24]   'John V. Brennan', New York Post online, 16 April 2002.

[25]   Abbé Sicard, *Course of Instruction* in Lane (ed.), *The Deaf Experience* (Cambridge, MA, 1984), p. 85.

[26]   *Langue Signe Française.*

[27]   Pierre Desloges, 'A Deaf person's observation about *An elementary course of education for the Deaf*' and Ferdinand Berthier, 'The Deaf before and since the abbé de l'Epée' in Lane (ed.), *The Deaf Experience*, pp. 43 and 167.

'natural morality' is also strongly apparent in England; William Wilde in 1854 argues that it is difficult to impress upon the Deaf and Dumb a just idea of right and wrong, especially as they are 'degraded by uncontrolled passions'.[28]

Comparing Deaf people to beasts and savages does recede as times change, but they continue to be likened to children and represented as 'backward' in their psychological and moral development in many writings on the welfare, spiritual and educational needs of the Deaf. For example in the 1960s Canon E. R. Sowter, chaplain to deaf people in Canterbury, suggests that few Deaf persons become 'adult' before the age of 30, that in Deaf adults there is a high degree of aggression and hostility to any sort of teacher, that due to the 'close link between the mouth and sexual stimulation' they are easily aroused by lip-reading.[29] In the 1970s Brian Murray, secretary of the central Church of England committee for work with deaf people, and the Roman Catholic Bishop of Kilkenny use more technical, 'scientific' psychological language: 'The Deaf show certain psychological similarities such as egocentricity and lags in conceptualising resulting in much impulsive behaviour',[30] and 'severely deaf people are liable to poor interpersonal relationships, to emotional under-development, to this egocentricity',[31] but the implication is the same. Deaf people are not able to behave according to hearing standards of morality without drastic intervention on the part of those hearing people who work with them.

With such an extreme construction of what it means to be deaf, it would seem the only way a d/Deaf person can come to God, or 'grow' in moral terms, is by being cured or healed. The link between forgiveness and healing (and by implication between sin and those considered in need of healing)[32] is perpetuated in many writers on issues of healing and the Christian faith. Morris Maddocks takes care to expand the concept of health and wholeness to include more that just physical wholeness.[33] However, in his discussion of the many roots of the concept of healing in the Bible, he equates 'wholeness' with 'holiness' and appears to be

---

[28]   William Wilde, *The Physical, Moral and Social Condition of the Deaf and Dumb*, quoted in Lysons, *Voluntary Welfare Societies for Adult Deaf Persons in England, 1840–1963* (Liverpool), p. 29.

[29]   Canon E. R. Sowter, 'Health and Welfare of the Adult Deaf'. Appendix to Church Mission to the Deaf and Dumb in Walsall, Wednesbury and Mid-Staffordshire, *Annual Report*, no. 74 (1960–61).

[30]   Brian Murray, *... and no birds sing* (*c*. 1978).

[31]   Peter Birch, Bishop of Kilkenny in J. van Eijndhoven (ed.), *Religious education of the deaf* (Rotterdam, 1973).

[32]   Which includes people with disabilities as the construction of disability in the church largely reflects the dominant medical model. Writers on Christian healing ministry such as Maddocks and MacNutt tend to mention disabilities in the same sentence as disorders such as depression and arthritis. None of them claims to have actually 'healed' a person with a life-long disability though.

[33]   Morris Maddocks, *The Christian healing ministry* (London, 1990), p. 7.

referring at least implicitly to physical wholeness.[34] As a natural corollary to this, when discussing the healing of the paralysed man in Mark 2:1–12, he suggests that Jesus treats the physical condition as a symptom of a deeper sickness and suggests that physical healing is a part of the total gift of salvation.[35] His underlying argument seems to relate to his understanding that God means for all people to be 'whole' and this is the meaning of salvation. In this understanding, Jesus' most important work was as a healer: 'Jesus sought out the marginal people of society … the sick, the underprivileged, the sinful … he healed broken bodies, forgave guilty consciences, restored people to wholeness which the creator meant for them'.[36] John A. Sanford is another writer on the Christian healing ministry who explicitly associates healing with wholeness;[37] being healthy means to become whole, which does not mean being perfect but being 'completed' in the sense of developing and purifying the soul.[38] He concludes that many illnesses, having deeper 'psychic' roots, need therapy as well as medication for restoration to health.[39] He does not specifically discuss disability at all (except in terms of illness-related disabilities such as arthritis) but his thesis appears to state that someone who is not physically 'healthy' appears to have further problems in the 'inner person' that prevent them becoming whole. Francis MacNutt is another writer on the Christian healing ministry who associates sin with disability. MacNutt explicitly names disabilities as a sickness and goes on to say 'Our physical sickness, far from being a redemptive blessing, is often a sign that we are not totally redeemed, not whole at a spiritual level'.[40] This suggests he constructs people with disabilities as people who cannot truly be 'saved' without physical healing.

Stephen Pattison produces a critique of this particular construction of sickness and disability on two grounds, one practical, and one theoretical. In practical terms he fears for the harm done to people by Christian healing ministry because of the association of sin and sickness. He argues that if someone is not healed, they often go away with the sense they have not enough faith, that they have too much sin, that the God they were told could forgive all has abandoned them.[41] His second criticism refers to the uncritical use made of the biblical texts on the construction of sin and sickness, use that does not attempt to engage with contemporary biblical scholarship. What he does not refer to, and in fact does not engage with at all, is the effect this construct has had on the lives of people with disabilities, who may

---

[34]   Maddocks, *The Christian healing ministry*, p. 13.

[35]   Ibid., p. 38.

[36]   Ibid., p. 68.

[37]   John A. Sanford, *Healing and Wholeness* (New York, 1977), p. 6.

[38]   Ibid., p. 20.

[39]   Ibid., p. 21.

[40]   Francis MacNutt, *Healing* (London, 1989), p. 177.

[41]   Stephen Pattison, *Alive and kicking: towards a practical theology of illness and healing* (London, 1989), p. 70.

be thought of as 'permanently unhealable'. Does this suggest that we are unforgivable and unable to engage with the experience of salvation? The commonly found indifference as to whether people with disabilities can access worship and the sacraments and word of God may suggest this construct underlies more than might be thought.

Pattison also has problems with the idea that 'healing' can be equated with 'wholeness' as in the arguments of Maddocks and Sanford. His criticism is based on the grounds that focusing on 'wholeness' as the aim of the Christian healing ministry trivializes and spiritualizes the real struggles and conflicts surrounding and expressing themselves in illness and healing;[42] and that this 'ethereal' understanding can serve as a hollow ideology encouraging Christians to opt for vague future dreams rather than engaging with what it means to be ill or disabled in a broken and complex world.[43] In other words, arguing that there is a necessary link between sin and disability, and that this link can only be broken if a disabled person is healed and becomes 'whole' puts the whole focus on the transformation of the individual, like the medical model, and does not consider that the person's real 'suffering' or need for healing may be caused by political considerations and unjust power structures rather than the impairment itself.

As well as being related to questions of sin and salvation in this life, this particular construction of disability also raises questions about the life to come. In Matthew 11:2–6, where John's disciples ask Jesus if he is the harbinger of the kingdom of God, Jesus' answer is 'go and tell John what you see and hear; the blind recover their sight and the lame walk, lepers are made clean and the deaf hear'. It is possible to read the implication that the coming of the kingdom of God will mean all people with disabilities will be physically healed, that if you are not healed, you cannot be a member of the kingdom of God. This is certainly an assumption that appears to be operating in Danker's discussion of the significance of Jesus 'the bringer in of the kingdom' and the 'healer of the blind and deaf' when he concludes, 'we await the full consummation [of the kingdom] and on that day the deaf <u>shall</u> hear'.[44] This raises a number of questions. Not least is the fact that it can be used to construct the concept of healing as something that all people with disabilities should desire as part of their spiritual 'growth' or 'sanctification'. Maddocks, MacNutt, the medical profession and the general population have a habit of suggesting that people who do not want to be 'healed' do not want to lose their position as the recipients of sympathy and the centre of attention.[45] Pattison points out that all such writers stress that you need to want healing; this is one way of covering their tracks if healing does not take place,[46] and as such is linked with

---

[42] Pattison, *Alive and kicking*, p. 76.

[43] Ibid., p. 77.

[44] Danker, 'Deafness and hearing in the Bible' in Pokorny (ed.), *The Word in Signs and Wonders*, p. 37. His emphasis.

[45] See Maddocks, *The Christian healing ministry*, p. 48 for example.

[46] Pattison, *Alive and kicking*, p. 54.

other causes such as not having sufficient faith or unconfessed sins as reasons why people are not healed.[47] It also firmly constructs the expectations of people with disabilities in that they are told they should not expect life to be easier until the next life, the kingdom of God. The kingdom of God cannot be coming in the here and now for people with disabilities.

The medical model may not explicitly state d/Deaf and disabled people are inherently less moral, but its emphasis on (hearing) doctors, audiologists, teachers, social workers and missioners/chaplains who know best what is right for d/Deaf people certainly suggests it is operating on an assumption that d/Deaf people naturally need guidance from hearing people. In addition, the strength of feeling found in conflicts between the medical and cultural/social models, for example, in the arguments over whether deaf children should receive cochlear implants, would seem to suggest that some very deep-rooted emotions are being touched. The assumption in the medical model seems to be that the consequences of being d/Deaf are so bad, in other words, that the consequences of deafness in their minds are so awful, that submitting deaf children to a major interventionist, possibly unnecessary and inefficient operation is perceived as better than the alternative: an educated, articulate, confident, signing Deaf child, who still cannot hear a sound.

Travesty of Divine Image

Eiesland's second suggestion of the way in which disability has been constructed in the Bible,[48] like the first construct, is also talking about a world where an individual affects the community just by who they are. It may be argued that the need to segregate people with disabilities, or heal them, as well as being an expression of their moral impurity, can also be constructed as expressing the perversion of the image of God in them. God is Holy, which is understood to carry the implication of physically unflawed.[49] The physically flawed are unclean. It is not merely their supposed sins that mean they are excluded but also their actual physical appearance, somehow deviated from the usual physical make-up of human beings. It is this concept that there is one 'divine image' to be a travesty of, that there is such thing as a norm against which we are all measured, which constructs the concept of disability as abnormal, a perversion of or deviation from the norm. People with disabilities cannot be created in the image of a 'perfect' God

---

[47]   MacNutt, *Healing*, Chapter 18, 'Eleven reasons why people are not healed'.

[48]   Eiesland, *The Disabled God: towards a liberatory theology of disability* (Nashville, 1994), p. 72.

[49]   See for example John Hull's identification of the God of the Bible as largely sighted in Hull, *In the beginning there was darkness*, p. 73. For argument, see also Horne, *Injury and Blessing*, p. 294 in which he argues that impairment imagery was applied to God in the Hebrew Bible and in early Jewish tradition with no sense of profaning God, but rather to express paradox about God.

and therefore are somehow less 'human' than non-disabled humanity. In this construction, people with disabilities are indeed 'children of a lesser God'[50] because there is no way they could be created in the image of 'our' God. This division of the world into 'normal' and 'abnormal' is very significant in the lives of disabled people. Mary Weir suggests that it may even be the major theological basis for the medical model, with its 'seemingly benevolent aim of fixing what is "wrong"'.[51]

Hull, in discussing Malachi 1:8, identifies two assumptions underlying this construction: firstly it is assumed disabled means useless, like 'someone offering for the ministry of the church who had already proved that he or she was incapable of doing anything else'. The second assumption is that God's handiwork is perfect, that any created thing with a blemish cannot come straight from the hand of God, but must embody the imperfections of a sinful world. 'Such people cannot stand before God because God is perfect, and it would insult God's handiwork if that which deviates from it were to be presented right in front of God's own altar'.[52] Again, Horne argues that this is a relatively modern reading of such passages; whatever the statements made by verses such as Malachi 1:8 and Leviticus 21:17–23 (which states that no priest with an impairment should approach the altar of God) there are records, in the Bible, of priests with impairments (for example Eli, Moses, Jacob, Zechariah) who did serve at the altar.[53] This ruling was not applied in the early church; Jerome and Augustine did not consider that their impairments, caused by old age, disqualified them from serving at the altar and there exists a specific canon law from the fourth century stating that impairment of the body does not exclude a candidate for the priesthood, but only pollution of the soul.[54]

Again, it is not until the growth of the medical model in the nineteenth and twentieth centuries that the assumption is made that disabled people are perversions of the norm and cannot therefore be allowed to serve God as priests. George Healey records that the canons of the Church of England in 1905 'do not admit the setting apart for the ministry of any man physically disqualified such as the blind, the deaf and dumb, and the lame' and cites diocesan bishops who admit the intellectual and spiritual competence of Deaf aspirants to the priesthood, but who always explain that they are bound to obey the church canons.[55] The more recent struggle for ordination by Deaf people will be discussed in the next chapter,

---

[50] Quote from Tennyson, *Idylls of the King*, 'as if some lesser God had made the world and not had force to shape it as he would'. Also the title of a play by Mark Medoff about the Deaf community and its relationship to the hearing world.

[51] Weir, 'Made Deaf in God's Image' in International Ecumenical Working Group conference, *The Place of Deaf people in the Church*, p. 6.

[52] Hull, *In the beginning there was darkness*, p. 72.

[53] Horne, *Injury and Blessing*, p. 297.

[54] Ibid., p. 298.

[55] George Healey, 'The difficulties of the British Deaf' in British Deaf and Dumb Association, *Proceedings of the ninth biennial conference* (London, 1905).

but Hull can instance Jane Wallman, a blind ordinand, who was only able to be ordained in the year 2000 after the principal of her theological college appealed to the Archbishop of Canterbury after two bishops turned her down as having a defect.[56] It would seem that this construction might still be one of the reasons for refusing Deaf people ordination to this day.

This construction of Deaf people (and their sign language) as 'abnormal' is visible in many writings about them. For example, Mary S. Garrett, a proponent of the oral system of education in early twentieth-century USA, refers to the 'unnatural' language of gestures,[57] a way of understanding sign languages that was not refuted, even by proponents of the manual method of education, until Stokoe in the 1960s.[58] Sutcliffe argues that signing and fingerspelling 'are radically different from the normal; they are abnormal ways of thinking and praying' and therefore it may be more difficult to teach a Deaf person to pray.[59] Sowter in the 1960s seems to argue that Deaf people are 'abnormal' in their immaturity, and often have 'unpleasing physical characteristics due to their physical disability'.[60] Finally, in 1997, the Committee for Ministry Among Deaf People, despite its affirmation of BSL as the natural language of Deaf people,[61] is still comparing Deaf people to hearing people and using assumptions that there is such a thing as normality. For example in discussing what it means to be Deaf the report states

> vision is a focussed sense, and only operates where a person looking, and is awake with eyes open ... a consequence of this is weaker bonds of contact between people ... Once a/Deaf person looks away, or goes out of sight of another person, contact is almost totally lost ... [this may affect] self-perception and feelings of wholeness.[62]

In other words, Deaf people are seen as being bound to have abnormal relationships with others because they are only aware of people if they can see them. This is making assumptions about 'normal ways' of forming and sustaining human relationships, through hearing and sight, which do not correspond to Deaf experiences of relationships.

It is this construction of people with disabilities that has preferred to keep them out of sight and argues that the presence of people with disabilities disturbs them. Webb-Mitchell suggests that able-bodied people are made uncomfortable by the

---

[56]   Hull, *In the beginning there was darkness*, p. 73.

[57]   Mary S. Garrett, *Possibilities of Deaf Children* (Philadelphia, 1906).

[58]   For further discussion of the way sign language has been constructed see 'Faith Comes by Hearing' below.

[59]   Canon T. H. Sutcliffe, 'Psychological difficulties in prayer as a consequence of deafness' in Pokorny (ed.), *The Word in Signs and Wonders*, p. 249.

[60]   Canon E. R. Sowter, 'The Health and Welfare of the Adult Deaf', appendix to Church Mission to the Deaf and Dumb in Walsall, Wednesbury and Wolverhampton, *Annual Report*, 74 (1960–61).

[61]   *The Church Among Deaf People* (London, 1997), p. 65.

[62]   Ibid., p. 7.

presence of people with disabilities because they are uncomfortable with the differences, and want to make such people like us: 'We [the normal community] are so uncomfortable with what someone cannot do we fail to appreciate who the person is'.[63] In Webb-Mitchell's argument, this is a problem with acceptance of individuals by individuals. We, as Christians, should be able to learn to accept people with disabilities for what they are, rather than reject them for what they are not. This rather over-optimistic and idealistic programme illustrates how widespread the construction of disability as an abnormality is without engaging with the structures that make such a construction possible. It is a question that requires tackling at a much deeper level than the level of individuals accepting individuals.

The construction of disability as something 'abnormal' suggests that a 'solution' is to render disabled people 'normal' and 'fit to be seen'. The importance of this construct in the life of the Deaf church can be seen in the adoption and perpetuation of St John of Beverley as the patron saint of Deaf people by the late nineteenth-century Deaf church. He is variously referred to in church publications as the first teacher of the deaf[64] and as taking a special interest in the poor and disabled,[65] but what St John of Beverley actually is reported to have done is to have restored speech to a dumb boy by making the sign of the cross on his tongue and then teaching him to speak the alphabet.[66] Jonathan Rée points out that not only does Bede describe the boy as dumb prior to his encounter with John of Beverley, he is also described as 'having scabs and scales on the head so that no hair ever grew on the crown' and that after miraculously being made to speak, he is also treated for these scabs and sores so he is restored to his people with a 'clear complexion, readiness of speech and a beautiful head of hair, whereas he had formerly been deformed, destitute and dumb'.[67] Rée suggests that John of Beverley is revered among those who work with d/Deaf people because he made a dumb boy look and behave 'normally', which is the ultimate aim of this very significant construction of disability.[68] Again, physical healing is seen as a major theological reaction to this concept of disability. If healing is not possible, the modern theory goes, then make people as near to normal as possible. Thus d/Deaf people must be taught to speak and lip-read and be 'integrated' and spend all their lives trying to be like hearing people.

David Pailin attempts to criticize the concept of a 'norm' to be measured against by comparing it to seeing our own taste in food, for example, as 'normal'.

---

[63]   Webb-Mitchell, *Unexpected guests at God's banquet*, p. 72.

[64]   Selwyn Oxley, *Work for the Deaf* (London, 1925).

[65]   'St John of Beverley Feast Day', Tees Valley Deaf Church Newsletter, Issue 2 (May 2000).

[66]   Bede, *Ecclesiastical History of the English People*, trans. Leo Sherley-Price, rev. edn, D. H. Farmer (Harmondsworth, 1990), chapter V.2, p. 268.

[67]   Ibid.

[68]   Jonathan Rée, *I see a voice* (London, 1999), p. 95.

If handicap (his word) means not being able to do the same as a non-handicapped person can, then we are all handicapped in some way because we do not all share the same skills and interests.[69] His suggestion is that there can be no theology of the handicapped as a distinct group, but only a theology of humanity that takes into account the handicapped state.[70] This is in part because there is no way to define 'handicap' without the unwarrantable comparison to a 'norm'.[71] Pailin seems to wish to dismiss the concept of a norm without quite knowing how to do it. He ignores the question of who defines the norm and its association with power and the maintenance of the dominant group in their position of dominance. By constructing people with disabilities as abnormal, it is possible to argue they do not have 'normal' desires for education, marriage and employment and so justify keeping them in ignorance and poverty. Saying 'we all are handicapped in some way' ignores the experience of systematic oppression in the lives and history of people with disabilities.

Pailin concludes that any theology relating to handicap cannot be a theology of liberation because 'the handicapped generally remain handicapped'[72] and as such he seems to be subscribing to the concept that liberation of people with disabilities is to be equated with healing. This is a construction of healing in general, and the healing miracles of Jesus in particular that is more generally acceptable in contemporary society than the previous construction that equates healing with forgiveness of sins. This view argues that Jesus, by healing people, was simply restoring them to society and in doing so was demonstrating the glory of God. Graham Monteith is one who interprets the healing of the blind man in John 9:1–12 in such a way.[73] This passage does specifically reject the concept of sin as the cause of the blindness, but is 'to reveal God's glory' any more positive a construction of disability? As Hull expresses it 'the man has been born blind to provide a sort of photo opportunity for Jesus'[74] or in other words, this interpretation of the text still presents the blind man as a passive object, rather than an active subject; he has been blind all his life merely so Jesus has someone so demonstrate his power on. Monteith argues that the blind man in John 9 is no longer bound by the restrictions imposed on him by society and the law as a result of his blindness but is freed to live within society. He associates this with Jesus' proclamation of himself as the one who comes to bring good news to the poor in Luke 4:16–19 and names the healing of the blind man as 'liberation'.[75] Stewart

---

[69]   David A. Pailin, *A gentle touch: from a theology of handicap to a theology of human being* (London, 1992), preface.

[70]   Ibid., p. 15.

[71]   Ibid., p. 29.

[72]   Ibid., p. 23.

[73]   W. Graham Monteith, *Disability: faith and acceptance* (Edinburgh, 1987), p. 29.

[74]   Hull, *In the beginning there was darkness*, p. 49.

[75]   Monteith, *Disability: faith and acceptance*, p. 30.

Govig is another who constructs the healing miracles of Jesus as 'liberation'.[76] However, he too suggests that those healed are liberated by being restored to 'normal' society; in his example, the 'deaf and dumb' man in Mark 7:31–8 was freed to join with others in praise of Jesus. This suggests that there is a 'normal' way to express praise and that is in verbal terms. In the first chapter, I defined liberation as having full access to the world as we are; as being about a change in society not the change in individual as liberation appears to be understood by the above authors.

Govig also suggests that the subject of the healing miracles is the mission of Jesus rather than the human condition of disability.[77] Horne seems to support this view when he suggests that the biggest significance of the impairment healings by Jesus is in the way they demonstrate his divine nature.[78] However, it is still the case that practically the only mention of disabled people in the Bible is as recipients of healing, even when they are given subject status by being affirmed as demonstrating key discipleship qualities and effectively act as evangelists.[79] Jesus may restore disabled people to society and enable them to be free to worship God in the temple once more, but the focus is still on an individual who needs correcting and restoring or on the individual as an object for demonstrating the divinity of Jesus. This construction, despite its connotations of 'common sense' and 'natural order', is in no way liberating for Deaf or disabled people; in fact its ability to be represented as common sense ('of course someone with only four working senses must be abnormal when compared to the majority of humankind with five') gives it the potential to be extremely dangerous and damaging to d/Deaf and disabled people in society.

Virtuous Sufferers

A third construction of disability identified by Eiesland in the Bible is the concept that if you are disabled you are suffering, and this suffering is somehow good for you.[80] This is less about the primary cause of disability and more a reflection on its purpose. For example, Paul's thorn in the flesh[81] is usually interpreted as a material 'thorn' or some sort of disability. Paul interprets it in his letter to the Corinthians as something sent by God to test his faith, and that the most appropriate response to such divine testing is righteous submission, which reveals the grace of God in

---

[76] Govig, *Strong at the broken places*, p. 99.

[77] Ibid., p. 100.

[78] Horne, *Injury and Blessing*, p. 331.

[79] Ibid., pp. 355 and 359.

[80] In this construction disability is assumed to be a cause of suffering, either directly through being unable to hear or indirectly through the consequences (for example social isolation, lack of education, underemployment) of being deaf.

[81] 2 Corinthians 12:7.

action.[82] Horne suggests that the testing of faith (and development of the soul) by the giving of impairment was understood in the early church as only being given to those with the potential to make use of them.[83] In other words, impairment as virtuous suffering was understood as a tribute to a person's potential for achievement rather than as a form of punishment or divine torture.

This construction of disability has appeared time and again in history, and unlike the previous two constructions, is not restricted to the late nineteenth and twentieth centuries. Webb-Mitchell, in a brief historical survey of the place of people with disabilities in history, speaks of the early and medieval church as caring for people with disabilities partly because such people were especially blessed. MacNutt also speaks of the history of the special place of suffering. He traces the change from the perception of sufferers as people to be healed in the early church to the perception of suffering as preferable for the sake of the soul. He relates this to the contribution of 'pagan' (Greco-Roman) thought that constructed the body as the enemy that got in the way of the perfection of the soul, so the more the flesh was mortified, the more the soul could be freed.[84]

Another perspective on suffering in the Christian tradition is the idea that suffering can have redemptive value. For example, many in the Black churches argued that while God did not want his people to suffer, that is that suffering and oppression was intrinsically bad, suffering could have secondary benefits.[85] Anthony Pinn suggests that this understanding of their suffering, known as redemptive suffering, was a major strand in black thought.[86] One black theologian who argued for such a view was Martin Luther King Jr. His argument was that as long as unmerited suffering was encountered and dealt with non-violently, it could be redemptive because it led to the reconciliation of black and white Americans, and also because God was on the side of those who suffered.[87] James Cone is another who, while arguing that black suffering is not ordained by God, and should not be accepted as the will of God, suggests that the connection to Christ's suffering on the cross through the suffering of Christ's followers can transform suffering into something that is redemptive and positive.[88] Pinn, however, is only one of several black people who have questioned whether suffering can have any redemptive value; he suggests that redemptive suffering and liberation are diametrically opposed ideas: 'one cannot embrace suffering as redemptive and effectively speak of liberation'.[89] While I would not accept Pinn's humanist

---

[82]   Eiesland, *The Disabled God*, p. 72.

[83]   Horne, *Injury and Blessing*, p. 167.

[84]   Francis MacNutt, *Healing* (London, 1989), pp. 65, 66.

[85]   Anthony B. Pinn, *Why Lord? Suffering and Evil in Black Theology* (New York, 1995), p. 10.

[86]   Ibid., p. 16.

[87]   Ibid., p. 75.

[88]   Ibid., p. 87.

[89]   Ibid., p. 16.

solution to the problem of unmerited suffering,[90] I agree that constructing the unmerited suffering of oppressed groups, such as Deaf and disabled people, as 'redemptive' in any shape or form is inimical to the enterprise of liberation. It carries with it the danger that all unmerited suffering should be passively accepted rather than protested against, because, while it may not be the will of God, it will help bring us closer to God.

One passage of particular significance in this construction is Mark 8:34, 'If any want to become my followers let them deny themselves and take up their cross and follow me'. Interpretations of this verse in writings on disability and healing struggle with it. Leslie Newbiggin identifies it with the essential paradox of Christianity; that of ministry through weakness, with the authority of the message certified by sharing in the suffering of Christ.[91] He recognizes that this image may also be used as a means of ensuring disabled people acquiesce in their own oppression.[92] To engage with this either/or picture, he can only suggest the gifts of people with disabilities are recognized and affirmed,[93] that such people have a specific part to pay in their weakness in society as it is constructed. This picture is still about disability as the affliction of an individual, and constructs the person with a disability as one with special gifts as a result of their 'weakness'.

Accounts of the lives of Deaf people written by hearing people abound in such constructions of Deaf people as being blessed with special gifts as a result of their deafness. For example, Dr William Sleight, headmaster of the Brighton and Sussex Institute for the Deaf and Dumb, wrote a memoir of a Deaf boy, John William Lashford, a pupil at the school who died young.[94] He represents Lashford as having because of his 'affliction' a great and simple faith in an age of rational doubt. Firth represents deafness as rendering certain ways of behaving acceptable when he says of Leslie Edwards, a notable Deaf missioner:

> In a strange way, Edwards' deafness provided a special opportunity for him to express his individual personality. His drive and enthusiasms might merely have encountered a rebuke had he been an ordinary hearing citizen. It was because of his deafness that people took him seriously and accepted his sometimes blunt behaviour.[95]

The Committee for the Spiritual Care of Deaf Mutes argue in conclusion to their report 'Mercifully, as some compensation for their pathetic infirmity, the deaf and dumb are nearly always gifted with special acuteness of vision'.[96] M. F. Washburn concludes that the little deaf child is able (despite their abnormality) to manifest

---

[90] Pinn, *Why Lord?*, p. 157.
[91] Leslie Newbiggin, 'Not whole without the handicapped' in Müller-Farenholz (ed.), *Partners in Life: the handicapped and the church* (Geneva, 1979), p. 18.
[92] Ibid., p. 20.
[93] Ibid., p. 24.
[94] Dr William Sleight, *A Voice from the Dumb* (London, 1848).
[95] Firth, *Chosen Vessels* (Exeter, 1988), p. 33.
[96] Committee for the Spiritual Care of Deaf Mutes, *Spiritual Care of Deaf Mutes*.

the glory of God by teaching us lessons of patience and courage.[97] Sutcliffe, quoting Jesus' dictum that we must become like children to enter the kingdom of heaven, argues 'Some of the deaf [although only "the best of them"], backward in education and general knowledge, have an amazingly simple childlike trust in God'.[98] This argument is very similar to the concept presented by Anthony Russo that their 'primitive thinking' leaves the deaf with a 'simple and beautiful faith, unencumbered by the accumulated layers of western man's religious controversies'.[99] Finally, the Church of England at the end of the twentieth century is still objectifying Deaf people as people with 'special gifts' as well as 'special needs',[100] people whose faith in God, 'untrammelled by the complexities of knowledge and understanding ... is direct, clear and simple (although very powerful)' and 'childlike in its openness and trust'.[101] This construct of Deaf people as possessing special gifts is an example of what Monteith calls the 'songs of praise syndrome'.[102] Deaf people blessed with such 'gifts' are expected to spend their lives inspiring and encouraging others rather than getting on with whatever they want to do.

Historically, this construction of disability has served to keep disabled people, along with other oppressed groups, in their subordinate positions. It also causes the perception of disability as abnormality to be internalized by disabled people themselves; suffering is interpreted as being simply about an individual's relationship with God. Is being 'divinely blessed' any more positive and truly liberating for the lives of those so affected? The seeming power of the powerless in the glorification of their suffering may be understood as one more means of and justification for active discrimination against people with disabilities, and one more excuse for not remedying the injustices that Deaf people and people with disabilities face in every aspect of their lives.

Faith Comes by Hearing

This fourth construct is specifically about Deaf people as users of sign language rather than English. The history of Deaf people indicates that for a long time they were widely constructed as being incapable of communication, except by use of simple gestures for concrete desires such as 'food', and therefore incapable of being educated. Such a perceived lack of language helps to explain why Deaf

---

[97] M. F. Washburn, *The educational mission of the deaf* (Chicago, *c.* 1920).

[98] Sutcliffe, *Soundless Worship: Spiritual care of the deaf and dumb*, report from the Central Advisory Council for the Spiritual Care of the Deaf and Dumb (*c.* 1950).

[99] Revd Anthony Russo, CSSR, 'The God of the Deaf Adolescent' in Pokorny (ed.), *The Word in Signs and Wonders*, p. 154.

[100] *The Church Among Deaf People*, p. 57.

[101] Ibid., p. 61.

[102] Monteith, *Disability: faith and acceptance*, p. 45.

people were long considered 'feeble minded and legally incompetent'.[103] Stewart Govig and Dorothy Miles both briefly discuss the legal and religious status of Deaf people in Judaism during the reign of Habakkuk and around the time of Christ. Govig mentions a question that arose of how much observance of Sabbath law was to be expected of Deaf people; if such people were not in full control of their minds, then they had reduced legal responsibility.[104] He says that the question was never settled one way or the other, but the query remains, if Deaf people did not have to observe the Sabbath and so obey the Jewish law, was this because God asked less of them than he did of those who could hear, or because God excluded them from the covenant with his people?

Whether or not they were fully part of the covenant, it still seems Deaf people were excluded from many religious and legal ceremonies as 'speech was held to be sacred ... [in such ceremonies] ... if someone could not "recite the formulae", they were not eligible to participate'.[105] This is despite the fact that Deaf people were common enough in society to have their right to marry by use of gestures discussed in the fourth-century Talmud.[106] This association of the ability to speak with legal and religious rites is also to be found in Roman practice, the legal codes of Justinian in the sixth century for example.[107] Many of the uses of the word translated 'deaf' in the Bible associates it with dullness of mind; the inability to hear is linked with the inability to think and the inability to conceive of language that is not spoken.[108] Muteness too is often used in negative ways throughout the Bible; idols made of silver and gold have mouths but make no sound in their throats,[109] and this inability to speak is taken as proof of their general incapacity to help people in the way that God can.[110]

Danker asks whether the resistance to deaf people and signs in Old Testament times was not just about the need for speech, but also because Israel had an ingrained resistance to the use of visual symbols due to their 'dreadful experience with idolatry'.[111] Whether or not this is a valid reason for the Old Testament view of deafness, it certainly can be argued that it is a factor in the response of Protestant churches to any visual representation of the Gospel. As a hearing biblical scholar, Krister Stendhal says 'Protestantism has a tendency to be a religion of the ears ... because only one cultural expression of the faith is permitted

---

[103] Dorothy Miles, *British Sign Language: a beginner's guide* (London, 1988), p. 10.

[104] Govig, *Strong at the broken places*, p. 24.

[105] Miles, *British Sign Language*, p. 10.

[106] Ibid.

[107] Ibid.

[108] See Hebrews 5:11 for example. *New Revised Standard Version* (*NRSV*) 'dull of understanding' is literally 'dull of hearing' and is so translated in the King James Version.

[109] For example Psalm 115:6–8 and Jeremiah 10:4–5.

[110] Horne, *Injury and Blessing*, p. 215.

[111] Danker, 'Deafness and hearing in the Bible' in Pokorny (ed.), *The Word in Signs and Wonders*, p. 29.

and that is music ... somehow things received through the ears are seen as less tainted by the devil than those received through the eyes'.[112] Protestantism, as exemplified by Calvin, certainly has always placed a high premium on the need for knowledge of the word of God coming before faith. This is because he is arguing against the scholastic concept of faith that is implicit and for the use of liturgy, preaching and scriptures in the vernacular. The subsequent development of church services in the language of the country would I suggest have suddenly revealed a division between those who could hear it and those who could not.

This inability to conceive of a full and legally competent language except in terms of speech and hearing is reflected in the language used in much of the New Testament about the word of God. Romans 10:17 for example says: 'So faith comes from what is heard and what is heard comes from the word of Christ'. This verse read literally suggests that the writer did not include d/Deaf people who communicate visually as being able to develop a personal faith in Christ in response to the grace mediated through his word. Augustine is one early theologian who appears to interpret this passage to argue that d/Deaf people cannot become believers, 'for what great fault innocence is sometimes born blind, sometimes born deaf, which blemish indeed hinders faith, as witness the apostle who says: "faith comes by hearing"'.[113] This belief of Augustine, referred to in every major work on Deaf people, has always been seen as either justifying the prioritizing of teaching of speech and lip-reading to Deaf children above all else,[114] or as an insurmountable obstacle for Deaf people in their relationship to Christianity.[115] However, Per Erikson, citing the work of Christer Degsell, an Augustinian scholar, concludes that what Augustine really meant was that d/Deaf people could not acquire faith by listening to spoken sermons the way hearing people did (and which was the major form of knowledge transmission in a world where almost no one could read); they had to find alternative means for accessing and transmitting the Gospel.[116] In another place, he goes on to say, Augustine refers to gestures and signs as *verba visibilia* or visible words, so presumably he thought deaf people could be saved if the Gospel was transmitted to them through signs.

Whatever Augustine really intended, the consequence of this oft-quoted interpretation of Romans 10:17 has been a dismissal of sign either as a language or as an adequate means of communicating with God or transmitting the Gospel.

---

[112] Krister Stendhal, 'Words, signs and wonders in the Bible' in Pokorny (ed.), *The Word in Signs and Wonders*, p. 22.

[113] Augustine, *Contra Julianum Pelagianum*, 111.10, quoted in Marilyn Daniels, *Benedictine roots in the development of deaf education* (Westport, CT, 1997), p. 4.

[114] See Abraham Farrar, *Arnold's Education of the Deaf* (London, 1901), revised edition of 1888 original (and reprinted as recently as 1954).

[115] See John Vickrey van Cleve and Barry A. Crouch, *A place of their own: creating the Deaf community in America* (Washington DC, 1989), p. 4.

[116] Per Erikson, *The history of deaf people: a source book* (Sweden, 1993), p. 18.

Oralists,[117] such as Thomas Arnold, even felt justified by this construction of sign in punishing Deaf children for signing because he believed that spiritual and intellectual development (and hence salvation) required spoken language; in his understanding sign could only express commonest physical wants.[118] Even the most fervent hearing manualist does not seem to support sign language as anything other than the most efficient means of teaching English, and once English is learnt, sign can be discarded. Samuel Smith, for example, who can be taken as representative of the chaplains and missioners at the end of the nineteenth century who supported the use of the manual method, writes 'signs are only the scaffolding by means of which a knowledge of language is erected; therefore when the building is finished let the scaffolding be removed; and the best educated Deaf are those who can communicate with their friends in correctly written language, without any reference to signs, through they may use them for brevity's sake among themselves'.[119] Sutcliffe, the organizing secretary of the Central Advisory Council for Spiritual Care of the Deaf, has a similar view in the 1950s,

> when a person cannot benefit from a hearing aid and finds lip-reading difficult, the medical profession generally has no further treatment or suggestion to offer. The Welfare officer to the Deaf has his solution to the problem and IT WORKS … in communicating with the deaf, he uses … finger-spelling and gesture … in conjunction with lip-reading … The method may not be liked, it may be objected to as seemingly ugly or being distasteful to many hearing people – but IT WORKS.[120]

A more recent example of how sign is ideally seen only as an accessory to English is in the work of George Firth, a chaplain with deaf people from the 1940s to the 1980s. He describes how those Deaf people who only used sign were referred to as 'dummies' in the 1930s and how this attitude has changed in recent years. 'Now, however, sign language has become much more acceptable. It is realized that a combination of lip-reading and speech, plus an elegant and judicious use of an occasional sign – or even a natural gesture – can greatly ease the strain on a person with severe deafness … one does not need to launch out into horse-bookies "tic tac"!'[121]

Many reasons are given over the years for the inadequacy of sign as a language for theology or talking about God. This is similar to the way the written word has been considered superior to the spoken word in theology; Jacques Derrida, for example, identifies this trend based on the grounds that the written word lasts

---

[117] Those who argued deaf children should not be taught or use any sign, but should be taught to speak and lip-read, that is the oral method of education.

[118] Cited in Rée, *I See a Voice*, p. 225.

[119] Smith, *The Deaf and Dumb*.

[120] Revd T. H. Sutcliffe, Foreword to Church Mission to the Deaf and Dumb in Walsall, Wednesbury and Mid-Staffordshire, *Annual Report*, no. 70 (1956–57).

[121] Firth, *Chosen Vessels*, p. 108.

longer.[122] In the nineteenth century with the growth of Darwin's theories, sign was understood as a language at a lower stage of evolution than spoken language. This theory appears in an article by a (hearing) missioner in 1963 who comments that 'the natural means of communication for a DEAF child, who racially is forced back to that dim period in prehistory when Man sought a means of communication, is a gesture or sign language'.[123] Griffiths goes on to say that sign possesses serious grammatical faults because it has never been taken seriously by educators of the Deaf 'who might have lifted this natural language from its crude patterns to the level of an efficient and grammatical means of communication'.[124]

The inefficiency and general vagueness of sign as a means of communication is another theme in arguments against sign as a language suitable for use in the church. The abbé Deschamps, an oralist rival to the abbé de l'Epée in the education of Deaf children in France, contended, 'gestures [sic] are vague and equivocal ... in sign we point to the sky, where the All-Powerful lives. Who can assure us that the deaf-mute does not take the sky to be God himself?'[125] The objectors (the hearing management committee) to the Deaf committees' proposal for building a separate church for Deaf people in London in 1864 argued that 'the vague language of signs' was not a suitable means for the administration of Communion 'except under special circumstances in which no church is required'.[126] Brian Murray (secretary of the General Synod Council for the Deaf in the 1970s) is one of several who write of how sign language is 'sublime' in the presentation of poetry, scripture and prayer. However, even at this stage, after Stokoe's proof that sign was a true language, Murray is still arguing sign is inadequate alone: 'it is more usual to combine the language of signs with the manual alphabet so that English language patterns may be presented and a proper sequence of ideas structured'.[127]

A particular inadequacy of sign language in a church context is in its perceived inability to represent abstract ideas; a perception that has continued within the church despite many assertions by linguists that sign is capable of expressing everything that a spoken language such as English does. Deschamps, in eighteenth-century France, asserts that signs are concrete and therefore severely limited, especially in developing any form of abstract ethical and religious understanding. 'Reduced almost entirely to an animal existence' he said, 'they have only their passions for a guide'.[128] Thomas Arnold, the leading British oralist of the late

---

[122] Jacques Derrida, *Writing and Difference*, trans. Alan Bass (Chicago: Chicago University Press, 1978).

[123] Christopher Griffiths, 'The deaf child – His problems and education' in Church Mission to the Deaf and Dumb of Walsall, Wednesbury and Mid-Staffordshire, *Annual Report*, no. 76 (1963). Author's capitalization.

[124] Ibid.

[125] Quoted in Lane, *When the mind hears*, p. 96.

[126] Quoted in Lysons, *Voluntary Welfare Societies*, p. 42.

[127] Murray, *... and no birds sing*.

[128] In Lane, *When the mind hears*, p. 97.

nineteenth century, argued at the Milan conference in 1880, 'no doubt signs are often animated and picturesque, but they are absolutely inadequate for abstraction'.[129] A more recent example, from the Annual Report of Walsall Mission in 1960, refers to the use of special film strips to help prepare younger deaf people for confirmation: 'visual means of instruction can be of great help to the deaf, as the deaf have great difficulty in understanding abstract ideas'.[130] The incapacity of sign (and therefore Deaf people) to cope with abstract ideas (such as the idea of God for example) is a constant theme in the writing of Tom Sutcliffe. At one international conference for all pastoral workers among the Deaf he talks about the problems of the use of metaphorical language in the Bible and in worship. In his paper, the problems are presented as 'both linguistic and psychological'; hearing people can abstract the meaning from the metaphor, but deaf only see a concrete, literal meaning that makes for absurdity. Even if the meaning of the metaphor is then explained to Deaf people 'it is in concepts that are not easily visualized, and therefore not easily explained to the deaf'.[131] In a paper published by the Central Advisory Council for the Spiritual Care of the Deaf and Dumb, Sutcliffe spells out the practical problems created by the supposed inability of sign to represent abstract ideas. He is describing how the missioner, reader or chaplain preaching to Deaf people has to simplify their sermons for a congregation of Deaf people to make them more concrete and childlike, because the 'abstract can rarely be gestured ... we cannot put forth delicate shades of meaning for the deaf, because they would not be seen ... [the sermon] is not an artist's painting but a cartoon'.[132] This idea that sign language cannot cope with abstract concepts persists to the present day. The 1997 report *The Church Among Deaf People* in its section on learning about faith [specifically referring to children] says 'Concrete facts are, for the most part, easily absorbed but an appreciation of the abstract and the spiritual is much more difficult due to the limitations in language development'.[133] This persistence of the belief that 'faith comes by hearing' as expressed in the inadequacy of any alternative means of transmission of faith is despite a refutation offered in mid nineteenth-century France. Pierre Desloges, Deaf and using sign language as his means of communication, points out that the sign for God may be the concrete sign for 'above', but that does not mean he thinks that the sky is God! His attitude and expression (the 'non-manual' features of the

---

[129] Ibid., p. 391.

[130] Church Mission to the Deaf and Dumb in Walsall, Wednesbury and Mid-Staffordshire, *Annual Report*, no. 73 (1959–60).

[131] Canon T. H. Sutcliffe, 'Psychological difficulties in prayer as a consequence of deafness' in Pokorny (ed.), *The Word in Signs and Wonders*, p. 249.

[132] Sutcliffe, *Soundless Worship*.

[133] *The Church Among Deaf People*, p. 40.

sign) show quite clearly that he understands the difference, that sign is capable of expressing abstract concepts.[134]

Sign language is a feature of the Deaf church in this country but it is largely used to translate the liturgy of the hearing church (Common Worship: services and prayers for the Church of England for example) and its hymns. Relatively few attempts are made to incorporate cultural aspects of sign language into services and teaching appears to remain at a very simplified level so I would argue that Deaf people are still constructed as being unable to fully engage with God's word. In the 'mainstream' church, sign language continues to be constructed as inferior to spoken language. Webb-Mitchell, for example, suggests that 'gestures' (in which he includes sign language as 'highly formalized and iconic') can be a way for all the Christian community, whether able-bodied or not, to communicate and worship together. Following Calvin's edict 'sacraments are God's word made visible', he suggests that everyone can move as appropriate in the service (sit, stand, kneel and so on) receive the bread and wine and see it being broken, and act out God's love in visiting.[135] Such inclusiveness is not possible if, for example, the congregation stands as a 'gesture' to acknowledge the importance of the Gospel reading, those in wheelchairs are excluded. This attitude also constructs sign and gesture as something that is a lowest common denominator and therefore something that the able-bodied are kindly reducing themselves to if that is all they share. For a Deaf person in an oral service, standing, sitting, kneeling, moving are all possible, but hearing people also have the words, the prayers and so on. To suggest that the movement alone is sufficient for Deaf people is to suggest that the construction of such people as being unable to fully participate in the worship of the community of God continues.

The belief that 'faith comes by hearing' is not only a factor in the construction of sign language as unworthy or unable to communicate faith (and therefore Deaf people as unable to engage with the word of God except in English), it is also a strong element in the way the ability and inability to speak has been constructed. Heinicke, one of the earliest proponents of oralism, claimed speech was God's gift, and that abstract concepts were only accessible via the spoken word.[136] In fact, as was later argued at the congress on the education of the deaf in Milan in 1880, signing was 'devil inspired nonsense'.[137] After this conference Farrar (the most famous pupil of the English proponent of oralism, Thomas Arnold) quoted Dr Zucchi, Board President at the Royal School for the Deaf in Milan (a leading oralist establishment), when he proclaimed, 'Speech is the light of the soul and the soul on earth is the light of the divine idea'.[138] At this same congress, the president,

---

[134] Desloges, 'A Deaf person's observation about *An elementary course of education for the Deaf* in Lane (ed.), *The deaf experience*, p. 37.

[135] Webb-Mitchell, *Unexpected guests at God's banquet*, Chapter 7.

[136] Dimmock, *Cruel Legacy*, p. 18.

[137] Ibid., p. 30.

[138] Quoted in McLoughlin, *A history of the education of the deaf*, p. 18.

Guilio Tarra, another Italian oralist, contends that 'Oral speech is the sole power that can rekindle the light God breathed into man when, giving him a soul in a corporeal body, he gave him also a means of understanding, of conceiving and of expression'.[139] In other words, the delegates at the Milan congress were agreed that speech was necessary for Deaf people to be able to claim to have been made in the image of God and therefore necessary for Deaf people to be accorded the status of full human beings. Aude de Saint Loup reaches a similar conclusion about the medieval view of deaf-mute people; their inability to speak raised doubts about their status as human beings because when God created Adam he 'blew his Spirit into him' which is what gave him life. Iconography connects this 'divine breath' directly with speech as God's word (which is the only thing that maintains divinity in humans after the Fall) is always presented as being spoken and heard. 'Faith comes by hearing' or the 'Word is received through the ear'.[140] This direct link between speech and the divine nature is discussed by Jonathan Rée. He suggests that in late medieval times, speech impediments were seen as an appalling spiritual calamity since the voice was the 'breath of human life' and the 'embodiment of the divine power'. 'Even God had to use voice to make the world, and Christ used vocal means for his miracles'.[141] This being so, 'creatures formed in God's image ought, of necessity, to be able to speak' and so those who were altogether incapable of speech or vocalization must be beyond the reach of comfort and assistance. It is not until the fifth century that Deaf people were granted the sacrament of baptism, the eleventh that they were allowed to marry and the thirteenth before it was acknowledged that they could make confession to a priest by signs (and therefore be admitted to Holy Communion for which the sacrament of penance was obligatory).[142] It could be argued that this view is only of historical interest, but responses to the report of the Deaf lesbian seeking a Deaf sperm donor to try to have a Deaf baby reveals that hearing and speech are still seen as a 'blessing' from God and the lack of them as a major obstacle in life and in faith.[143]

---

[139] In Lane, *When the mind hears*, p. 393.

[140] Aude de Saint-Loup 'Images of the Deaf in Medieval Western Europe' in Fischer and Lane (eds), *Looking Back: a reader on the history of Deaf communities and their sign languages* (Hamburg, 1993), p. 389.

[141] Rée, *I See a Voice*, p. 89.

[142] Aude de Saint-Loup, 'Images of the Deaf', p. 390.

[143] Jeanette Winterson, 'How would we feel if blind women claimed the right to a blind baby?' in *The Guardian*, Tuesday 9 April 2002 (online article), Patricia Pearson 'Deafness: a gift no child should be given' in *The National Post*, Ontario, Wednesday 10 April 2002 (online article) and Sheenagh Pugh, email to *The Guardian*, Thursday 11 April 2002 (online letters page).

Conclusion

These constructions may not have been universally accepted in the ancient world, but I have shown they exist in the present day in the way Deaf people have been treated by and discussed by the church, including by those who work with them. Given that all work with Deaf people historically arose from a Christian context, I would suggest that these constructions must, together, provide the basic conceptual roots of the oppressive medical model. Until these constructions are uncovered and explicitly rejected, we cannot hope to eliminate the medical model from theology no matter how well meaning our intentions are. Deaf Liberation Theology must formulate its own theological constructions of Deaf people before it can truly be said to be working for the liberation of the Deaf children of God.

Chapter 5

Deaf People Constructed in the Church as an Organization

The persistence of the four constructs identified in the previous chapter, and consequently, of the medical model in the face of the strong alternative cultural construction of what it means to be Deaf and a radically changed and rapidly changing world suggests that some strong forces are acting to preserve the status quo. I argue, along with Nancy Eiesland, that one of these forces is the potential for power and control over d/Deaf people's lives created by seeing d/Deaf (and disabled) people as objects of charity.[1] This particular construct has been the basic principal behind the organizational structures of the Deaf church over the years, both up until the 1970s when it was primarily a welfare agency with religious involvement and from the 1970s onward when the focus shifted to a more specifically religious organization. This construct is at the roots of the institutionalized oppression of d/Deaf people within the structures of the church; and therefore to transform the Deaf church into an organization truly working for the liberation of Deaf people we need to deconstruct this edifice, to tear down whatever prevents d/Deaf people from realizing their full potential before we can rebuild. Looking at the experiences of users of secular charities in the third world and d/Deaf charities in the UK can help us understand how the Deaf church operates as an organization, where it continues to fail Deaf people and how it could be improved.[2]

Construction as Objects of Charitable Giving

The Deaf church as an organization, originated as, and to a large extent still operates as, a charity, divided into those who give or do and those who receive. Understanding d/Deaf people as objects of charity means that there must be people who are constructed as the subjects who give to charity; this construct requires both donors and recipients to operate. Despite their fundamental interrelatedness,

---

[1]   Eiesland, *The Disabled God: towards a liberatory theology of disability* (Nashville, 1994), p. 73.

[2]   Structures in the Church of England in general and the Deaf church in particular have changed in the few years since this was written. The structures as described are correct in 2001.

being the 'donor' (of money or time or skills) is valued much more than being a 'recipient'. Stewart Govig, an able-bodied American theologian who chaired a committee made up of disabled and non-disabled people to formulate the response of the Lutheran Church to the UN 'International Year of the Disabled' in 1981, discusses some of the effects that being perpetually 'objects of charity' has on people with disabilities. Such people are always on the receiving end of favours and kindness and feel constantly obliged to be grateful and tend to think of self as a non-producer and therefore a burden on society.[3] Being the object of charity is inevitably associated with a second-class status in a society that glorifies achievement and work. Peter Beresford, a disabled man, argues 'Individual reliance on charity is personally demeaning, inadequate and unreliable. It is out of people's control, inherently patronising and substitutes personal dependency for disabled peoples individual and collective rights'.[4]

In addition to being experienced as personally demeaning, being constructed as an object of charity can also be experienced as extremely disempowering. As Alker argues 'once perceived to be "in need" we might well as well be',[5] or in other words, constantly being constructed as being in need of help means that we experience ourselves as needing that help. An example of this was seen when the post of secretary to the Committee for Ministry among Deaf People (effectively the 'head of the Deaf church' as it is structured today) was frozen on the retirement of the previous incumbent of the post. Instead of seeing this as an opportunity to examine whether this post really served the needs of Deaf people in the church (especially as it is currently structured so as to effectively exclude a d/Deaf person from doing the job) a campaign was instantly mobilized to agitate for the 'unfreezing' of the post on the grounds that 'we need someone in that position to fight on our behalf'.[6] The Deaf members of the NDCC have, for so long, seen themselves as dependent on the help of others they cannot see how things could be done any other way.

This is just one of many examples of d/Deaf people not seeing the possibilities of taking up options of gaining control over their own organizations and churches because of a fundamental lack of confidence in their own capabilities. Moving from a donor–recipient relationship between hearing and d/Deaf people to one that is more equal is a more complex process than hearing people resigning en masse and saying to d/Deaf people 'here you are; you do it'. There is a delicate balance to be drawn here between supporting d/Deaf people to do their own thing and being over-paternalistic and arguing they still cannot cope.

---

[3]   Govig, *Strong at the broken places*, p. 41.

[4]   Peter Beresford, 'Poverty and disabled people: challenging dominant debates and policies', *Disability and Society*, 11/4 (1996): 558.

[5]   Doug Alker, *really not interested in the Deaf?* (Darwen, 2000), p. 105.

[6]   Reports from 'NDCC Autumn Conference 2001' and Ven. Gordon Kuhrt's talk to the NDCC committee on 'Future of the Church's Ministry Among Deaf People' in *Signs* (Spring 2002): 5, 7.

The attitude that Deaf people cannot do it for themselves is common in many authors writing in the area of theology and disability. *The Church Among Deaf People* prioritizes the need to do things for Deaf people. Its first recommendation to the General Synod of the Church of England is 'that the Church of England at national and diocesan level *takes responsibility for* helping people to appreciate the gifts and to understand the needs of all deaf people, and for putting energy and resources, people and finance, into using these gifts and meeting these needs'.[7] Despite the reference to the gifts of Deaf people as well as their needs, this recommendation is still perpetuating the image of Deaf people as those who need to have things done for them, thus dividing the Deaf church into those (mostly hearing) who do and those (d/Deaf and deaf-blind) who receive. Alker identifies this division as 'organizational paternalism', which he defines as 'the control of power by organizations that purport to 'speak for Deaf people', enabling them to get what they want in order to maintain or enhance their organizations ... regardless of whether or not it is actually what Deaf people want'.[8]

Webb-Mitchell attempts to provide an alternative construction than that of helping disabled people as objects of charity. He uses the parable of the great banquet in Luke 14:15–24 and argues that we are all invited to join with God in the banquet as equals in the common life of the spirit.[9] He suggests that people with disabilities are especially wise in the parable as they graciously accept the invitation extended by God when others are too busy to do so.[10] This leads him to formulate a grand vision of inclusiveness acted out in the life of the church; we must invite, welcome and care for 'guests' representative of all human conditions including disability.[11] The basic difficulty with the image of the banquet is that people with disabilities are still objectified as people to be invited and welcomed; 'inclusion' is a wonderful idea, but it still carries the implication of a group inviting individual others to join in with their way of doing things. It is not until page 124 of his book that he suggests asking people with disabilities themselves what they experience and feel. The other difficulty is the idealization of people with disabilities, as he seems to think they will be as glad to accept the invitation as the guests were at the original 'great banquet'. He does not seem to consider the possibility that those who came to the banquet in the end were likely to have been those desperate for food and bored with nothing to do. People with disabilities are as likely to be preoccupied with worldly concerns as any other. This construction continues to objectify people with disabilities as people who will be glad to be invited anywhere and happy to respond positively to such an invitation. The possibility that many people with disabilities are so excluded and alienated by the

---

[7]   *The Church Among Deaf People*, p. 53 (my emphasis).
[8]   Alker, *really not interested in the Deaf*, p. 106.
[9]   Webb-Mitchell, *Unexpected guests at God's banquet*, p. 84.
[10] Ibid., p. 91.
[11] Ibid., p. 107.

church that they are unlikely to perceive any such invitation as anything but patronizing pity is not considered in this construction.

This effort, along with other similar ones, to do away with the construction of d/Deaf and disabled people as objects of charity condemns the stereotype of the pitiful object of charity, but this condemnation is not sufficient for d/Deaf and disabled people to be liberated from this particular construct. To do this, the underlying structures and assumptions also need to be questioned or else, as happens here, the arguments end up perpetuating and justifying the stereotype in different terms and continuing to disempower d/Deaf and disabled people within the life of the church.

This well-meaning disempowerment of people with disabilities is illustrated in the access policies in many churches today. Eiesland details the case of the American Lutheran Church (the committee chaired by Govig) that adopted an access policy in 1980 in preparation for the UN International Year of the Disabled in 1981. This policy ignored the burgeoning disabled rights movement and continued to place able-bodied people at the speaking centre, speaking of doing things for disabled people.[12] The fundamental flaws in this policy are shown up in a later section of the document. It argues that not all disabled people can be considered for ordination or public ministry because of congregational discomfort with persons of visible disabilities and the need to maintain religious rituals in the way they are done by able-bodied clergy.[13] John Hull agrees with this assessment of the access policies of the church as being more about the needs of the congregation than the disabled individual. He quotes Deuteronomy 27:18 'cursed be anyone who misleads a blind person' and argues from the experience of blind people seeking ordination that behind this apparent compassion, encouraged by the church, is a deep failure to offer full and real acceptance and inclusion of blind people in the structures of the church.[14] Deaf people seeking ordination face similar obstacles, despite the rhetoric on the part of the mainstream Church of England of 'access for all' and the CMDP 'welcoming the development' of the growth in the numbers of ordained Deaf people.[15] For example, one Deaf ordinand[16] had to have his wife act as a sign language interpreter throughout his training because neither his diocese nor the central church training body would fund interpreters. Other Deaf ordinands and clergy who have faced difficulties related to lack of deaf awareness either in their training or in their job hunting have had to solve these difficulties alone. The support they might have hoped for from the CMDP was never forthcoming. Those Deaf people who have managed to overcome these obstacles did so because they had a good relationship with their own diocesan officials, not because those with influence in the Deaf church supported them. Yet

---

12   Eiesland, *The Disabled God*, p. 75.
13   Ibid., p. 86.
14   Hull, *In the beginning there was darkness*, p. 73.
15   *The Church Among Deaf People*, p. 29.
16   'Ordinand' refers to priests in training.

other Deaf people do not even get the opportunity to go forward for selection to the ordained ministry because their chaplain will not recognize that they might have a calling and they do not have an independent relationship with any other clergy who might support them in exploring their sense of vocation. The obstacles placed in the way of the ordination of people with disabilities by a church which promotes a policy of access hints at the power dynamics underlying this construction of disability: keeping people with disabilities as silent objects and passive recipients of charity rather than recognizing them as subjects calling for justice that might shake up the structures and rituals of the church. This construct is visible in much of the work done to make churches more accessible to people with disabilities; work such as ramps and loops rarely extend to include the sanctuary, thus effectively stating that people in wheelchairs or using a hearing aid will not be in the 'active' area round the altar, the symbol of authority in many churches. People with disabilities are expected to be passively receiving the ministry of others, or ministering to others 'in their own special way'. They are not expected to be holding the positions of authority within the church structures as reflected in the understanding of the ordained ministry.

The importance of the access of d/Deaf and disabled people to positions of power and authority within the church cannot be overstated. If d/Deaf and disabled people cannot become church leaders and have real influence over structures and policies that affect their own lives and their own faith, then no matter how well they can access the church building and worship, it is not a liberating church.

Models of Charity

It can be argued that while Deaf people were once regarded as objects of charity, this is no longer the case in the church as d/Deaf people are no longer reliant on the missions for welfare and interpreting support, and also due to increased opportunities to participate in the life of the church.[17] I would suggest that this argument depends on a particular view of charity as exemplified by the model of charity as a 'moral economy' described below. Similar arguments can be found for the idea that organizations in the 'third world' are no longer charitable organizations, but 'development agencies'. Sarah White and Romy Tiongco disagree with this assessment and have identified three other models, 'liberal development', 'taking responsibility' and 'liberation', of which only the last one does not continue to divide people into 'donors' and 'recipients', and thus perpetuate the basic assumptions behind the idea of charity. All four models are to be found in the world of today at many different levels; it is not a question of current and past models. It is not always easy to discern which the dominant model in each situation is. What follows below is my attempt to apply these models to the experience of Deaf people in the Church.

---

[17] *The Church Among Deaf People*, p. 13.

The Moral Economy

Perhaps the first model of charity to be found historically, and the only one until late in the nineteenth century, may be called 'the moral economy'. This model understands poverty or disability as something that just happens. God has created us all different: some to be rich, some poor; some to be able bodied and some disabled; some to hear and some to be deaf; some who 'have' and some who 'have not'. The relationship between those who 'have' and those who 'have not' is one of mutual rights and obligations. The 'haves' are to behave towards the 'have nots' with fairness and compassion, expressing their thanks to the God who has given them what they have by sharing it with those who have not. In return, the 'have nots' have the responsibility to accept their God-given lot, being humble, hardworking, loyal and grateful for what they are given from the 'charity of the rich'.[18]

This model in one form or another dates back to Old Testament times, as formalized in the Deuteronomic law.[19] Helping your neighbour in the shape of the widows and orphans was your religious obligation and responsibility and their right. The ancient Israelites had a vision of a society where all things came from God; the people were merely stewards to oversee the harvest and distribution of God's gifts. The responsibility for distributing the harvest – sharing their good fortune – did not rest specifically with individuals, but with the community. For the people of Israel to be righteous in God's eyes, they had to take good care of the have nots dwelling with them to the social and spiritual benefit of them all. As White and Tiongco express it 'caring for the poor is actually built into the political framework'.[20] The book of Leviticus classifies people with disabilities as being recipients of the same kind of 'justice' as the poor, widows and orphans,[21] so we can justifiably assume that they had the same rights to glean food from the fields after the harvest and so on.[22]

The ideal of the moral economy is probably the original hearing model of welfare in the Deaf church, as references by wealthy philanthropists such as Selwyn Oxley to 'the Englishman's way' of helping those who need practical assistance and cannot help themselves make clear.[23] In fact, giving to charity was

---

[18]   Sarah White and Romy Tiongco, *Doing theology and development: meeting the challenge of poverty* (Edinburgh, 1997), p. 37.

[19]   See for examples Leviticus 19:9–10, 23:22; Deuteronomy 24:19–22. In these three extracts, the Hebrew people are commanded not to harvest their crops too thoroughly, but to leave corn and olives and grapes for the poor, the foreigners, the widows and the orphans to glean.

[20]   White and Tiongco, *Doing theology and development*, p. 40.

[21]   Leviticus 19:14.

[22]   It's worth noting that if we believe the strictures of the prophets such as Isaiah and Amos, the Israelites never achieved this lovely egalitarian vision.

[23]   Selwyn Oxley, *Ephphata Sunday and its meaning* (London, *c.* 1938).

an accepted responsibility and obligation of the wealthier classes for centuries. Peter Shapely analyses social structures in Victorian Manchester and concludes that:

> Charitable association allowed all individuals with the necessary capital to acquire or maintain symbolic power ... to transform economic power into symbolic power ... The notion of charity work as God's work was an essential component of the charity field ... obituaries portrayed such men as virtuous Christians who had fulfilled their duty to God through their charity to the poor.[24]

Whatever the motives for giving to charity, the construction of those in need of help remained one of objectifying such people and rendering them passive and silent. Records of charities usually refer to benefactors as individuals, recipients as an undifferentiated lump: 'the handicapped' or 'the poor'. The Annual Reports of the Church Mission to the Deaf and Dumb in Walsall, Wednesbury and Mid-Staffordshire name the hearing founders (who started the work), mostly hearing missioners (who do the work), the hearing management committee (who oversee the work) and the major (hearing) benefactors (who fund the work) but consistently refer to 'the deaf', 'the deaf and dumb' or 'the born deaf' as the people whom the whole mission exists to serve. Even the deaf boy who inspired the foundation of the mission (by Jane Besmeres) is never given the dignity of a name, but is always referred to as 'the deaf and dumb boy'.[25]

In this model the power and control of the Deaf church is in the hands of those who are 'fitted by birth' or position or status to be in charge. Historically, the Deaf churches were by and large run by a management committee made up of local clergy and businessmen, often with no experience of Deaf people, but who were major donors to the individual church missions. Deaf people were only trustees or on management committees if they themselves were born into the gentry (for example, Sir Arthur Fairbairn, born Deaf, founder and benefactor of the mission to deaf people in Southampton and treasurer of RADD)[26] and usually could only become missioners or be ordained if they were protégées of a churchman with enough power to get round the canon law forbidding ordination of people with a defect. The first ordained Deaf man in the Church of England, Richard Pearce, was one of many educated Deaf men who worked to preach the Gospel to Deaf people at that time, but he, alone, was lucky enough to attract the attention and support of the Bishop of Winchester who ordained him in 1885.[27] He is described as the 'deaf

---

[24]   P. Shapely, 'Charity, status and leadership', *Journal of Social History* 32/1 (1998): 162.

[25]   'The story of the mission', Church Mission to the Deaf and Dumb in Walsall, Wednesbury and Mid-Staffordshire, *Annual Report*, no. 73 (1959–60).

[26]   Arthur Dimmock, 'Sir Arthur Henderson Fairbairn' in Jackson and Lee (eds), *Deaf Lives: Deaf people in history* (Feltham, 2001), p. 62.

[27]   Geoffrey J. Eagling, 'The Reverend Richard Aslett Pearce' in Jackson and Lee (eds), *Deaf Lives*, p. 147.

son of a leading inhabitant of Southampton',[28] a fact which highlights the perceived need under this model for people to come from the 'right class' for leadership. Even then, he was only ever ordained deacon, which means that he was never able to pronounce the absolution of sins, to give a blessing or celebrate Holy Communion, all-important symbols of authority within the Church of England.[29] Pearce was not the only Deaf man to be ordained at that time. Edward Rowland was a self-taught Deaf missioner, influenced by Matthew Burns, who was ordained as a minister in the Congregational church in Wales in 1882. Being a nonconformist church, all that was required was that his Deaf congregation wrote a 'requisition' asking that Edward Rowland be formally ordained as their minister and be known as the Revd Edward Rowland.[30] We are told that Rowland went on to serve his Deaf congregation in exactly the same way as any other nonconformist minister served his. The 'moral economy' model of leadership in a charitable organization was very dominant, but it was not the only possible model available.

This model that those who control the work of charitable organizations such as the Deaf church are those who have the right status rather than those who have the right experience can still be found operating today. Doug Alker describes how, when he became chair of the East Lancashire Deaf Society (ELDS) in 1984 he was not only the first Deaf chair, he was the only d/Deaf person on the management committee.[31] His first move as chair was to amend the constitution so that 51 per cent of the management committee had to be d/Deaf. He writes that 15 years later, the ELDS is still the only Deaf charitable organization in the country that is d/Deaf controlled. The situation is similar in the church. One diocese, for example, has (as of 2001) a management committee for the work among deaf people. This committee is chaired by a prominent churchman from the diocese, a friend of the bishop, who cares about Deaf people but who still cannot use sign language after many years as chairman. At a national level, the chair and vice-chair of the Committee for Ministry among Deaf People (CMDP) are a bishop and a lay representative from the General Synod who are hearing and do not have any personal experience of working with d/Deaf people.[32] The same hearing laywoman from the General Synod chairs the training committee, responsible for the training of new chaplains and for meeting the training needs of d/Deaf people within the church. All these committees do have d/Deaf representatives serving on them, but

---

[28]   Committee for the Spiritual Care of Deaf Mutes, *Spiritual Care of Deaf Mutes*.

[29]   The Church of England has what is referred to as a threefold understanding of ministry, the lowest level being deacons, who may then be ordained priests. A very few are then chosen to be consecrated as bishops. Women followed a similar process to Deaf people: they could be ordained deacon in 1987, but had to wait until 1994 to be ordained priest. (The usual period of the diaconate is one year before being ordained priest.)

[30]   'Ordination of the Revd E. Rowland' in *A Magazine Intended Chiefly for the Deaf and Dumb*, no. 117 (September 1882), p. 102.

[31]   Alker, *really not interested in the Deaf*, p. 69.

[32]   Information from the 'Chaplains Mailing List', August 2001.

Alker argues strongly that a committee cannot really be said to be controlled by those whom it serves unless it is over 51 per cent d/Deaf people.

This model does not threaten, or even question the status quo either because there is no point in questioning something that is ordained by God or because the wealth and position of too many people is bound up in the social order as it is. This model is basically oppressive in that it states that d/Deaf people are born inferior, and they should accept that role under the control of those who were born with the advantage of hearing.

Liberal Development

The second model highlighted by White and Tiongco originated in the recognition that the moral economy just didn't work in a modern industrialized world. The amount given voluntarily was simply not enough to meet the needs of all the people who, for whatever reason, could not manage their lives without some outside help. Alker also suggests that this model deteriorated as 'charity' evolved from being about acts of kindness to being an institution or an industry – where 'charity' was no longer about simply alleviating pain or destitution, but involved taking control of people's lives.[33] As religion became less influential, the understanding of the causes of poverty and other needs also changed. Poverty and the consequences of being d/Deaf were now attributed to ignorance and lack of opportunities rather than simply being part of the natural order of things. During the late nineteenth century, a boundless optimism in technological progress suggested that if poor people and disabled people in the UK (and later, overseas) had more education and more technology, they could 'catch up' the rich, able-bodied, hearing people and countries and therefore poverty and oppression would eventually be eradicated. This reflected an assumption that history is a linear, evolutionary process in which individuals and societies evolve to higher levels of development over time. Western Europe and the USA were considered the pinnacles of human development and the white, educated, male, hearing, able-bodied middle or upper class being right at the top of the pyramid. This paradigm change in the understanding of the causes of poverty and the 'misfortune' of disability led to a new focus on 'development' as the aim of 'charitable' work. In the UK and the USA in the late nineteenth and the early twentieth centuries, charities began focusing on 'helping people to self-sufficiency'. Applicants for aid were interviewed and required to provide references to their 'respectability' and 'industriousness'. Grants were limited to specified needs and had limited time scales. Further help depended on the individual or family concerned fulfilling conditions and showing progress towards self-sufficiency. The 'objective' judgement of the 'charity workers' was always considered as being the final

---

[33] Alker, *really not interested in the Deaf*, p. 101.

word.[34] The idea that poverty could be a product of environmental factors also began to gain currency during this time. Charities began to work at improving housing and working conditions and providing Friendly Societies, and Ragged Schools and Settlements where poor people could improve their minds and their character and therefore their options in life by contact with their social betters. The Deaf missions and societies were also strongly affected by this model. Many of the schools for Deaf children were founded on this principle that education was the road to improved quality of life,[35] and an important aspect of welfare work in the missions was, as far as possible, finding employment for Deaf school leavers so that they could become self-supporting.[36]

Woodroofe argues that it was these developments in attempting to solve the difficulties of the poor and disabled by education and employment that led to the growth of social work as it is currently understood, where the professional social worker knows what is best for the families and individuals with which they work: 'the professionally qualified welfare worker, one must suppose … can administer grants of money more efficiently than the unqualified, and her training fits her to understand more clearly the common human needs and feelings to which public assistance programmes should be geared'.[37] George Firth, the hearing chaplain to the Church Mission to the Deaf in South Staffordshire and Salop, illustrates that this model is found, historically, in the Deaf church as well. In one essay he talks about the need for 'professional attitudes and ideals of service which should fit the needs of the customer'.[38] In another he warns of the dangers that might arise if there are not enough trained welfare workers among Deaf people; 'deaf people may have to go ahead and solve their own difficulties for lack of anyone qualified to help them'.[39] The fact that Deaf people could themselves qualify as welfare workers or missioners or church leaders of some kind does not seem to have occurred to him; he refers to Deaf people being 'allowed' to have a greater part to play in the management of their own local societies but specifies that this involvement is restricted to 'general policy, the care of buildings and furnishing, employment of staff and so on'.[40] There is no mention of them actually being employed as staff themselves. Sutcliffe argues that he cannot see how Deaf people could have the capacity for leadership either in the 'normal world' or 'in the

[34]   See Kathleen Woodroofe, *From charity to social work in England and the United States* (London, 1961), p. 44 for example.

[35]   See, for example, Raymond Lee and John A. Hay, *Bermondsey 1792* (Feltham, 1993).

[36]   See, for example, Objects of the Mission' in Church Mission to the Deaf and Dumb of Walsall, Wednesbury, and Mid Staffordshire, *Annual Report*, no. 44 (1930), p. 2 and Chris Griffiths 'Missioner and Welfare officers report', ibid., no. 81 (1967–68).

[37]   Woodroofe, *From charity to social work*, p. 217.

[38]   Firth, *Chosen Vessels*, p. 127.

[39]   Firth 'Recruitment to Deaf Welfare Work' in Church Mission to the Deaf and Dumb in Walsall, Wednesbury and Mid Staffordshire, *Annual Report*, no. 80 (1966–67).

[40]   Firth, *Chosen Vessels*, p. 124.

smaller world of the Deaf' due to their limited education, limited experience, inability to think clearly (that is in English) or to express their thoughts clearly (in English) and the inability of sign to express precise thoughts and thus substitute for English.[41] Many within and without the church regarded Sutcliffe as an expert on the needs and abilities of Deaf people.[42] It is hardly surprising that with this view of Deaf people, they never had any real opportunities for control under his tenure.

This focus on 'trained professionals' who know what is best for their clients has a major impact on who has power in any charitable organization. Mike Oliver points out that key decision makers in traditional charities are: 'usually salaried professional staff who articulate their own assumptions about the needs of disabled people'.[43] In theory, the 'objectivity' of this model means that Deaf and disabled people themselves can become leaders if they can acquire the professional qualifications. However, due to unstated assumptions that leaders are hearing and able-bodied, Deaf and disabled people often have to cross additional barriers to obtain these qualifications or to get a suitable job. For example, Doug Alker in describing his first bid to become chief executive officer (CEO) of the RNID[44] describes how the interviewers for his first round interview (experienced workers with Deaf people) failed to ensure there was an interpreter present. Having successfully negotiated this obstacle, he then had to undergo psychometric tests biased against a Deaf person (they used hearing norms for assessing social behaviour for example). At length, having made it to the final shortlist, the one trustee he had confidence in was all but excluded from his interview. Alker did not get the CEO job that year. Three years later, he applied for the vacant CEO job again. In the intervening period he had obtained an MBA and additional targeted experience and was thus better qualified than any other candidate. In addition, there had been a very public set of campaigns and two TV programmes asking why such a suitably qualified Deaf man was not able to become CEO of the major deaf charity in the UK. This time, he did get the job.[45]

---

[41]   Canon T. H. Sutcliffe, 'Can the Deaf be Trained for Leadership?' in Pokorny (ed.), *My eyes are my ears: a collection of papers* (New York, 1974), p. 193.

[42]   Revd Tom Sutcliffe was deafened as an adult, after being ordained priest. He was a chaplain with RADD from 1935 to 1942, chaplain to the deaf in Blackburn diocese from 1942 to 1952, secretary to the CECD (that is effectively 'head' of the Deaf church) from 1952 to 1974. He was also on the committee for the International Seminar for the Pastoral Care of the Deaf and its successors during the 1970s. During his period as secretary to the CECD he managed the training of chaplains and lay people to work in the Deaf church, and was involved with the training of social workers for deaf people and interpreters. Throughout his working life he was also involved with the RNID, BDA and the World Federation for the Deaf.

[43]   Robert Drake, 'Charities, Authority and Disabled People: a qualitative study', *Disability and Society*, 11/1 (1996): 11.

[44]   Royal National Institute for the Deaf. The initials also, in Deaf folklore, stand for Really Not Interested in the Deaf, hence the title of Alker's book.

[45]   His experiences are described in Alker, *really not interested in the Deaf*, pp. 89–99.

Within the church, Deaf people have experienced similar obstacles to gaining the 'professional qualifications' (training and recognition) required to obtain positions where they might have power over the work of the Deaf church. For example, Vera Hunt, the first Deaf woman priest, writes of her feeling that she has had no choices in her life, 'no choice to follow a vocation ... no choice to serve Jesus'.[46] Even once her vocation to the ordained ministry was recognized by her chaplain, she was not given the choice of going for selection as a stipendiary (paid) priest, but had to become an NSM (non-stipendiary minister or unpaid priest) under the control of the stipendiary chaplain in her diocese.[47]

White and Tiongco argue that this liberal development model does contain within itself the seeds of liberation with its emphasis on the need for education (with the associated result of equipping individuals with the tools and concepts with which to question the status quo) and the rights of the individual to more than basic subsistence.[48] This assessment would probably be accepted by Deaf people who honour those, such as the abbé de l'Epée, who first recognized in the mid-eighteenth century that Deaf people could be educated by means of their own language of signs. However this model has failed to provide any long-term solutions to poverty or the inequalities experienced by Deaf and disabled people either in the UK or on a global scale or indeed in the church. Power and control are still in the hands of an elitist group; the 'recipients' still have no power to challenge or change anything.

Taking Responsibility

The liberal development model just described and criticized is not the only model with a strong hold in the circles of power and influence in the North. Another model emerged, first in the USA and is still gaining ground in the UK. It is in part a reaction to the liberal model described above, but also, more emotionally, a backlash against the liberation model described in the next section. This is the model that says along with liberals that individual rights and the dignity of humans are important, but argues, '[the market economy] is a system that pays respect to human dignity because it allows human freedom. It permits individuals the freedom to buy and sell, save and invest, choose preferred forms of employment and develop the skills they feel appropriate and it allows minorities the same rights too'.[49]

---

[46]   Vera Hunt, 'The Place of Deaf People in the Church: My Story' in International Ecumenical Working Group Conference, *The Place of Deaf People in the Church*, p. 25.

[47]   The training for both is exactly the same.

[48]   White and Tiongco, *Doing theology and development*, p. 48.

[49]   Brian Griffiths, 'Christianity and Capitalism' in Digby C. Anderson (ed.), *The kindness that kills: the churches' simplistic response to complex social issues* (London, 1984), pp. 105 and 113.

This model grew particularly strong during the 1980s and early 1990s when the political scene was dominated by the then 'New Right'. It understands each individual as being morally responsible for the choices they make in their own lives and in consequence for their own circumstances which arise from these choices. Peter Bauer includes even people in the 'third world' in this category. They are poor because they have overspent their income, or because there are natural circumstances beyond their control, or because they are materially unambitious and culturally conditioned to accept their life as inexorably ordained by fate and therefore do not seek to develop their full potential. In fact, as he argues, many people in the 'third world', such as 'Indians' and 'Negroes' in Latin America, are no worse off and in many ways better off than their ancestors ever were.[50] The answer to poverty is for individuals to pull their fingers out to provide for their own and their families' needs. If they really can't feed themselves and their families, for whatever reason, then private charity distributed to the 'deserving' poor is the answer.

In part, this model depends on the developments in psychology that suggest material help alone is not sufficient to change individuals or society for the better. The individual had to take the responsibility for their own lives.[51] This, combined with the political commitment to the sanctity of business and profit and economic growth, strengthened the idea that poverty and oppression were the result of moral and psychological inadequacy. The aim of charity, social or welfare work was focused on the individual to strengthen their moral fibre and force them out of 'dependency' and into work.[52]

In similar terms are arguments that d/Deaf people are better off today than they have ever been, with hearing aids and cochlear implants and subtitled TV and improved diagnosis of deafness in infancy and all the other technologies available to help us to 'live a normal life'. If we don't achieve a 'normal' life despite our opportunities then that is our own choice. For example many contemporary discussions of Deaf education represent it as a progress towards increased use of speech and lip-reading by Deaf children, aided by the development of audiological technology, and argue that Deaf school leavers are better fitted for life in the hearing world than ever before.[53] This perspective ignores the existence of many Deaf teachers and professionals in the late nineteenth century, before the 'developments' of technology, who were educated through sign language and who used sign language to communicate all their lives. In this argument, those Deaf people who are not able to communicate adequately through speech and lip-

---

[50] Peter Bauer, 'Ecclesiastical Economics of the Third World: Envy Legitimized' in Anderson (ed.), *The kindness that kills*, p. 34.

[51] Woodroofe, *From charity to social work*, p. 132.

[52] Ibid., pp. 134–5.

[53] See, for example, Wendy Lynas et al., 'A critical examination of different approaches to communication in the education of deaf children' in Gregory and Hartley (eds), *Constructing Deafness*, pp. 125 and 127.

reading (in which category I would include myself in any context larger than a group of about four or five people, all of whom I know) simply do not try hard enough. This argument dismisses many Deaf people who choose to use BSL as 'doing so for political reasons' simply because their speech and lip-reading are adequate in one-to-one contexts.

In this model, the control of any organization goes to those who have the 'savvy' to develop the skills and contacts required to become a leader. The argument runs that the system rewards those who have earned their place and does not encourage or support those who, for whatever reason, fall behind. Alker worked hard and overcame many obstacles to reach the position of CEO of the RNID under the chairmanship of a man who saw his job and that of the board of trustees as setting the objectives for Alker to achieve and not interfering in the process. The results, as discussed in the next section, probably illustrate a move from a 'liberal development' ideal to an organization that was well on the way to being truly 'liberating'. However, under an increasingly right-wing political climate, this chair was replaced with an oralist[54] who undermined Alker's authority and generally made it impossible for Alker to function efficiently as a Deaf CEO. Under this new regime, the board of trustees, previously encouraging, withdrew their support and, as Alker says, he found himself in 'free fall', despite having achieved, and in some cases exceeded his targets for his first year as CEO.[55] In the end, Alker resigned rather than be 'kicked upstairs' to a purely nominal post. He minded desperately, not only for himself, but also for the way it was apparently 'proved' that a Deaf person could not do the job of CEO of the largest deaf organization in the UK.[56]

I would argue that the present Deaf stipendiary clergy within the Church of England (half of the total number of Deaf clergy/church army officers in the church) have achieved their present positions under the influence of this model. We were given the chance to prove we could do the job, often overcoming obstacles alone, and now we are experiencing the freedom to attempt to challenge the structures of the Deaf church and the church at large. If this model of 'taking responsibility' continues to operate in the church then Alker's experience suggests that we too are vulnerable to backlash and might find ourselves in 'free fall', unsupported by those who might help and thus 'prove' that Deaf people cannot lead their own church.[57]

---

[54]   'Oralist' refers to people who think that the most important thing in the development of deaf children is to teach them to speak. They are against the use of sign language in education, and often against its use in any situation.

[55]   Alker, *really not interested in the Deaf*, p. 154.

[56]   Ibid. The current CEO of the RNID is technically 'deaf' in that he wears a hearing aid; however, he does not use sign language but relies on amplification, speech and lip-reading and thus communicates 'normally'.

[57]   Clergy are not subject to employment law, so Deaf clergy cannot even claim the partial protection of the Disability Discrimination Act.

This model is the harshest on those constructed as recipients of charity. Rather than merely unlucky or unfortunate in their birth and life as in the previous two models, they are actively considered as responsible for their own problems. This model not only objectifies recipients and denies them a voice; it is responsible for actually constructing those in need of help and support of whatever kind in a very negative light. Even if it superficially 'liberates' those who prove their worth, such 'liberation' is very much on the surface, leaving those individuals vulnerable to being undermined and brought down. Those who are not able to 'liberate' themselves because of their circumstances receive no encouragement, support or opportunities; they must simply accept what they are given. Alker argues that despite the presence of Deaf people on management committees, this model is basically the paternalism of the 'moral economy' in a new and virulent form.[58] The only protection against its operation in the life of the Deaf church is in a recognition and rejection of its values wherever they occur and the establishment of structures to ensure that no competent Deaf person in the leadership of the church ever loses their position purely because they are Deaf.

Liberation

There is however a fourth approach to understanding the relationship between the rich and the poor, the able-bodied and the disabled, hearing and Deaf which does give all people dignity and choice and which does at least challenge the status quo. This approach first encroached on the consciousness of those from the North at the SODEPAX[59] conference in 1969. A Catholic priest from Latin America, Gustavo Gutiérrez, read a paper on the meaning of development that he later published as *Theology of Liberation*. In it, he argued that poverty could only be eradicated if the poor were free to make their own decisions and that the cherished liberal concept of objective judgements was fundamentally invalid. Neutrality is impossible, any understanding of a situation is always shaped by experience of that particular situation or in other words 'where you stand depends on where you sit'.[60] Another feature of this model is the way in which material benefits are simply part of the whole package instead of being the only measured criteria. The impact that poverty has on civil, political and social rights in addition to the material cost is highlighted and the education of people in their rights is an important part of the programme. The poor themselves were to be the agents of their own destiny and the voices of their own experience. The job of outside agencies was to provide tools for the poor to analyse their own contexts and formulate their own solutions.[61]

---

[58] Alker, *really not interested in the Deaf*, p. 105.
[59] Joint Committee on Society, Development and Peace – a WCC and Roman Catholic collaboration.
[60] White and Tiongco, *Doing theology and development*, p. 64.
[61] Ibid., p. 65.

In recent years, this model has been refined, partly to try to explore why it does not always act as predicted. The world is no longer understood simply as a matter of the 'dependent' poor and the 'oppressive' rich. The role of the poor in colluding with the system for their own security and the complexity of the economic and power relationships involved have begun to be more fully realized. Also, the fact that no population is homogenous has been identified as a factor in the operation of this model; within any country is to be found women, ethnic minorities and disabled people for example, who are likely to be objects of further discrimination and oppression from their own people and governments.[62] Similarly, within any oppressed group, such as Deaf people, there are likely to be those from ethnic minorities as well as women and others who experience further discrimination within their own world.

In the Deaf experience, Alker's appointment as CEO of the RNID sparked off an intended shift in organizational ethos from the 'liberal development'/'taking responsibility' model to a 'liberation' model. As he says, his intention was to make the RNID into an organization that used 'its power and influence, its position and its resources to make things as they should be ... to truly lead when it came to Deaf rights and have the Deaf "on board"'.[63] He intended that the RNID should both lead in 'campaigning to challenge society's attitudes and influence policies' and in 'providing services, which enable the achievement of the vision'.[64] In other words Alker envisioned the RNID as both creating opportunities and equal access for Deaf people through its campaigning work and providing the services such as improved interpreter provision and better education that would enable Deaf people to fully take up these opportunities. For the first time an organization working for d/Deaf people was to attempt to earn the recognition of d/Deaf people by evaluating themselves according to standards that d/Deaf people themselves defined.[65] Alker then proceeded to establish a mechanism by which the views of deafened, Deaf and hard of hearing people were consulted at every level of policy making and evaluation[66] and to begin a shift in ethos by which rights based services, such as the provision of interpreters, were funded by statutory funds rather than charitable income.[67] If an organization or a company refused to provide interpreters, he saw the role of the RNID as applying moral and political pressure for them to do so rather than 'letting them off the hook' by subsidizing the provision of interpreters through charitable funds. This was not simply a

---

[62] White and Tiongco, *Doing theology and development*, pp. 72–4. Gutiérrez also writes of his recognition that the 'dependency' model of the relationship between rich and poor oversimplifies issues in his introduction to the second edition of *Theology of liberation: history, politics and salvation* (London, 1988).

[63] Alker, *really not interested in the Deaf*, p. 99.

[64] Ibid., p. 126.

[65] Ibid., p. 127.

[66] Ibid., p. 129.

[67] Ibid., p. 132.

commercial decision to save money; if interpreters were provided by right, rather than as a charitable favour, then Deaf people would not be in the demeaning position of being dependent on qualifying for help and feeling obliged to be grateful for whatever was provided. At the same time, Alker set out to revamp the staffing structure of the RNID to bring in a more participatory style of management where individuals had more freedom and more responsibility.[68] It was at this point, having achieved all the targets for the first year, despite a drop in income due to the recession, and put structures in place that would make the RNID a truly liberating organization for d/Deaf people that the oralist backlash began, which resulted in Alker resigning as CEO after a tenure of only two years and the participation and service rhetoric of the RNID under its new management sounding rather hollow.

Despite Alker's bad experience, and the fact that he did not have time to fully reach his potential as CEO, it is helpful to look at the RNID under his leadership to see some hints of what a liberating Deaf organization might look like. A key feature of this 'liberation' model is the fact that it tries to look at the whole situation rather than focusing on the needs of individuals. It tries to ask what the roots of the problem are instead of simply patching up the symptoms – backing up 'aid' and support with political action to remove the need for 'aid' in the future. This model also calls for a fundamental shift in the understanding of how power works and where power is to be found. Alker's restructuring of management was intended not only to make the RNID more efficient as an organization, but, in due course, to ensure it remained d/Deaf controlled. Significant phrases that have been bandied about to refer to this change of relationship are 'shared decision-making', 'participation' and 'empowerment'.[69] For example, Taylor argues, 'The poor and oppressed are not the objects of development … but its main agents. It is they who bring justice about, not the rich and powerful who are unlikely either to change significantly their attitudes or relinquish their privileges'.[70] White and Tiongco agree, 'Bottom up people participation is the key to long term, sustainable changes'.[71]

The increasing emphasis on 'participation' in decision-making by users of charities, and the growing use of the word 'empowerment' to describe the work of charities and an increased role of charities in campaigning for changes in attitudes and laws is a mark of the liberation model active in charities. There are many new 'user' agencies and charities set up by disabled people using the 'social' model of disability and with aims relating to working for political action and social change

---

[68] Alker, *really not interested in the Deaf*, p. 136.

[69] Michael Taylor, *Not angels but agencies: the ecumenical response to poverty – a primer* (Geneva and London, 1995), pp. 82–5; White and Tiongco, *Doing theology and development*, pp. 99–102.

[70] Taylor, *Not angels but agencies*, p. 84.

[71] White and Tiongco, *Doing theology and development*, p. 102.

to improve access and campaigning against discriminatory practices.[72] These agencies make a distinction between 'charity' as something that attends to individual needs and sees disability as being about a personal tragedy or an individual issue amenable to an individual solution and universal 'rights' which focus on the need for disabled people to have the same access to economic and social structures as any other citizen.[73] They advocate what they refer to as a 'development' model based on the full involvement of disabled people in the conceptualization and analysis of their needs, and the decision on how to meet them: 'Disabled activists argue that governments and non-government agencies should base aid policy and practice on a development, not a charity model, working to involve and empower disabled people'.[74] The question that really needs to be asked at this level is how much the rhetoric of 'participation' and 'empowerment' is actually reflected in practice and also how users or clients themselves see the work of the organization.

The Deaf church is one such organization that has begun to use the language of 'participation' and 'empowerment' over the past 20 or so years. As stated above, the NDCC is run by an all-Deaf committee. There are Deaf representatives on many management committees including the CMDP itself; Deaf people have had increasing opportunities to participate in leading worship in church services. *The Church Among Deaf People* states that a 'top-down approach is no longer adequate ... Chaplains should seek to encourage these attitudes of independence and self-determination among deaf Christians ... seek to enable them to become full members of the church and to obtain equality of opportunity, as well as developing leadership and ministerial training'.[75] However, I would question how far this rhetoric extends to Deaf people actually having control over their own church. For example, the NDCC, or other Deaf people on committees have no real power and influence in key areas such as the appointment and training of chaplains; there is no mechanism for 'feedback' and evaluation from Deaf people in the church to the CMDP and the wider church. Deaf people are asked to contribute to the annual chaplains training conference, but, as Alker highlights in his own contexts, they are usually merely asked to speak about themselves and their personal experiences rather than being given the opportunity to participate in the process of converting their experiences and view of what Deaf people need into public policy. Rather ironically, Alker himself was invited to speak at the chaplains training conference in June 2001 on 'The Present and Future Deaf Community', a primarily descriptive brief. Strong and inspiring as his talk was, there was no suggestion that we might use his political and organizational expertise to restructure the Deaf church, either

---

[72] Robert Drake, 'The exclusion of disabled people from positions of power in British voluntary organizations', *Disability and Society*, 9/4 (1994): 476.

[73] Beresford, 'Poverty and disabled people': 560.

[74] Ibid.: 563. The word 'development' is understood and used in a different way from the liberal usage.

[75] *The Church Among Deaf People*, p. 24.

nationally or at diocesan level, to make it a more liberating organization for all Deaf people.

'User participation' is the language of a liberating organization, but it does not automatically transform an organization into one that is working for the liberation of its users. Beresford, in arguing for what he calls a 'rights based' approach to issues arising out of poverty and disability, points out that poor and disabled people in both North and South continue to be marginalized in debates and developments around poverty, despite a rhetoric of consultation.[76] Drake, in his 1992 survey on the participation of disabled people in authority structures and as the voice of 'traditional' charities, concludes that despite all the rhetoric in favour of powerful roles and positions for disabled people, neither the purposes nor the structures of voluntary agencies have actually been affected so as to change the role of disabled users of the charities from one of subordination and powerlessness.[77] White and Tiongco highlight the different ways in which user participation can be found in the practice of organizations and argue that only where there is a clear shift in power relations can 'user participation' be considered as truly empowering.[78] This shift in power relationships is more than a different use of words or a change of mind; it involves a whole 'paradigm shift' or a 'conversion experience' in which a whole way of relating to the world is changed.

In a Deaf context, one way of enabling this power shift to occur is to make sign language the only language in use, forbidding the use of voice and thus ensuring that visual communication dominates the gathering. Marilyn Daniels describes the results when Gallaudet University's department of education faculty meetings, with 35 per cent Deaf faculty members, adopted such a *voice off* policy. This policy meant that the seating arrangements changed (so that everybody could see everyone else), that the time spent in meetings was reduced (since there was only one, instead of two languages in use) and illustrated how strongly the balance of power had previously been located with those who spoke and heard English, despite the fact that every hearing member of the faculty board was expected to be bilingual.[79] Another example of the power shifts associated with a *voice off* policy was at a recent Chaplains Training Conference for chaplains among Deaf people. They had with them for one day a Deaf BSL trainer. She asked them all to 'switch off' their voices for the day and only use sign language, (supplemented by finger spelling and paper and pen for those who were still learning). The Deaf chaplains came away from this conference saying that it was the best one they had ever attended (previously they had all experienced feeling left out by the hearing chaplains not using sign language when they spoke among themselves), and hearing chaplains

---

[76] Beresford, 'Poverty and disabled people': 555.

[77] Drake, 'The exclusion of disabled people from positions of power in British voluntary organizations': 477.

[78] White and Tiongco, *Doing theology and development*, pp. 106–109.

[79] Marilyn Daniels, *Benedictine Roots in the development of deaf education: listening with the heart* (Westport, CT, 1997), p. 113.

came away saying that it had been the most challenging conference they had ever been to. 'Real' power shifts such as these can be experienced as very threatening by both Deaf and hearing people.

Liberation in Action

Constructing d/Deaf people as objects of charity, whether under a model of a 'moral economy', 'liberal development' or 'taking responsibility', is ultimately oppressive as all three models are basically rooted in the medical model of what it means to be d/Deaf. A fourth model of charity 'liberation' is more liberating in its approach. With its emphasis on consultation with those constructed as 'users', and tackling the causes of the 'needs' rather than just meeting them, it is well placed for taking on board the alternative cultural and social models of what it means to be d/Deaf. However, the 'liberating' model is fundamentally counter-cultural, which has an impact in terms of the forces acting on organizations operating under this model. Voluntary groups led by disabled people and using a rights-based approach and with a more informal and less hierarchical structure tend to have far fewer resources in terms of money, people with time and administrative facilities than the more traditional charities. In fact, the traditional 'big boys' offer little or no support to local users groups and utilize their greater expertise in fundraising and more professional approach together with their historical links and perceived credibility to compete successfully for government and local authority grants for their own use with the small, local, user controlled organizations.[80] The backlash against any seemingly successful counter-cultural organization appears to be severe, as illustrated by Alker's experience at the RNID. These forces mean that 'user participation', no matter how well intentioned, all too easily becomes nominal, a way of putting a new face on an organization that stays basically the same. The challenge for the Church of England and the Deaf church is not how d/Deaf people can have access to the hearing church, but how the church can become an organization that contributes to the liberation of all d/Deaf people.

---

[80]   Robert Drake, 'Charities, authority and disabled people': 15.

Chapter 6

DEAF-WORLD, Sign Language and the Bible: Is There a Deaf Liberation Hermeneutic?[1]

The Bible remains normative for all Christians at all places and at all times.[2]

The first source of theology is the Bible ... because it is the primary witness of God's revelation in Jesus Christ. No theology can retain its Christian identity apart from Scripture.[3]

These two quotes, the first from an Indian theologian and the second from a Malawian, illustrate the fact that it is impossible to do Christian theology without, at some point, engaging with the Bible. For 2,000 years and through several major shifts in worldview and schisms in the Christian church it has been the primary source from which all theology has developed. Even the liberating and decolonizing trends in theology of the past 20 or 30 years, which have challenged every aspect of theology, including biblical studies, to the core, have not rejected the use of the Bible as a source. In fact, it has often been used as a major resource for encouraging resistance to oppression and dehumanization and for sustaining hope in an alternative future.

Acceptance of the Bible as a primary source in Christian theology does not mean that it needs to be accepted as the unchallengeable, immutable word of God and nor does it mean arguing that it the sole source of revelation. For liberation theology it means developing an ongoing, dynamic, critical conversation with the text in the context of both the time it was written and the time it is being read.

---

[1] Hermeneutics may be defined as the science of methods of explaining the meaning of the biblical text in a contemporary context.

[2] Stanley J. Samartha, 'Scripture and Scriptures' in R. S. Sugirtharajah (ed.), *Voices from the Margin: Interpreting the Bible in the Third World* (London, 1995), p. 32.

[3] Ecumenical Association for African Theology (EAAT) inaugural declaration quoted by Patrick A. Kalilombe, 'A Malawian Example: The Bible and Non-literate Communities' in Sugirtharajah (ed.), *Voices from the Margin*, p. 421.

Some Methodological Questions

The first thing to consider is where I am coming from as a theologian and how my situation might impact on my perception of the Bible and the use of the Bible as a source. I am a practising Christian, and while not uncritical in my approach to the text, I would situate myself in what can be called a 'confessional' approach. Anyone studying the Bible is working on the same material, but believing Christians are likely to have differences in methodology, aims, practices and presuppositions from non-believers. For example, a confessional approach is likely to begin with the assumption that the biblical text, in one way or another, is inspired by and is the revelation of the one true God. A non-confessional approach is more likely to be agnostic about the existence of God and therefore begins with the assumption that the biblical text is simply a collection of writings from ancient times. It has been suggested by some people that the only true liberating approach is a non-confessional one, prepared for a possible outcome that sees the biblical text as irredeemably patriarchal and therefore of no use to women or other oppressed groups.[4] I would imagine many non-Christian Deaf would agree, and so I need to ask if so how has the Bible and my work any relevance for the wider context of a Deaf community struggling for liberation?

Segovia suggests that it is not quite as simple as a choice between a non-confessional approach that is liberating and a confessional approach that is not. He argues that all approaches to the text, whether 'confessional' or not, are theological one way or another.[5] In other words, starting with the belief that the Bible is a purely human, literary construction and the word 'God' refers to a human projection will influence the outcome of biblical study as much as starting from the opposite position. In fact, as this question does not seem to be discussed at all among third-world and black theologians, I would argue that the distinction between confessional and non-confessional approaches to the Bible is a western philosophical distinction. Asian and African theologians, whatever their faith, seem happy to both regard the Bible as sacred scripture, revealing the word of God, and also to acknowledge and work with the fact that it was written by humans and has been interpreted by humans and so reveals human prejudices as much as it reveals the word of God.[6] What is necessary is that any reading of scripture must be a

---

[4]   Milne, 'Towards Female Companionship' in Athalya Brenner and Carole Fontaine (eds), *A feminist companion to reading the Bible: approaches, methods and strategies* (Sheffield, 1997), p. 59.

[5]   Fernando F. Segovia, *Decolonising biblical studies: a view from the margins* (Maryknoll, NY, 2000), p. 49.

[6]   See for example Sugirtharajah (ed.), *Voices from the Margin*. The status of the Bible in relationship to the sacred scriptures and ancient texts of other faiths and cultures is extensively discussed, but at no point is the Bible considered as anything other than the revealed word of God. The central issue here is not whether God exists, but how different faiths relate to God and to each other, and how the Bible functioned under colonialism as a

critical reading and that any appropriation of biblical elements must be a *critical* appropriation in the context of a commitment to the struggle.[7] Acknowledging a confessional starting point is a statement of position, necessary in the context of a western theologian, rather than something that automatically negates my reading of the Bible in the context of the Deaf liberation struggle. The consequent tension between questions of faith and belief on the one hand and the secular questions of liberation theories on the other is, I would argue, a necessary tension. Just as we use liberation theories to critique readings of the Bible, so do we need to use faithful readings of the Bible to critique 'secular' theories and so trust that in the midst of this struggle we come up with ideas that are of significant benefit to the lives of Deaf people.

It is possible to argue that the Bible is irredeemably anti-Deaf, written by hearing people for hearing people and only including Deaf people as passive objects for controlling, or negative subjects for elimination. However, this approach ignores the history of the Bible as a liberating text for many minorities, not least Deaf people in history. It also assumes that there is only one meaning to be found in any text, an assumption that is difficult to defend in a post-modern worldview. Segovia, for example, suggests that the meaning of any text is in the interaction between a text and a reader, so there is not one single meaning, or one single text, but many 'texts'.[8] This means that 'plucking positive images out of an 'anti-Deaf' text' is not only possible, but also valid; it is allowable that the meaning of the text can shift. The original intention or meaning (as far as we can reconstruct it) is part of the interpretation, but not the whole; there are other considerations to be taken into account.

One oppressed group that has attempted to tackle the ambiguity of the Bible is poor black women. Elsa Tamez, from Costa Rica, points out that the Bible is well accepted as containing a liberating message for the poor and is considered a subversive book by those sections of society or the church that do not have a preferential option for the poor. At the same time it contains clear and explicit cases of the marginalization or segregation of women.[9] One response, from grassroots communities, to these texts has been to argue that those were different times; that reality is different today and that God is the God of life and therefore cannot favour discrimination against women. Tamez agrees with this, suggesting that the Bible is a 'testimony of a Judeo-Christian [*sic*] people with a different culture, for whom holy revelation always works in favour of those who have least' and always needs to be interpreted in any situation. Women can therefore include

---

way of legitimizing discrimination against faiths other than Christianity with the consequent oppression of the people.

[7]   Gerald O. West, *Biblical hermeneutics of liberation* (Maryknoll, NY, 1995), p. 172. His italics.

[8]   Segovia, *Decolonising biblical studies*, p. 43.

[9]   Elsa Tamez, 'Women's Rereading of the Bible' in Sugirtharajah (ed.), *Voices from the Margin*, p. 49.

themselves among the oppressed and favoured by God and so contextualize the segregation texts. In the same way, it is possible to argue that what it means to be Deaf has changed so much since the Bible was written, that it is possible for us to identify with other groups in the Bible and so find a positive value in the text for our liberation. The difficulty with this position is the way that these texts have led men and women to internalize the inferiority of women and the fact that the Bible not only legitimates but also legislates for the marginalization of women (and also d/Deaf people). Having said this, Tamez still finds the Bible of use for women, and criticizes first-world women who reject the Bible altogether as assigning too much importance to peripheral texts and not enough to the profoundly liberating central message; from her point of view 'it is precisely the Gospel's spirit of justice and freedom that neutralizes anti-female texts'.

This argument that the Bible is at heart a text that is positive for all marginalized people, whether poor, or female, or black, or disabled or Deaf, is a commonly used one. George Koonthanam, a Dalit (outcaste) biblical scholar in India, suggests that all the beneficiaries of the saving acts of God in history are the poor and powerless; that the Bible tells the stories of a tribe of landless and rootless people who begin the history of God's people, of a band of slaves liberated from Egypt, of prophets who thundered against the silent agony of oppressed masses, of a smitten remnant brought back from exile in Babylon and of God's own self clothed in flesh and walking on earth as the friend of the discriminated and marginalized sections of Palestine.[10] Kwok Pui Lan, a Chinese woman and biblical scholar, writes in very similar terms of the way that historically marginalized people have continued the story begun in the Bible of God's acts for the liberation of the powerless.[11] The Bible has not only been used as a tool for oppression, but also as a tool for liberation on many different fronts.

Renita Weems, a womanist scholar from America, uncovers many metaphors of sexual violence in the Bible, and their damaging applications, and acknowledges that some stories in the Bible are hopelessly irredeemable. She also argues, however, that 'as long as there are women and men … who have found in its pages the impetus and courage to resist oppression, then there remains … the responsibility to help contemporary readers to read the Bible with a suspicious hope, careful of the Bible's distortions and mindful of its possibilities'.[12] She suggests that we deal with the negative texts of the Bible by acknowledging their existence and deconstructing their effect (or, in other words, claiming our rights as readers to differ with the authors) but also recognizing and affirming their positive

---

[10] George Koonthanam, 'Yahweh the Defender of the Dalits: A Reflection on Isaiah 3:12–15' in Sugirtharajah (ed.), *Voices from the Margin*, p. 107.

[11] Kwok Pui Lan, 'Discovering the Bible in the Non-Biblical World' in Sugirtharajah (ed.), *Voices from the Margin*, p. 303.

[12] Renita J. Weems, *Battered love: marriage, sex and violence in the Hebrew Prophets* (Minneaolis, 1995), p. 123.

side.[13] We need to do this because of the history of the liberating use of the biblical text. It was the revolutionary text of the black people who rebelled against slavery and fought for civil rights in the USA as well as the text legitimating such practices. It has also been used as a text in support of women's emancipation as well as a way of propagating their subordination and it has been used by Deaf people in support of their full dignity of people made in the image of God as well as against Deaf people as travesties of the Divine image. If we reject the text as irredeemable, we are also rejecting a significant part of the liberation history not only of the ancient people in the Bible, but in the lives of our own people as well.

Weems highlights two issues that need further discussion. The first is the fact that the Bible and also individual texts within it can be read in both negative and positive ways, which do not necessarily balance each other out. In other words, the Bible does not consist of one voice; it is a collection of many voices, some of which contradict others. If we treat it as if it were a single voice, whether positive or negative, we are doing violence to the text and also to the context of the liberation struggle. If we accept that there is no 'single voice' in the Bible to be accepted or rejected, we cannot argue that the Old Testament is basically positive for Deaf people and the New Testament (and therefore Christianity) is basically negative as contended by Van Cleve and Crouch.[14] Their argument is based on the existence of three passages which can be read as positive about Deaf people in the Old Testament,[15] and only oppressive passages in the New.[16] This is reading the Bible in a very simplistic way, assuming that single verses taken out of context say everything that there is to be said about deaf people in the Bible. It also ignores the fact that the New Testament is based on the Old, that they are seen as two parts of the same story, and cannot be separated in this way.

Segovia argues that postcolonial Bible study needs to renounce the idea of a 'master narrative' itself as a construct and take the diversity of texts, readers and readings to heart as well as recognizing the reality of imperialism and colonialism in both ancient and contemporary times. He suggests that there is a multiplicity of voices preserved in the text, however faintly, dissenting, suppressed and contradictory voices as well as those that became the authoritative, accepting ones. Other voices may be totally absent, but can be identified through their silence or because they are repudiated by the text. The goal in working with this multiplicity of voices is not some 'antiquarian interest' in who said what, and who thought what, but a living dialogue and struggle with the text in the light of reality and

---

[13] Weems, *Battered love*, p. 10.

[14] John Vickrey Van Cleve and Barry A. Crouch, *A place of their own: creating the Deaf community in America* (Washington DC, 1989), p. 2.

[15] Exodus 4:11 (people are deaf because God made them that way), Leviticus 19:14 (deaf people are to be treated with respect) and Isaiah 29:18, 35:5 (the day of the Lord will mean there are no limits on human fulfilment, including disability).

[16] Matthew 11:5, Mark 7:31–7 (deaf people as objects to demonstrate the power of Jesus) and Romans 10:7 (faith comes by hearing).

experience. If the text is not seen as an unanswerable monologue, but as full of multiple voices in dialogue with each other, we, as readers, can take an active and critical part in the discussion and 'add ones own voice to the overall din of a very different time and a very different culture'.[17] We, as Deaf people, need to take our part in this active and critical discussion with the Bible; otherwise we perpetuate our absence from the ancient texts into the present.

Kwok Pui Lan is another who rejects that idea that the richness of the Bible can be boiled down to one voice or critical principle, She argues a feminist interpretation of the Bible that must 'sort through particular biblical texts and test out in a process of critical analysis ... how much the content and function legitimates and perpetuates patriarchal structures'.[18] For Kwok Pui Lan, the critical principle by which all texts are read is the community of those who read the Bible and appropriate it for their own liberation. In other words, what she seems to be suggesting is that 'minority' interpretations need to take seriously the multiple voices of the text and the readers, and accept that some texts are irretrievably negative from some points of view, and that others are affirming and positive for some and assess these readings by reference to a norm worked out by the 'minority' community. This is not replacing one oppressive norm by another because, in Kwok Pui Lan's eyes, the community norms must be accountable to other communities; truth claims must be tested in public discourse, in constant dialogue with each other. The norms of different communities may not be fully compatible, but if one norm is perceived as damaging to another community then that would, at very least, throw up some serious questions that need to be answered. In other words, the Deaf community needs to work out its own norm for engaging with the different voices in the Bible, but it needs to do so in dialogue with other minority communities as part of the wider liberation struggle.

Speaking of the community or the readers as the locus of a critical principle for biblical hermeneutics brings us to the second point highlighted by Weems and this is the issue of the biblical text being legitimated by the history of its use as a liberating text by those struggling for their freedom in the past. Weems will not give up on wrestling with the text as long as her people, black women, are finding in it the impetus and courage to resist oppression. Can we say the same about the Deaf community? Is there any evidence that Deaf people in the past and present have found in the Bible texts and beliefs to give them motivation for and courage in their struggle for liberation from hearing norms and affirm their uniqueness as Deaf people rather than sub-standard hearing people? Deaf people's egalitarian and liberating readings of the Bible will be discussed in more detail later in the chapter, but it seems that we can answer this question in the affirmative. Deaf people have survived over one hundred years of discrimination and oppression firmly convinced of their dignity as human beings made in the image of God. This belief

---

[17]   Segovia, *Decolonising biblical studies*, p. 98.

[18]   Pui Lan, 'Discovering the Bible in the Non-Biblical World' in Sugirtharajah (ed.), *Voices from the Margin*, p. 302.

did not come from the hearing people who worked with them, but is rooted deep in the psyche of the Deaf themselves. For example, two presentations at the 9th Biennial Conference of the BDDA in 1905 refer to the condition of uneducated deaf people.[19] One presentation, by the hearing president, William Sleight, likens uneducated deaf people to animals, in worse condition even than savages who have communication to lift them above the status of beasts. W. Eccles Harris, a Deaf member, by contrast simply states that education is necessary for all people to learn about God and develop their 'moral nature'; that uneducated deaf people are not fundamentally different from uneducated hearing people in their ignorance of the world, but contain within themselves the potential, shared by all God's children, of developing a 'moral nature' and knowledge of God. Harris appears to be convinced, in opposition to Sleight, that whether educated or not, Deaf people are fully human and this humanity is guaranteed by their creator.

Evidence that this conviction, authorized and perpetuated by the Bible, has helped Deaf people to survive and resist oppression can be seen in many Deaf subalterns in the church today. These strong Deaf working-class men and women may not have much 'Bible knowledge', they may not be able to tackle the English of the Bible and read it easily for themselves, but they do hold to an oral tradition that the Bible says that God loves everybody exactly the same, and that everybody has been made in the image of God and shares the dignity of human beings.[20] This oral tradition comes out in writing in the NUD's 1982 *Charter for the Rights of the Deaf*;[21] the authors of this pamphlet would all identify themselves as agnostic, but they begin with a quote from Exodus 4:11: 'Who hath made man's mouth? Or who maketh the dumb, or deaf, or the seeing, or the blind? Gave not I the Lord?'[22] In other words, the conviction that God made Deaf people to be Deaf, as expressed in this quote, underlies what has been called the most radical Deaf document of all. This is a powerful conviction in a world that sometimes seems to say exactly the opposite. However, it did not prevent the damage to Deaf self-esteem and the Deaf community caused by the more negative uses of the Bible to legitimate oppression, particularly in the context of the 'spiritualized gospel' of the Deaf church under the missioners and the chaplains. This spiritualized gospel, common in the Deaf church for most of the twentieth century, did not seek to apply this principle of essential equality to life in the world or the church. In other words, while all d/Deaf people and those who work with them would affirm that all d/Deaf people are

---

[19]   Revd W. Sleight, 'Presidential report' and W. Eccles Harris, 'Paper on the history of the Deaf' in British Deaf and Dumb Association, *Proceedings of the ninth biennial congress* (London, 1905).

[20]   An example of this 'oral history' is in the response of one Deaf subaltern, a 'reader' in the Deaf church to a member of his congregation who signed '*GOD NOT LOVE ME WHY? MADE ME DEAF.*' The response was along the lines of '*STUPID – BIBLE SAYS GOD LOVES EVERYBODY, DEAF, HEARING EVERYBODY, SO GOD LOVE YOU.*'

[21]   National Union of the Deaf, *Charter of Rights of the Deaf* (London, 1982).

[22]   Kings James Version.

made in the image of God and loved by God equally with hearing people, this has not always been considered relevant to issues such as the education of d/Deaf children or the social position of d/Deaf people; nor has it always been apparent in the attitudes within and without the church towards such things as 'genetic counselling' and medical 'treatment' of d/Deaf people. However, when it is put into action in the world, the conviction, shared by Deaf Christians and non-Christians alike, of the essential equality of Deaf people in a hearing world was the seed from which the modern Deaf liberation movement grew.

This Deaf oral tradition about the Bible suggests a critical principle: that the Bible must be read to affirm the full humanity of Deaf people in a world that has so often denied it. Modern Deaf liberation would also add that for the Bible to be working for liberation, it must also be read in a way that affirms the distinctive language and culture of Deaf people. Beginning with the real questions and concerns and norms of real Deaf readers rather than with the text is one way of approaching the difficulty that the text does not speak of Deaf people's language or culture. This is an example of the well-documented method of Liberation Theology known as the hermeneutical circle. In Asia for example, whose culture and traditions did not grow from the Jewish/Christian roots of western European culture, this method is in common use. George Soares-Prabhu points out that if a reading of the Bible starts with the text, all dialogue will circle around the narrow confines of the text and will not affect the 'carefully insulated reader'.[23] If, however, a reading starts with the reader's concerns then it will evoke a response from the text that affects the reader's situation and gives rise to new questions and so set in motion the dialogue that is a mark of a 'genuine hermeneutical circle'. What legitimizes this way of approaching the text is what he calls the 'post-modern recognition of the real reader' or, in other words, the post-modern recognition that there is no text without a reader, and that there is no possibility of an 'idealized objective reader', but that every reader of the text reads subjectively, according to their own context. Sugirtharajah describes the book of third-world biblical reflection he edits as being authored by 'real readers' trying to make sense of their context and the text and who are deconstructionists, not from the logic that leads others from structuralism to post-structuralism, but 'from the experience of divided, uprooted and unassimilated lives' and also reconstructionists because 'for those genuinely threatened by chaos the logic of survival requires some new order, even if only provisional'.[24] This focus on real readers and their concerns not only maximizes the liberation potential of the text, but also contributes to the liberation of the reader. Essentially all readings of the text have validity, whether they are

---

[23]   George M. Soares-Prabhu, 'Two Mission Commands: An Interpretation of Matthew 28:16–20 in the light of a Buddhist Text' in Sugirtharajah (ed.), *Voices from the Margin*, p. 322.

[24]   R. S. Sugirtharajah, 'Introduction: The Margin as a Site of Creative Re-visioning' in Sugirtharajah (ed.), *Voices from the Margin*, p. 3.

academic or popular, trained or not.[25] In fact, all readings of the text are needed – the research and detailed analysis of the academic dialogue with the force and dynamic criticism of the popular readings to produce a reading that has been tested as much as possible in the light of the questions of the struggle for liberation. There are few Deaf academic readings of the Bible to which we can refer, but there are many popular, oral readings by Deaf people who live their lives in one long struggle for liberation. Ultimately, it is their questions and their concerns that determine the starting point for reading the text and assess whether there really can be a Deaf Liberation hermeneutics.

Text and Context: Reading the Bible as a Deaf Person

Deaf Liberation hermeneutic therefore needs to begin by tackling some of the questions and concerns that Deaf people have in relation to the Bible. These fall into two different groups. The first set of questions is related to the fact that the Bible is a written text. This is a significant issue for a people whose first language is a visual language that cannot be written down and in an environment where only an educated elite can comfortably read the English translation of the Bible. How can we talk about the concerns of 'real readers' in a context where many cannot read the text for themselves? The second set of questions is located around the fact that the Bible only sees deafness as signifying something negative, as a lack of hearing. In other words, the only understanding of deafness in the Bible is the medical model of deafness. No concept of a Deaf community, with a distinctive language and culture is to be found within the text. We need to identify particular strategies that might help to bridge this gulf between the biblical and the contemporary worlds for Deaf people before we can read the text in a liberating way.

BSL and the Bible

For a true liberation hermeneutic, the Bible must be read and interpreted by the people, and most of the time liberation theologians assume that the text itself is available to people and can therefore become the object of interpretation.[26] It can also be argued that a post-colonial, liberating reading of the Bible needs to be in the language of the people rather than the language of the colonists. In other words, for a true Deaf Liberation hermeneutic, Deaf people need to be able to encounter and theologize on the text in their own language of BSL rather than in English. Paddy Ladd, who discusses this issue in his own context of academic Deaf Studies, suggests that while the use of English is necessary to be part of the wider academic

---

[25]   Segovia, *Decolonising biblical studies*, p. 46.

[26]   As suggested by Patrick A. Kalilombe, 'A Malawian Example: The Bible and Non-literate Communities' in Sugirtharajah (ed.), *Voices from the Margin*, p. 423.

(and, in this case, Christian) community, those who are bilingual need to take the responsibility of ensuring that those who cannot use English are not excluded from the discourse.[27] One of the ways we can do that is by making sure our work is presented and discussed in a BSL context as well as in English, and that, despite the methodological challenges of working in two languages and two different media, we incorporate BSL perspectives into our work.[28]

One of the reasons the issue of language is so important for Deaf Liberation hermeneutics is the fact that many Deaf people cannot easily read the text of the Bible for themselves. Literacy and reading levels among Deaf people vary a lot. Particularly among the older generations (that is those educated 'orally' once the Milan conference recommendations had been fully implemented), inadequate oral education focused on attempting to teach speech and lip-reading rather than the acquisition of skills in reading, writing and arithmetic mean that for many Deaf adults, written English is still very much a second language. A report published by the British government in October 2000 suggests that there has been no overall improvement in the achievement of deaf pupils in the 20 years since Conrad's report on the literacy of Deaf school leavers was published, and therefore 'most children with severe to profound hearing losses do not reach functional language or literacy levels'.[29] There has been no published research into literacy among Deaf adults. Experience suggests that while some Deaf adults continue to improve their reading levels after school, it remains a second language that must be read with the aid of a dictionary. It has been argued that this illiteracy has been a direct consequence of the dominance of 'oral' methods of education over 'manual' since the Milan conference of 1880. Prior to that, literacy varied among Deaf people much as it did among the hearing population at that time. Deaf people who had a good (usually 'manual') education could read and write; those who had not had any such education could not. The existence of highly literate Deaf people in this pre-Milan world is why we can refer to Deaf people in the past as having read and interpreted the Bible for their own liberation, because Deaf people who could read the text and share it with others did exist.

This discussion of literacy and reading levels within the Deaf population suggests that, by and large, the text of the Bible is not easily available to Deaf people for them to interpret themselves in their own context. This is a situation that can also be found in countries like Malawi, where lack of meaningful education has resulted in 50 per cent or more of the adult population being functionally

---

[27] Ladd, *In search of Deafhood: towards an understanding of British Deaf culture* (Bristol, 1998), p. 238.

[28] An increasingly common way of doing this in the Deaf world is to release videos of conference presentations as well as a book of written papers. Doug Alker published *really not interested in the Deaf?* as both a book in English and as a BSL video translation, so that Deaf people could choose the language in which they wanted to encounter the book.

[29] Felicity Fletcher-Campbell, *Literacy and Special Educational Needs: a review of the literature* (London, 2000), p. 16.

illiterate. In the context of Malawian society, reading and writing are marginal channels of learning, communicating and assimilating knowledge and values. In a faith based on written scriptures, this has a very great impact on the distribution of power within the churches. Patrick Kalilombe suggests that those who cannot read the Bible are at the mercy of their literate neighbours, who can pick and choose what to read, leaving out what they think are useless, dangerous or ambiguous parts.[30]

In the modern (Anglican) Deaf church, access to the text of the Bible for the majority is usually via the 'readings' that are part of the liturgy of the service. Due to constraints of time, there is usually only one reading chosen from a published 'lectionary' or list of readings to be used on each day. If it is a communion service (as most are), the reading will most likely be from the Gospels[31] (as is 'required' by Anglican liturgical rules). The reading will be signed, either by the chaplain or a member of the congregation. In a minority of cases, the 'signing' will be a clear and adequate translation of the text. Often the 'signing' is the English/BSL amalgam known as Sign Supported English (SSE) which consists of signs from BSL presented in the English word order, with a great deal of fingerspelling for the parts of sentences without a direct sign equivalent. Peter McDonough, a Deaf Roman Catholic priest, argues that SSE 'translations' are fraught with conflicts, aberrations and ambivalences, usually unintelligible and onerous to the majority of Deaf people.[32] The use of SSE by hearing chaplains usually represents either an inadequate mastery of sign language (in 1997 only eight of a total of 48 chaplains could be said to have 'fluency' in sign language)[33] or, for more fluent chaplains, a desire to speak and sign at the same time – which is impossible if BSL, with its own grammar, is used. Deaf people, who are native signers, use SSE for 'reading' biblical texts as a general rule because their English reading skills are not good enough to understand the text sufficiently well to translate it into clear BSL.

This issue has been recognized for a long time. In 1978, the World Bible Translation Centre published a new translation of the Bible designed especially for deaf people in the USA. This *English Version for the Deaf* was neither a revision nor a paraphrase of English versions; rather the translators consider it a serious translation, from the original Greek or Hebrew into the 'closest natural equivalents in English for the Deaf community'.[34] The intention behind this translation was twofold. Firstly, the vocabulary used is fairly simple and reflects the then average

---

[30] Kalilombe, 'A Malawian Example' in Sugirtharajah (ed.), *Voices from the Margin*, p. 427.

[31] The books of Matthew, Mark, Luke and John, telling the story of the life of Jesus.

[32] Peter McDonough, 'The Place of Deaf People in the Church – a Deaf Priest's View' in International Ecumenical Working Group Conference, *The Place of Deaf People in the Church*, p. 47.

[33] 'Fluency' is taken to mean has passed CACDP Stage 3 or above. *The Church Among Deaf People* (London, 1997), p. 83.

[34] *The Holy Bible: English Version for the Deaf* (Michigan, 1978).

reading level of Deaf people in the USA; words or phrases that are considered to need further explanation are expanded in footnotes. However, the translators claim that the text is more than a simple English version, and that they have 'learned to appreciate the unique thought patterns of the deaf person's mind and to respect the intricate structure of his [*sic*] independent language' with the result that the text can be signed without the need to 'translate' the English text into sign. The intention behind this Bible, to make the text accessible in English to Deaf people as a people with a distinct language, was praiseworthy. However, it has never fully achieved this aim for at least three reasons. The translation is still basically readable as an English text, it uses some elements of sign language grammar, such as proper names throughout instead of pronouns, but it is not possible to sign from it word for word and produce clear, understandable sign language, whether ASL[35] or BSL. In other words, it is effectively a translation from Greek or Hebrew into written SSE, with all the problems of SSE as described above. The second difficulty with this translation is the fact that it was done by hearing people. They have tried to speak primarily to the Deaf and not to the hearing, but as I have said above, hearing English thought forms and structures still predominate. The final difficulty preventing this translation from achieving its aim is its reception by Deaf people and those who work with them in the English Deaf church. Many Deaf people like the text because its simple English and explained words mean it is more understandable than other English translations, but still do not have the skills or confidence to translate it into clear BSL. Many of the hearing chaplains, and some of the more educated and literate Deaf people, do not like or use this translation because they do not seem to trust that such a Bible, with such a limited vocabulary, can actually contain the meaning of the Greek and Hebrew text. This distrust appears to arise from a familiarity with Bible translations that are as much a piece of English literature, using the full richness of the English language, as they are a rendition of the meaning of the original languages. Or in other words, existing English translations are being set up as a 'norm' to which the *English Version for the Deaf* is being compared to its detriment.[36]

What is needed to render the Bible text fully accessible to Deaf people is a good BSL translation on a visual medium such as video or CD-ROM. Peter

---

[35] American Sign Language, which would have been the sign the translators used as their basis for the structures and thought patterns of Deaf people. The signs used are different to BSL, but the underlying grammatical structure is very similar, which is why the American translation has been helpful in a British context.

[36] It is worth noting that Peter McDonough recently published a 'Lectionary' or selection of Bible readings for each Sunday on the same principle of English that could easily be translated into BSL. This lectionary for Deaf people is a paraphrase from English, referring to the original language where necessary. It is too soon to assess its value and reception, but the fact that it has been produced by a 'native' Deaf signer suggests it should be much better than the *English Version for the Deaf*. Unfortunately, it only covers selected passages from the Bible, so its use in Bible study will be limited. Peter McDonough, *Signs of God: Lectionary for deaf people* (Chawton, 2002).

McDonough, with the organization Visible Communications, is attempting to produce a BSL Bible on video. So far (2001), this translation covers chapters 1 to 7 of the Gospel of Luke on three videos at £10 each. There is also a video of parables from Matthew and John, 18 of the Psalms on two videotapes and a video of the story of David and Goliath in BSL and cartoon animation at the same sort of price per tape. These videos are all translations by Deaf people into BSL and represent a vitally important project for Deaf people's access to the Bible. However, the price of this access is too high for most Deaf churches and Deaf people and is unworkable for the purposes of easy reference. At this rate, the Gospel of Luke will require a total of eight or nine videotapes, and so it will cost a Deaf church or individual £80 or £90 to buy just the one Gospel. Even if the whole Gospel were owned, running through the many volumes of the videotape to find a particular reference would be a slow and inefficient process. CD-ROMs and DVDs can hold much more data than videotapes, and may be able to hold the whole signed Bible in an easily referable format. However, the cost of getting such a project off the ground would be prohibitive. To date, the only country attempting such a project is Norway, where the National Bible Society is working with funding from the government.[37] It would appear that the ideal of an affordable BSL Bible is some way in the future. One day Deaf people may be able to sign the texts from a computer screen on the lectern, or watch the text as part of a Bible study group or in their own home without having to deal with issues of English use and translation, but this dream is not sufficient for a liberation theology now.[38]

The net result of these factors is that the vast majority of Deaf people only have access to a small number of texts, selected first by a distant hearing committee and secondly by hearing chaplains according to their own judgements, interests and objectives. The texts chosen are often presented in a form that is unintelligible, and does not make the meaning of the texts clear. This structure gives the literate, educated chaplains a great deal of control over Deaf people's encounter with the Bible and therefore over their capacity to reflect on it and use it for their own lives. As Kalilombe asks of the Malawians 'Are they [the illiterate or Deaf people] reduced to having others do theology for them?'[39]

If this is not to be the case, alternative ways of presenting and interpreting the text of the Bible need to be found. An important point here is that the written text is only one way of transmitting the contents of the Bible; other media, more familiar and more effective in a non-literate society, can be found. Kalilombe suggests that media such as these are already present in societies where reading and writing are marginal to the culture. These media include hearing and seeing the message rather

---

[37] Sue Dyson, 'IEWG at Tallinn, Estonia, September 2000' in *Signs* (Spring 2001): 6.

[38] It is interesting the compare this with Kalilombe, who talks of the use of the Bible on tape for Malawians, but who feels that the potential benefits of an oral Bible are outweighed by the cost of the equipment.

[39] Kalilombe, 'A Malawian Example' in Sugirtharajah (ed.), *Voices from the Margin*, p. 423.

than reading it, utilizing mnemonic devices such as repetition and variation of analogous visual aids to memorize the text.[40] Storytelling, a form of oral transmission of texts, is a traditional art in many cultures, including Deaf culture, and in the hands of a skilled practitioner accurately transmits what is seen as the essence of the narrative.

Peter McDonough has explored the use of storytelling as translation, in his MA thesis on issues of translating the Bible into BSL.[41] He asked seven Deaf people to sign selected passages from the Gospels and then analysed the results in terms of how they accomplished the same purpose [or, in his words, aroused the same effect] in BSL, as was accomplished/aroused in the 'original' English.[42] In other words, what McDonough was trying to establish was some principles to assess whether BSL translations were 'good' translations or not. What he found in the course of his study was that what was considered a 'good' translation by Deaf people (or the meaning transmitted in natural sign, 'embodied in its own culture and colloquial idiomacy')[43] was not always seen as a 'good' translation by hearing people, who seemed to be looking for a 'direct and true translation of the biblical text'.[44] McDonough concluded that this mismatch was largely due to the nature of BSL as used by Deaf people and the fact that the process he was studying was one of *translation*, with plenty of time to present the passage, as opposed to one of *interpretation* (with which the hearing people who could sign would be familiar), which attempts to sign the passage simultaneously with it being read aloud by someone else. BSL, as used by Deaf people, contains a large proportion of non-manual features as part of its innate grammar, such as facial expressions and body language that appeared, to hearing viewers, to lead to the generation of meanings that were not alluded to by the biblical texts. There was also the fact that many of the hearing viewers were uncomfortable with some of the signs used, which were not considered 'polite' or 'appropriate' in English culture and were therefore condemned as 'not correct'. However, to Deaf viewers, these non-manual features were an essential part of the biblical text in their language; as McDonough expresses it 'If we were to translate the biblical texts literally, there would only be half the language or even less. Our culture and the nature or the syntactic of our language, demand that we have to use our language in its totality'.[45] These non-manual features are not in fact adding meaning to the text. They are grammatical features, integral to the meaning of BSL, using the tradition of storytelling in the Deaf community, with a delight in exploiting the resources of the language and

---

[40]   Ibid., p. 427.
[41]   Part of which was published in Peter McDonough, 'Presenting the Word of God in Sign Language' in Peter McDonough (ed.), *Ephphata: Proceedings of the International Catholic Deaf Religious Conference 1996* (Monmouth, 1998).
[42]   Ibid., p. 59.
[43]   That is in the traditional storytelling format.
[44]   Ibid., p. 60. See also p. 71.
[45]   Ibid., p. 73.

manipulating it to dramatic effect, together with background knowledge of biblical history, culture, medicine and common sense to embellish the story so as to provide the non-manual elements required by the culture and language of Deaf people. This gives us translations that engage our interests and our lives with the living word of God in the Bible.

In fact, instead of adding meaning that is not there, sometimes the demands of BSL clarify the meaning of a particular passage for all, hearing and Deaf, who can understand the signs. One example of this is in the translation of the concept 'shepherd', which is frequently used in both the Hebrew and the Christian Bibles. In twenty-first century England, we envisage shepherds as people who basically chase sheep with the aid of dogs and curly topped sticks. This was reflected in translations of 'shepherd' as *SHEEP-CHASER-AND-HERDER* or *PERSON-WITH-CURLY-STICK*, both rather authoritarian signs. In ancient Israel, rather than chasing unintelligent sheep into sheep pens and fields, the shepherd knows each sheep and calls to them to follow him and in this way leads them to where he wants them to be.[46] This concept of shepherd can be translated as *SHEEP-LEADER* and signed in a very gentle way indicating the nature of the relationship between the shepherd and the sheep. So, the concrete nature of BSL that needs to look at the original actions to produce a translation that is true to the original concept of the shepherd texts has also shown the way to a new and deeper understanding of the power relationships we are referring to when we talk of Christ the Good Shepherd.

Another significant way of 'translating' the biblical text is by the use of dramatized retellings of the story. A dramatized retelling can be said to apply 'the meaning of the text to a familiar world in a familiar idiom'[47] or, in other words, the essence of the story as seen by the participants in the drama is presented in the culture and language of Deaf people. This is basically the same process as discussed above with reference to storytelling, but is perhaps even more engaging for the viewers who get drawn into the drama in the character of the 'crowd'. One example of a dramatized retelling was seen at 'The Way to the Stable': A Christmas Celebration in Sign Language led by a Deaf priest, Bob Shrine.[48] The dramatized retelling of the birth of Jesus really did take the events described and move them to twentieth-century Deaf culture. For example, Luke 2:1–3 explains the move of Mary and Joseph from Nazareth to Bethlehem by saying that Augustus Caesar had announced a census and all must travel to their own town to be registered. In the section of the drama entitled 'Announcing the Census' a man playing a Roman soldier announced to the congregation, in the manner of a Deaf club secretary, that everyone would have to go to their town of birth to be registered. By this, I mean that the man signed directly to the congregation, he

---

[46] I am indebted to Donald Read for bringing this particular point to my notice.

[47] Kalilombe, 'A Malawian Example' in Sugirtharajah (ed.), *Voices from the Margin*, p. 431.

[48] This service, in December 2000, was videoed, and it is this video that provides the substance for the following paragraph.

explained what was meant by 'census' or 'registration' in the way a Deaf club secretary would explain voting procedure, for example. He also ad-libbed and involved members of the congregation in spontaneous improvization when, after signing *CAESAR SAY WHAT? ALL MUST GO TO PLACE BORN THERE*, he signed to one person *YOU – BORN WHERE? MANCHESTER – YOU GO TO MANCHESTER* and to another *YOU – BORN WHERE? LEEDS – YOU GO TO LEEDS* before continuing with his explanation of the census.[49] This brief extract illustrates not only how the biblical text can be appropriately presented in BSL using the cultural forms and idioms of the Deaf community, but also suggests a way that the Deaf community already does hermeneutics in a non-written form. By representing the announcement of the census as evoking the Deaf club secretary in this way, the dramatized retelling is also making a statement about the power dynamics implied in the text. Just as Deaf people were traditionally often at the mercy of the whims of the Deaf club secretary,[50] so were Hebrew people such as Joseph and Mary at the mercy of the Roman government. This is a form of hermeneutics that we can name 'oral hermeneutics' in a term first used by Kwok Pui Lan in discussing the interpretive style of Indian women.[51] She suggests that a characteristic of an oral hermeneutic is the freedom to reappropriate the text to the context. Sometimes the story is framed in a new context, or the ending changed, or variants are suggested alongside the original story. Sugirtharajah, in commenting on a dramatized retelling of the story of the birth of Moses produced by Asian women, says that 'in the hermeneutical tradition of the West, the biblical documents are studied in silence and it is assumed that only the printed word can communicate the authentic meaning'.[52] However, these dramatized retellings illustrate how 'hermeneutics can use not only philosophical tools, but also the medium of the performing arts to unlock the biblical narratives'.

Other traditional forms for transmitting narrative in both Malawian culture and also the western church tradition are music, singing and dancing. Large parts of the Bible have been transmitted in the psalms, hymns and canticles that are sung in churches all over the world.[53] Kalilombe argues that songs are effective vehicles

---

[49]   Questioning the audience is a major strategy in Deaf cultural discourse and is also related to the grammatical structure of BSL questions and answers. For example '*ME GO OUT WHAT FOR? SEE DOCTOR*'. See Lorna Allsop, *British Sign Language style in lectures: a comparison of deaf and hearing lecturers* (Dip. SS thesis, University of Bristol, 1995).

[50]   Usually based on carrying out the demands of the missioner.

[51]   Kwok Pui Lan, 'Overlapping communities and multicultural hermeneutics' in Brenner and Fontaine (eds), *A feminist companion to reading the Bible*, p. 212.

[52]   Editor's introduction to an Asian group's work, 'An Asian Feminist Perspective: The Exodus Story' in Sugirtharajah (ed.), *Voices from the Margin*, p. 255.

[53]   Canticles are portions of scripture that are paraphrased and sung in the same way as the Psalms. A well-known example of a 'canticle' is the Magnificat or Song of Mary from Luke 2: 46–55 which is often sung in the form of the hymn 'Tell out my soul'.

for information and teaching, easy to remember and to reproduce.[54] While the idea of setting parts of the Bible to music is not relevant to Deaf culture, the basic concept of biblical texts, presented in a rhythmic form of BSL for all to sign together in the form of 'BSL hymns' created by Deaf people, could be a powerful way of spreading biblical texts in a form that is both easy to access and straightforward to memorize. If we can develop enough 'portions' in BSL hymnody, the 'biblical song' could replace the reading in both liturgical and Bible study settings, thus enabling everyone to encounter the text.

Finally, in Kalilombe's example, there is the existence of 'visual-media' as a way of circulating information and important messages in a non-literate society. He argues that the visual objects of African societies are a medium for 'expressing values, recalling stories, fables or parables ... for evoking meaningful history'.[55] Such visual objects do this through evocative and associational powers of their shape, design, textures and colours, and this associated symbolism can be explored and extended into the world of the Bible. In Deaf culture the power of visual symbols is already part of our daily life experience. For example, pictures of biblical scenes have a long history in the development of Deaf people's spirituality and knowledge of the Bible; and recently, the *Lion Graphic Bible*[56] has replaced the old *English Version for the Deaf* as a favoured 'translation' for use by Deaf people because signing the story by describing the depicted scenes has the potential to overcome many of the issues raised in attempting translation from English to BSL, not the least in meaning that any native signer can read the Bible, whatever their knowledge of English.

A particular way in which pictures can be used as a means of engaging with the text of the Bible occurred at a workshop at an NDCC conference. On this occasion, the picture used was an illustration of Psalm 23 produced by the nuns of Turvey Abbey. Having a rough idea of the psalm, a group of Deaf (and hearing) people were asked to look at the picture and produce a BSL 'hymn'. The result is very much a truly BSL paraphrase of the psalm rather than an attempt at translation. Another example of the use of visual symbolism as an aid to reading the Bible was observed at a recent NDCC conference. One workshop, run by a 'moderately literate'[57] Deaf woman was on 'colour and the Bible'. She encouraged the participants to associate events in the life of Jesus with coloured items in everyday use in the garden, so that when they encountered these coloured objects in the future, they would bring into their minds a particular text or story in the life of

---

[54] Kalilombe, 'A Malawian Example' in Sugirtharajah (ed.), *Voices from the Margin*, p. 428.

[55] Ibid., p. 429.

[56] Jeff Anderson, *The Lion Graphic Bible*, illustrations Jeff Anderson, script Mike Maddox, lettering Steve Harrison, 1st paperback edn (Oxford, 2001).

[57] I would define a 'moderately literate' Deaf adult in this context as someone who has a functional knowledge of English, but who still struggles with the very specialized language of the Bible.

Jesus associated with those colours. In other words, in our Deaf British culture, colours already have meanings and symbolism, both abstract and concrete, associated with them.[58] For example, the colour blue is associated with water, red with blood or love and green with grass or growth, regardless of the actual colours of an object or concept. What this workshop leader did was to encourage the participants to use the pre-existing symbolism of colours, and search in the Gospel for events in Jesus' life and aspects of Jesus' character with the same kind of symbolism; for example, looking at the colour blue led to exploring the story of Jesus' baptism, or the encounter with the woman at the well. In the future, for these participants, the colour blue can be used as an aide-memoire in the telling of these stories, and a tool for exploring and explaining their meaning. This is one example of the way we Deaf can use visual symbolism to present the Bible in an accessible way, but what is necessary is that Deaf people themselves work out the associations and establish connections between their understanding of visual symbols and the text of the Bible. The Deaf artist, Niall McCormack, has also used colour to reflect on biblical and theological ideas; his depiction of the Trinity uses the easily accessible symbolism of colour as a way of exploring this particular concept.[59]

Presenting the Bible in BSL and Deaf cultural forms, whether via storytelling or dramatized retelling or 'BSL hymns' or visual-media, inevitably involves a process of interpretation of the biblical text. At some point someone who can read the text and who can be trusted by Deaf people to transmit the meaning without too much distortion, preferably a Deaf person, is needed. However, as these examples have shown, once given the outlines of a text, Deaf people can take the stories and characters and teaching of the Bible and transmit them in a vivid and appropriate form to spread the word of God among the Deaf community.

It is possible to criticize these presentations of the text as moving too far from the written text, as containing too much interpretation and therefore not being sufficient to transmit the text of the Bible as we have it in printed books. In other words, the variation between one 'text' (signed or acted or whatever) and another is too great. I have discussed one or two criticisms such as this above with reference to the issues of storytelling and dramatized retelling in BSL, but there is one more point to make in response to this issue. That is the concept of a fixed, written text is a very recent one. Prior to the invention of printing, for the first 1,500 years of transmission of the Bible, it was in manuscripts copied from other manuscripts. As David Parker points out, this meant that every copy was different, both unique and imperfect. The further back we go, the greater the degree of variation between texts, so that the earliest substantial evidence for the New Testament in the citations of Justin Martyr bear very little resemblance to the text

---

[58]   This symbolism is not specific to Deaf people; it appears to be universal throughout the UK.

[59]   <www.niallmc.com/trinity.html>.

of the New Testament enshrined in print today.[60] It was the invention of printing, and the ability to produce large numbers of identical copies that led to what Parker calls the idolatrous idea that the written text itself was authoritative.[61] This is a concept that he suggests may be unravelling with the growth in the number of electronic texts of the Bible, which are more akin to the variability of manuscript copies than the fixed nature of the printed text. Once the electronic text is installed on the machine, it can be manipulated by changing readings, reordering the text, deleting or adding material and storing notes. The text of the Gospels is, and remains, a living text, subject to change, however it is presented – manuscript, print or electronically.[62] I would argue that the growth of 'oral hermeneutics' and visual ways of presenting the text are part of this process of freeing the readers of the Bible from the tyranny of a written text that claims it is the only authoritative word of God. Deaf people, no matter how good or bad their English is, *can* directly encounter God's self-revelation through the storytelling, dramatized retellings, BSL hymns and visual media that make up the 'text' of the Bible in BSL.

Deaf People in the Bible?

I have discussed the potential liberating value of the Bible and ways in which the text can be encountered and explored using methodologies that are independent of English. I have concluded that the Bible is of value for Deaf liberation and that there are a large number of very creative methods for exploring the meaning of the texts. However, there is still one major issue that needs to be discussed before we can claim that there is a Deaf Liberation hermeneutics, and that is the issue of the total absence of positive portrayals of d/Deaf people in the Bible, which makes it hard for us to find our place in the dialogue between the voices in the text and in the contemporary world. One passage that is particularly experienced as anti-Deaf is Leviticus 21:16–23. This passages states that d/Deaf people (like anyone who is physically 'imperfect') are 'impure' and cannot therefore fully participate in the religious ceremonies that were at the heart of the relationship between God and Israel and therefore were necessary for full membership of the nation of Israel. There are a number of tactics developed by feminist biblical scholars for dealing with anti-women and anti-deaf texts such as this. Heather McKay summarizes these tactics as being either reactive, proactive or inclusivist, with no single approach solving the all problems raised by the text.[63] As will be seen, I do not see these tactics as being mutually exclusive and comprehensive approaches, but rather as avenues that lead to fruitful encounters in a multivalent approach to the Bible. Reactive tactics are used by those who are convinced that the Bible text is basically

---

[60] D. C. Parker, *The living text of the Gospels* (Cambridge, 1997), p. 188.

[61] Ibid., p. 190.

[62] Ibid., p. 213.

[63] Heather McKay, 'On the future of feminist biblical criticism' in Brenner and Fontaine (eds), *A feminist companion to reading the Bible*, p. 70.

liberating for women. These tactics focus on criticizing the historical exegesis and modern interpretation of the anti-female texts and argue that the continued use of these texts against women is contrary to God's desire for the modern world.[64] What this results in is the creation of a 'canon within the canon', which says that the anti-female texts are not relevant to the modern world so they must be ignored. A reactive approach to the anti-Deaf passages could argue that the purity laws of Leviticus, which defined who could and could not be saved by following the law; belong to a very specific social, political and economic culture. This text, part of the existing canon of the Bible, was selected from a much larger body of literature.[65] The process of canonization, or declaring which of the existing texts were deserving of being collected together and designated 'the word of God', was as much affected by the social, political and economic purposes of the final text as it was by a belief that these texts, uniquely among the texts of the time, reflected the word of God. The particular section we are interested in, the Torah, or books of the law that include the book of Leviticus, was canonized around 400 BCE. In the history of Israel, this was the time when the Persian king was allowing the Hebrew people to return to Jerusalem after 70 years of exile in Babylon. Banana suggests that the primary intention behind the selection of these particular texts as being worthy of canonization was because of their nationalistic appeal; in a time of exile and the chaos of the return to Jerusalem they helped to keep alive the nation and worship of Jehovah, or, in other words, they functioned to keep alive the identity of the Jews as a separate nation and prevent them from being totally assimilated into the Babylonian culture. These texts seem to use two strategies for this purpose. One is a focus on the identity of the Jews as the chosen people of God and their land as the kingdom of God on earth; the other is a focus on the purity of the Jewish people, on their separateness and difference from the people around them. This identity, purity, separateness and difference is established and safeguarded by the laws detailed in the Torah, which, it can be argued, were basically there to make quite clear who was in and who was out.[66] It is in the context of this time that we can read the texts from Leviticus that state physically 'imperfect' people such as Deaf people are impure. They must be cared for (Leviticus 19:14) but cannot fully participate in the religious life of the nation (as they cannot speak) and therefore must be excluded from the holy place in case they blur the clear boundaries set up to separate Jews from others. We are no longer in a socio-political context where we need to define boundaries in such a way as to decide

---

[64]   McKay, 'On the future of feminist biblical criticism' in Brenner and Fontaine (eds), *A feminist companion to reading the Bible*, pp. 71–5.

[65]   Canaan S. Banana, 'The Case for a New Bible' in Sugirtharajah (ed.), *Voices from the Margin*, p. 76.

[66]   N. T. Wright is an example of the many biblical scholars who understand the function of the purity laws and the Torah as primarily to aid the 'political struggle to maintain Jewish identity', *Jesus and the Victory of God* (London, 1996) especially pp. 378 and 388.

who is pure and who is not. This suggests that we need take no more notice of these passages in Leviticus than we do of those that instruct us to make grain offerings or specify dietary laws for us to follow.

Treating the purity laws of Leviticus as no longer relevant to our lives is not a purely modern phenomenon. Jesus' own relationship to the laws of his ancestors is complex and contentious, but it did not appear to involve slavish, unthinking obedience.[67] As has been suggested by many different commentators, from different contexts, he seemed in fact to openly undermine the purity laws and the traditions built up around them.[68] As Tom Wright puts it, for Jesus 'genuine purity is a matter of the heart, for which the normal purity laws – and hence one of the major definitions of Jewishness and Jewish loyalty – are irrelevant'.[69] Reactive approaches to anti-female texts often take this tack of illustrating how Jesus ignored social and religious laws of his own time in his relationships with women as a way of saying that proclaiming Jesus renders these texts irrelevant. Carole Fontaine defends the Bible against those who would reject it completely because of the anti-female bias in a self-proclaimed 'liberationist' reading of the Gospels. Jesus was a 'Jew who envisions a new humanity, demonstrating that there may be another paradigm of maleness, another way to be human', or in other words, if we women focus on a Jesus who challenged the social structures of his day, we can ignore much else in the Bible which sets up relationships of domination and submission between men and women.[70] Nancy Eiesland appears to take the same approach for disabled people in their relationship to the Bible. She has a vision of the disabled God in Jesus that becomes the yardstick by which we measure all other parts of the Bible.[71] In the same way, we d/Deaf can look at a Jesus who challenged and undermined the purity laws, and disregard other parts of the Bible that attempt to stigmatize us as impure.

Similar tactics of setting other anti-Deaf passages in their socio-historical contexts can be shown to render them all irrelevant in the light of the social and cultural understandings of what it means to be d/Deaf; but is this enough? McKay suggests that reactive tactics, establishing a canon within a canon, tackle only the symptoms of patriarchy in the texts rather than the root causes of their continued use against women.[72] In other words, those who argue with individual texts and

---

[67] This is discussed extensively within the perspective of western academic scholarship by Wright in *Jesus and the Victory of God*, Chapter 9; see especially p. 371f. where he summarizes the arguments.

[68] See, for example, Hisako Kinukawa, 'The Syrophoenician Woman: Mark 7:24–30' in Sugirtharajah (ed.), *Voices from the Margin*, p. 138.

[69] Wright, *Jesus and the Victory of God*, p. 396.

[70] Carole R. Fontaine, 'The Abusive Bible' in Brenner and Fontaine (eds), *A feminist companion to reading the Bible*, p. 112.

[71] Eiesland, *The Disabled God: towards a liberatory theology of disability* (Nashville, 1994), p. 87.

[72] McKay, 'On the future of feminist biblical criticism' in Brenner and Fontaine (eds), *A feminist companion to reading the Bible*, p. 74.

their applications in this way are simply solving problems created by others in their faith community and in the process colluding with 'textual oppressors' by not demanding any admission of guilt or asking for restitution. What this argument suggests to me is that by simply ignoring the anti-Deaf texts as I have suggested above, we are not grappling with the root causes of their use against d/Deaf people. This root cause can be identified as the conviction that the Bible is authoritative for all times and all places, and that anything else, whether rejection of individual passages as described above or retelling the story as discussed in the previous section, is not 'biblical': it is simply secondary literature or something that is tinkering at the fringes of the text and not to be taken seriously. To tackle these root causes, it appears that we need to go further than questioning the authority of individual texts; we need to question the authority of the Bible as a whole.

This course, which McKay labels a 'proactive tactic', can lead to total rejection of the Bible. However, this is not the only way forward. Both feminist and 'third-world' scholars who have attempted to move on this point have suggested we both question any a priori authority of the Bible as the word of God and also that we open up the canon of authorized scripture to include other texts. Carole Fontaine agrees that the first step in undercutting the seeming authorization in the Bible of the 'exploitation of any who are not in-group, elite males' is to acknowledge that it is a human product of elite males[73] rather than a text specifically authorized by God.[74] Women in Latin America and Asia have identified the same need to deny the authority of harmful texts (as opposed to simply ignoring them as irrelevant) and reject the sacrality of the Bible itself as a guarantee for truth.[75] Questioning the authority of the Bible does not, however, mean rejecting it out of hand; nor does identifying it as a product of elite males mean it does not contain anything of God. McKay suggests the Bible can still be regarded as authoritative, but it needs to be a deserved authority, an influence earned through relevance to women's [and Deaf people's] lives.[76]

As suggested above, we can argue that the canon of the Bible as we have it was the product of human decisions and was affected by political and social factors that are no longer relevant. What this means is that a number of scholars taking the 'proactive' approach argue not only for the lessening of the absoluteness of biblical authority, but also for the opening up of the canon to include other texts; or, in other words, rejecting not so much the authority of the Bible text per se, but simply the authority of the canon that separates the Bible as we have it from other writings

---

[73]   That is, it is the product of the only people who could read and write in those days.

[74]   Fontaine, 'The Abusive Bible' in Brenner and Fontaine (eds), *A feminist companion to reading the Bible,* p. 93.

[75]   Tamez, 'Women's rereading of the Bible' in Sugirtharajah (ed.), *Voices from the Margin,* p. 52 and Kwok Pui Lan, 'Discovering the Bible in the non-biblical world', ibid., p. 301.

[76]   McKay, 'On the future of feminist biblical criticism' in Brenner and Fontaine (eds), *A feminist companion to reading the Bible,* p. 77.

from the ancient world. This is a significant question for Asian scholars, who want to ask how their own ancient scriptures relate to the Bible,[77] and for women who want to use 'goddess' and 'sophia'[78] texts in apocryphal and other ancient Near East literature. While agreeing with the principle of reopening the canon to include as many voices, as many points of view as possible, and accepting that the more voices we can find the more everyone on the margins will benefit, much more research is needed to explore how, specifically, widening the canon can benefit Deaf people.[79] Can we, for example, include in the canon non-written texts such as icons, stained glass and other depictions of an encounter between God and humankind? Meanwhile, I would argue, the Bible as we have it includes in its many voices valid encounters with the reality of the living God; and in dialogue with our own experiences of God it is still the best way to learn who God is and what God wants for Deaf people.

The third approach to biblical texts identified by McKay is called the 'inclusivist' approach. I understand this to be similar to the 'proactive approach' in the way it approaches the whole of biblical texts and not just the 'female-friendly' ones, but different in the way it discusses how women's voices might be involved behind the text as well as looking for women's voices actually in the text. In other words, biblical scholars such as Athalya Brenner explore the possibilities suggested by the fact that women may have been involved in the production of the biblical texts as cultural products, that is that women were involved in the events narrated and the retelling of the stories even if they were not involved in the final process of writing the text.[80] John Hull, a blind scholar, has used tactics very similar to this in *In the beginning there was darkness*. He describes himself as entering into conversation with the Bible from his point of view as a blind person. His rereading of the text not only incorporates the places where there is a specific blind character, but also the references that arise from the fact the Bible was written by people who were 'embedded in the sighted world' and therefore uses metaphors and figures of speech from sighted experience that alienate him, as a blind reader, from the text.[81] In other words, he traces both the blind voices and the sighted voices in the text, showing how blindness in the characters is often, but not solely, a weakness or a punishment.[82] Samson, for example, after being blinded by

---

[77] Samartha, 'Scripture and Scriptures' in Sugirtharajah (ed.), *Voices from the Margin*, p. 21.

[78] Sophia is the Greek word for 'wisdom' personified in female form.

[79] Horne in *Injury and Blessing* explores apocryphal and classical literature looking for references to disabled people (including d/Deaf people). His work suggests that there is much of interest to d/Deaf people to be found from opening up the canon in this way.

[80] McKay, 'On the future of feminist biblical criticism' in Brenner and Fontaine (eds), *A feminist companion to reading the Bible*, p. 77.

[81] John M. Hull, *In the beginning there was darkness: a blind person's conversation with the Bible* (London, 2001), p. 3.

[82] Ibid., p. 65.

the Philistines, succeeds in killing more of them than he ever killed during his sighted years. Hull understands this story as an affirmation of the abilities of blind people: 'a determined and highly organized blind person, in the right place and the right time, can be most effective'.[83] The sighted nature of the text is examined, stories that are meaningless for or exclude blind people and the use of blindness as a metaphor for wickedness or folly are deconstructed. However, despite the overwhelming sighted nature of the Bible text, Hull finds metaphors that, whatever their original intention, can be read as having a special and affirming meaning for blind people. The most notable example of this is Psalm 139. In Hull's account of becoming blind and adapting to life as a blind person, he recounts how, when he first heard Psalm 139 read after his acceptance of blindness, he felt that it must have been written by a blind person because it so exactly described his experience in verse 12: 'the darkness and the light are both alike to thee'.[84] He develops this insight to suggest that only a blind person, to whom darkness and light are alike, can share this characteristic with God and for Hull this means that 'without blind people, the religious experience of sighted people is not complete'.[85]

As Deaf people, we need to reread the text in a similar way, looking for characters and metaphors that express Deaf experience as well as the use of deafness as a metaphor for stupidity and wickedness. This is a project that is yet to be done for the whole Bible, but I can give one brief example of a passage that hit me as hard as Psalm 139 ever did John Hull. This is from Psalm 141:1–2, which is often used at the beginning of evening worship. These verses plead that God will come quickly in response to the psalmist's call, and will listen to his voice, smell the incense that is burnt and see the lifting up of the psalmist's hands in the evening sacrifice. As a Deaf person, my use of BSL in the language of worship is affirmed in this passage and given a place of equal status with the use of the voice in the 'calling of God' at the beginning of worship. Even Deaf-blind people, who can smell the incense, are included in this multi-sensory call to worship.

Rereading the Bible in an 'inclusivist' way does begin the process of a mutually enriching dialogue with the text, and I look forward to a comprehensive encounter with the Bible from the Deaf point of view comparable to *In the beginning there was darkness*. However, it is limited from the Deaf liberation perspective in that it primarily uses the social model of what it means to be d/Deaf. In other words, using the 'inclusivist' methodology, we Deaf people are taking control of the construction of what it means to be d/Deaf in the Bible text, but we are doing so as individuals, who have BSL as our first language, and not as a Deaf community that has experienced oppression and discrimination at the hands of hearing 'colonialists'. One final question that needs to be explored and answered before we can delineate a Deaf Liberation hermeneutics is the question from the cultural

---

[83]   Ibid., p. 18.

[84]   John M. Hull, *Touching the Rock: an experience of blindness* (London, 1990), p. 51. The Bible quote is from the KJV.

[85]   Hull, *In the beginning there was darkness*, p. 132.

model: how can we interpret the Bible in a way that relates to our experience of oppression and our struggle for equality in a majority hearing world?

Asian biblical scholars explore a very similar question. Samartha, for example, asks 'how can the Bible, a Semitic book formed though oral and written tradition in an entirely different geographic, historical and cultural context, appropriated and interpreted for so many centuries by the West through hermeneutic tools designed to meet different needs and shaped by different historical factors, now be interpreted in Asia by Asian Christians for their own people?'[86] Samartha's essay is more about raising questions than answering them, but Kwok Pui Lan, in the same volume, suggests that a new image for the process of biblical interpretation in a world historically not shaped by the biblical vision might be what she calls 'dialogical imagination'.[87] 'Dialogical' because it involves constant conversation between several different religious and cultural traditions, both ancient and modern, and 'imagination' because it looks at both the Bible and the Asian reality anew to challenge the established order of things. It is a process that involves re-imagining what the biblical world was like so as to include our present-day reality in the text of the Bible – a process that places the people of modern-day Asia, and which could place the modern Deaf community, in the world of the Bible regardless of the distance of culture and time and exclusion from the 'original' world of the Bible. Kwok Pui Lan goes on to develop this process of dialogical hermeneutics with reference to her own Korean *Minjung* context. *Minjung* is a dynamic Korean concept that refers to the subjugated group in any relationship of dominance and subjugation; women subject to men, one ethnic group subject to another ethnic group or one race ruled by another race are all *Minjung*. The Korean nation, for much of its history, has been a *Minjung* nation in its Asian context, surrounded by the threat of larger surrounding nations and in its experience of colonization by the Japanese. This 'social biography' of the nation can engage in a fruitful dialogue with the 'social biography' of the ancient Hebrew people, surrounded by threats from and colonized by Egypt, Assyria and Babylon, which amplifies understanding not only of the text of the Old Testament but also the meaning of the Korean *Minjung* story itself.

Kwok Pui Lan has given a name to an intuitive process that has been used many times in liberation hermeneutics by oppressed people. African slaves in the Caribbean for example identified strongly with the Hebrew slaves; so strongly that 'Negro spirituals' based on biblical images such as *Let my people go*[88] are coded political songs – slaves singing their desire for liberation disguised as 'spiritual songs' about an event that took place maybe 3,000 years ago.[89] This can be said to

---

[86]   Samartha, 'Scripture and Scriptures' in Sugirtharajah (ed.), *Voices from the Margin*, p. 21.

[87]   Kwok Pui Lan, 'Discovering the Bible in the non-biblical world', ibid., p. 294.

[88]   Based on Moses' plea to the Pharaoh on behalf of the Hebrew slaves.

[89]   Iain MacRobert, *The black roots and white racism of early Pentecostalism in the USA* (Basingstoke, 1988), p. 32.

be a process of 'dialogical imagination' because the black slaves used their situation to illuminate the text of the Bible against the reading of the white slaveholders, and the text of the Bible encouraged the black slaves to see God as a God of liberation in this world and to imagine a different world where they would be free – the first step towards their rebellions that led to emancipation. This process suggests that we Deaf people can look in the text and find groups and people who we can instinctively relate to as having shared experience and dialogue with the stories they are involved in to illuminate both the biblical text and our own situation. The dynamic definition of *Minjung* can include Deaf people as subject to hearing people and so we, like *Minjung* theologians, can look for *Minjung* in the Bible as a people with whom we can identify and whose stories can engage with ours.

Ayn Byung-Mu is another *Minjung* theologian who operates using the process of dialogical imagination. He specifically looks at the Gospel of Mark to identify who were the *Minjung* in the world of first-century Palestine, the context in which Jesus lived as a human being.[90] He bases his analysis on the fact that Mark uses the Greek word *ochlos* to describe 'the people' or 'the crowd' rather than *laos* as in the other Gospels. *Ochlos* seem to have been defined in a similarly relational and fluid way as *Minjung*, in terms of domination and subjugation. For example, the poor in Mark are *ochlos* in relation to the rich, and the tax collectors are *ochlos* in relation to the Jewish nationalist establishment that rejected them as Roman collaborators. *Ochlos* also refers to 'sinners', which was not just those who deliberately broke the Jewish law, but included those who could not accomplish the duty of the laws of the Sabbath or cleanliness. This includes, for example, those who could not keep the law because of their occupation (for example they had to work on the Sabbath, or handle things considered 'impure') or because of poverty or sickness (which would include those we would call disabled). In other words, the *ochlos* includes all are those who are alienated, dispossessed and powerless in their society, with which category we could certainly identify ourselves as a Deaf community. Ahn Byung-Mu goes on to analyse Jesus' relationship with the *ochlos*, his preference for 'sinners' (according to the contemporary ideology) and children (who are also unable to keep the law), his opposition to the laws of cleanliness, which alienated and oppressed many, and his declaration of the kingdom of God which showed to the *ochlos* a new way of living and a new hope. We Deaf can also read the Gospel of Mark, and identify with the people, the *ochlos*, to find Jesus' message for us.

The *ochlos* in Mark are not the only people in the Bible we can identify with in a process of dialogical imagination. In the Hebrew Scriptures, there are many stories, songs and prayers from the times of exile when the Jews were a minority group, with their own language and culture, in a wider context that may or may not have been deliberately oppressive. One such example is the story of Daniel. Daniel was among the young men from the royal family of the Israelites who were

---

[90]   Ahn Byung-Mu, 'Jesus and the Minjung in the Gospel of Mark' in Sugirtharajah (ed.), *Voices from the Margin*, p. 101.

brought to the Babylonian court after the fall of Jerusalem. They were to be educated in the language and literature of the Chaldeans (or Babylonians), given new, Babylonian names and assimilated into the culture of the court.[91] Daniel led the group, who objected to this process despite the temptation of becoming part of elite and the risks of punishment, and maintained their own religion, language and culture in various ways with a few major confrontations. This story resonates with the experience of the Deaf community, who maintained their language and culture under the leadership of many brave 'Daniels' who refused to stop signing in schools despite the risks of punishment, and it resonates with the experience of the educated Deaf elite who face the temptation of assimilation into the majority English culture and consequent rejection of their own language and culture. We can sympathize with Daniel and enter into his feelings to produce a Deaf reading of the text and we can learn from and be encouraged by Daniel's fidelity to his God, his culture and his language, a faith that was always answered and was never in vain.

The conclusion of all this seems to be that a Deaf Liberation hermeneutic is not only possible, but also desirable. We can engage in an imaginative dialogue with the people of the Bible and learn much about God's desire for liberation of the oppressed people of the world and the ways in which this desire has been acted out in the past and can be acted out in the future and can help us, as Deaf people, in our struggle for a more just world.

---

[91]   Daniel 1:3–7.

Chapter 7

Can Jesus Sign?: Who is Jesus Christ for Deaf People Today?

The Word became flesh and lived among us.[1]
In Christ God was reconciling the world to himself.[2]
FEW DEAF-PEOPLE INTEREST COME TO THE CHURCH BECAUSE JESUS CHRIST WAS NOT DEAF.[3]

The first two of these quotes state the central mystery of the Christian faith: that Jesus Christ was the Word of God and lived on earth among us, and that through him God somehow became reconciled with the world. The second, an extract from a lament in sign language written down by the Deaf man who created it, states a central problem of many Deaf people today with the Christian faith, that they cannot see any relevance to their lives in a faith centred upon a hearing man. This chapter is an attempt to address these issues, to explore how we might be able to talk meaningfully about Christ to Deaf people today; or, in other words, just what does a hearing Jewish man who lived in first-century Galilee have to say to Deaf people in twenty-first-century Britain?

This question is central to the construction of a Deaf Liberation Theology. If we cannot respond to it in a way that relates adequately to Deaf experience of the world as it is and as we would like it to be, then it is difficult for us to claim Christ as our liberator and saviour. If we are not able to develop a distinctive understanding of Christ as our saviour, then it is difficult to see how we can claim to have a distinctive Deaf Liberation Theology. At the heart of this issue is the question that faces all who reject classical 'white, male, middle-class, western, able-bodied, hearing' theology as oppressive: is the oppression located in the formulation, the working out of the Gospel of Christ by humanity, or is it located in the Gospel itself? In other words, once we have deconstructed the church and removed all that is oppressive from its theology, is there anything left from which to rebuild? Can we Deaf find salvation, liberation and transformation in the person of Christ and in the Christian Gospel, or do we need to move on to some kind of post-Christian spirituality or faith?

---

[1]   John 1:14.
[2]   2 Corinthians 5:19.
[3]   Anthony Maciocha, 'Psalm 151 for the Deaf Community' in *Signs* (Spring 2000).

Jesus Christ, the 'poor, black, disabled woman'

'Christology', as defined by Kelly Brown Douglas, is 'to attempt to discern and define what it means for Jesus to be Christ "the bearer of God's rule, the mediator of God's salvation"'.[4] This task is one that has dominated much of Christian theology from the time Jesus asked his disciples 'Who do people say that I am?'[5] In the fourth century at the councils of Nicaea and Constantinople the results of the 'intellectual wrestling' with the concepts of Jesus Christ in the Gospels and the New Testament by many different people were codified in what is now known as the 'Nicene Creed'.[6] To use Douglas's paraphrase, the Nicene Creed states that Jesus is Christ because of his unique metaphysical make-up as God incarnate and the divine/human encounter.[7] Macquarrie and Douglas agree that the Nicene Creed has formed the basis for all subsequent western Christology, and that it is insufficient for the needs of modern-day Christology, but disagree on the question of how we should relate to it today. Macquarrie suggests that it is still a useful starting point for reflection, something with which Christological study still needs to engage.[8] He suggests that classical ideas need to be engaged with, even if they are ultimately discarded, and continues the age-old debate of whether Christology should begin with Jesus' origin in God (from 'above') or with his humanity (from 'below').[9] Douglas, in contrast, argues that the Nicene Creed does not, and never has, related to the understandings of Christ found in the lives of black men and women who confessed Jesus as Christ because of what he has done and is doing during his own time and in their lives.[10] In her view, the Nicene Creed is not just irrelevant, it is also deeply problematic as it jumps straight from the incarnation of Jesus to his crucifixion and resurrection, skipping over Jesus' ministry, diminishing his actions on earth and implying that Jesus' work on earth is unrelated to what it means for him to be the Christ.

R. S. Sugirtharajah argues that perceptions of Jesus are basically contextual, they are not validated by 'timeless claims or dogmatic soundness, but by the appropriateness of the image to a specific context'.[11] Sugirtharajah argues that the process of forming such perceptions is similar to that of the early Christians, who were trying to respond to the questions, priorities and needs of a specific community. There is really no reason why their formulations and insights should still be regarded as binding today, just as there is no reason why western understandings of Jesus should be imposed on Asian Christians.

---

[4] Kelly Brown Douglas, *The black Christ* (Maryknoll, NY, 1994), p. 111.
[5] Mark 8:29.
[6] John Macquarrie, in *Jesus Christ in modern thought* (London, 1990), p. 159.
[7] Douglas, *The black Christ*, p. 111.
[8] Macquarrie, *Jesus Christ in modern thought*, p. 172.
[9] Ibid., p. 342.
[10] Douglas, *The black Christ*, p. 112.
[11] Sugirtharajah, R. S. (ed.), *Asian Faces of Jesus* (London, 1993), p. viii.

Rosemary Radford Ruether in discussing the relationship between patriarchy and Christology argues for the importance of affirming the particularity of the historical Jesus as a first-century, Jewish, Galilean male and suggests that every person in every other time and place has to ask how Jesus, in all his historical particularity, can be paradigmatic of universal human redemption for all.[12] Macquarrie, along with other theologians in the western academic tradition, takes issue with this argument that the fact that Jesus was a man can be a problem for women. He suggests that the historical particularities of Jesus, specifically his maleness, are contingent, not essential parts of any discussion of who Jesus is, and therefore are of 'no theological importance'.[13] Eleanor McLaughlin argues that in a world where women (along with every other oppressed group) have never been included in 'generic' humanity without qualification, the idea that a representative (white, hearing, able-bodied) man implies the inclusion of all people in salvation is simply inadequate. She suggests that the more 'conservative' theologians who see Jesus' maleness as necessary may actually be more honest to the tradition as constructed and understood until very recently. They at least admit that there are differences in the way men and women are regarded in the world and that this difference is significant for theology.[14] This is true also of the experience of black and Asian people and disabled people, and is true also of Deaf people. The fact that Jesus, as presented in the Gospels, is hearing is a question that needs to be tackled for Deaf people. The view expressed in the quote that begins this chapter *'FEW DEAF-PEOPLE INTEREST COME TO THE CHURCH BECAUSE JESUS CHRIST WAS NOT DEAF'*[15] is not simply a view of radical Deaf people, prejudiced against anything hearing and irrelevant to d/Deaf Christians; it is rather a vital and important question for all d/Deaf people who want to follow Christ.

McLaughlin goes on to argue that it is not possible to address the problem of a male (white, hearing, able-bodied) Jesus by focusing on some kind of non-embodied Christ. The fact that Jesus was human, the 'Word made flesh', appears to be fundamentally part of God's revelation of God-self to humankind. The incarnation, the very idea that the divine could be embodied at all was a scandal to the first-century people among whom Jesus and his disciples lived and taught, both Jews and Greeks, and as such it seems to be an essential part of God's challenge to humanity.[16] Shocked reactions to pictures of Jesus as Asian, black or even female

---

[12]   Rosemary Radford Ruether, 'Can Christology be liberated from patriarchy' in Maryanne Stevens (ed.), *Reconstructing the Christ symbol: essays in feminist Christology* (New York, 1993), p. 23.

[13]   Macquarrie, *Jesus Christ in modern thought*, p. 360.

[14]   Eleanor McLaughlin, 'Feminist Christologies: Re-Dressing the tradition' in Stevens (ed.), *Reconstructing the Christ Symbol*, p. 121.

[15]   Maciocha, 'Psalm 151 for the Deaf Community' in *Signs* (Spring 2000).

[16]   McLaughlin, 'Feminist Christologies: Re-Dressing the tradition' in Stevens (ed.), *Reconstructing the Christ Symbol*, p. 127.

('Christa's') may very well be a vital reminder of just how scandalous, in human terms, the incarnation actually is.

A very particular focus on the significance of an embodied Christ comes from the work of the disabled theologian, Nancy Eiesland. She too argues that Christology is the natural domain of a contextual theology since 'the incarnation is the ultimate contextual revelation'.[17] For her, the issue of embodiment, the 'problem' of Christ as he is usually represented, is not so much his gender, but the fact that he is considered to have a 'normal' body, and that is part of what makes him a 'perfect' human being.[18] However, Jesus did not always have this 'normal' body; after his resurrection, he appeared to the disciples with 'both impaired hands and feet and pierced side'.[19] In the Gospels of John and Luke, they record that when Jesus appeared to the disciples after the resurrection, he showed them his hands and his feet, or his hands and his side, and asked them to touch him.[20] Pictures of this event tend to show Jesus as upright as ever, with red marks in his hands and feet and side, but otherwise unaffected, a depiction that is challenged by Eiesland as distorting the physical presence not only of people with disabilities, but of the incarnate God in Jesus himself. Eiesland envisages the physical presence of the post-resurrection Christ as the 'disabled God', God in a sip-puff wheelchair (used by quadriplegics to manoeuvre by blowing and sucking on a strawlike device).[21] It is in this symbol of God incarnate, neither as 'an omnipotent, self-sufficient God' nor a 'pitiable suffering servant' but as a 'survivor, unpitying and forthright' that Eiesland locates the transformative power of Christ for disabled people.

The key insight of Eiesland is that there are many different aspects of Christ in the Gospels, that Jesus' full humanness includes not only his experiencing growing from child to adult; it also includes his experiencing what Eiesland calls the contingency of bodies, the fact that part of human life is experiencing the pain and limitations of the body.[22] The blind theologian, John Hull, also perceives Jesus as changing through his life and experiencing the 'contingency of bodies'. He finds both helpful and unhelpful aspects of Jesus in his exploration of the Gospels from his specific context as a blind man. Among the unhelpful aspects is the fact that 'most of the sayings of Jesus indicate that his outlook is that of a sighted person addressing sighted people'.[23] He speaks to the sighted world in ways that seem to

---

[17]   Eiesland, *The Disabled God: towards a liberatory theology of disability* (Nashville, 1994), p. 99.

[18]   Ibid., p. 91.

[19]   Ibid., p. 99.

[20]   Luke 24:36–9, John 20:19–28.

[21]   Eiesland, *The Disabled God*, p. 89.

[22]   Ibid., p. 104.

[23]   Hull, *In the beginning there was darkness: a blind person's conversation with the Bible* (London, 2001), p. 150.

share the sighted prejudice against the blind world[24] and even uses 'blind' as a term of abuse.[25] Jesus speaks of the restoration of the sight of the blind as an integral part of his mission, and for Hull, raises the question of whether a blind person can be a disciple.[26] However, Jesus does include experiences and stories to which both blind and sighted people can relate. In particular, Jesus is a tactile man. He touches people and allows himself to be touched. Here, Hull, who experiences the world through touch, finds a Jesus to whom he can relate.[27]

However, incidental points of contact such as this are not enough to mitigate the offence to blind Christians of a Jesus who seems to only want disciples who can see. To Hull, this is a major stumbling block to blind people even though this feeling of offence is often not expressed or barely conscious. Often, rather than feel offended at Jesus, he suggests that Christian blind people turn the offence back on themselves and feel ashamed for having such thoughts, or even feel ashamed at being blind.[28] Like women, like disabled people and like Deaf people, Hull finds he encounters images of Jesus that are not only irrelevant to his life, but which are actually experienced as oppressive.

The tactile Jesus, who tells stories to which blind people can relate, is simply not sufficient to mitigate this offence; like Eiesland, Hull finds he needs to explore not only what Jesus said and did to others, but also what Jesus himself went through. Jesus himself briefly experienced what it was like to be blind in a very physical way. This occurred after Jesus' arrest and trial before the high priest as described in the Gospels,[29] when he was blindfolded by some of those present, who then proceeded to torment him by spitting on him and striking him and then mocking him: 'Prophesy! Who is it that struck you?' The significance of this passage is not that Jesus cannot see, but that in being mocked and humiliated in this 'sadistic game of blind man's bluff' Jesus enters into the experience of many blind people by being ignorant of what is going on around him.[30] For Hull, this moment of identification is what enables him to form a relationship with Jesus; 'it is because, however briefly, he shares our condition ... that we cannot be offended at him'.

Eiesland's disabled God, while continuing the challenge to oppressive images of Christ and acting as a reminder of the scandal and particularity of the incarnation, it can be argued, is of only limited relevance to Deaf people. Her perception of the disabled God is based on the social model of disability, the model that distinguishes between impairment (which is embodied) and disability (which is imposed by an able-bodied society). Thus the disabled God challenges the

---

[24]   Ibid., p. 154.
[25]   Ibid., p. 157.
[26]   Ibid., p. 160.
[27]   Ibid., p. 156.
[28]   Ibid., p. 161.
[29]   Mark 14:65, Luke 22:64.
[30]   Hull, *In the beginning there was darkness*, p. 165.

medical perception that it is the impairment itself that is the problem and states that bodies are made in the image of God whether they are 'normal' or not.[31] God can appear in any body, however unexpected.[32] However, except for recently deafened and hard-of-hearing adults, the physical aspect of impaired hearing is rarely seen as an issue for Deaf people. Exploring the idea that Christ may, at some point, have not heard or not fully understood what was said to him may help some Deaf people to relate to him, but does not address the central issue of this chapter, that Christ is not Deaf. Hull, who I would argue almost has a cultural understanding of blindness in addition to his identification of socially imposed limits,[33] recognizes that it is not enough for identification to be at a purely physical level. To truly experience what it means to be blind and therefore provide a moment of identification for blind Christians, Jesus must also experience the sheer helplessness of a blinded person in a hostile situation.

Both key images of the disabled God and the blinded Christ that challenge the image of the oppressive able-bodied and sighted Jesus are focused on incidents during the period of Jesus' arrest, crucifixion and resurrection. For Eiesland and Hull, as for so many theologians, the full significance of the incarnation is not realized until the end. No matter what Jesus says and does, no matter how much he does in fact include disabled or blind (or d/Deaf) people in his vision of the kingdom,[34] he remains an ambiguous figure for disabled or blind people until his crucifixion. Then and only then does the disabled God and the blinded Christ show such people that Jesus is indeed incarnate in the whole of their human experience and can transform their lives by taking their impairment and showing it is not a place of shame, but a place where God became flesh. This is an insight that Deaf people can share. Jesus at his trial and crucifixion was a figure of fun, despised or ignored for how he looked and behaved, helpless and unable to control the situation. Jesus after his resurrection was physically broken and bloodied, but not defeated. Thus Jesus can identify with both the negative and positive sides of being d/Deaf; with both the anger and frustration and pain of only having partial information, of being mocked for not knowing what is happening, and with the pride and joy of being able to say 'I have had a hard time, and I still can't hear, and I still get frustrated, but it doesn't matter, if you can't accept me, it's not my problem, but yours'.

---

[31]   Eiesland, *The Disabled God*, p. 104.

[32]   Ibid., p. 100.

[33]   For Hull, blindness appears to be a way of life; a way of behaving that could almost be described as an alternative culture. For example, Hull, *In the beginning there was darkness*, p. 35, describes a meeting of a committee in which every member is blind. As each member enters the room they call out 'Hi, is this xxx meeting? I'm N' and everyone will reply 'Yes, I'm M' and so on round the room. This seems to me to be describing a culture (in the sense of ways of behaving and relating to the world and each other) based totally on sound (as Deaf culture is based totally on vision), a culture that is, in an all-blind context, totally 'normal'.

[34]   See for example the parable of the great feast in Luke 14:12–14.

The ambiguity of Jesus for Deaf people nevertheless remains. The idea of a disabled Christ is a helpful, but not a sufficient response to the question that Jesus was not Deaf. Being Deaf is so much more than not being able to hear that approaches such as those from Eiesland and Hull based on the social model cannot fully answer the question; we must take on board the questions posed by the cultural model as well. The Jesus in the Gospels is usually a speaking Jesus; if we Deaf imagine ourselves into the Gospel stories, we can imagine feeling left out, unable to understand what Jesus was saying to everyone else. In these terms, Jesus is no different from all the teachers and preachers and colleagues and friends who have excluded us from discussions and stories and jokes by using speech. This feeling of exclusion from Jesus' circle of followers is reinforced by the fact that the Gospel is presented to Deaf people in English, the language of school and oppressive situations in the world. These questions from a cultural point of view can perhaps be summarized by one question: 'Can Jesus sign?' In other words, can we Deaf have direct access to Jesus and his message, or do we always need to go through hearing interpreters, something that increases the dependence of d/Deaf people on hearing people and perpetuates oppression. Ultimately, this question is about whether Jesus is on the side of Deaf people in their struggle for a more just world, or whether he, like so many hearing oppressors, is only interested in d/Deaf people who can speak and lip-read.

One way of approaching this question is seen in the work of Jacquelyn Grant, a 'womanist' theologian. She asks 'Is Jesus on the side of poor, black women?' and identifies the classical portrayals of Christ as a male, white king as having imprisoned Jesus in a sexist, racist and 'classist' framework. This framework she names as having been used as a way of keeping black women in their proper, subordinate position.[35] She goes on to explore how Jesus was actually experienced in a liberating way in the lives of black women, as expressed in their prayer and their songs, and later in their writings, which enabled them to meet Jesus as their saviour rather than their oppressor. This does not mean that Jesus was never experienced as oppressive by these women, but that black women had an experience of Jesus that could be set over and above the Christ presented by their oppressors. She identifies four main ways Jesus is seen, which progress from 'Jesus the co-sufferer' through 'Jesus the equalizer' and 'Jesus means freedom' to 'Jesus the liberator'.[36] Jesus the 'co-sufferer' enables them to dignify their unjust suffering by relating it to the unjust suffering of the divine and so giving them some of the self-esteem which their situation otherwise took away from them. Jesus the 'liberator', at the other end of the scale, is not just a Jesus who gives self-esteem, but also a Jesus who 'empowers African American women to be significantly engaged in the (political) process of liberation'. Beginning a Christology with the experience of black women, rather than with the 'titles' of

---

[35] Jacquelyn Grant, 'Come to my help, Lord, for I'm in trouble' in Stevens (ed.), *Reconstructing the Christ symbol*, p. 66.

[36] Ibid., p. 67.

Jesus in the Gospels as a 'classical' Christology or reading the Bible from a particular perspective, as do Hull and Eiesland (as well as white feminist theologians such as Rosemary Radford Ruether),[37] means that her Jesus, from the start, is one to whom 'ordinary' (or non-academic) black women can relate. More than that, Grant, by contrasting the way Jesus was presented by the white oppressors with how he was experienced by black women, shows how even at the least 'political' end of her scale, Jesus is a powerful influence on black women in enabling them to break out of the vicious circle of oppression that stripped them of their dignity and self-esteem as well as their freedom.

Grant's Christology is a good example of how the 'Christ symbol' has been reconstructed in the past, by ordinary Christians to be transformative rather than oppressive. Her work emphasizes the importance of understanding how Jesus has been presented to black women, or Deaf people in the past, and how they have experienced him as a way of counteracting the tendency to focus on a 'single-issue' Christ. A contextual, liberating Christology would seem to need to be rooted firmly in the lived experiences of Christ by a particular group and to be assessed according to the effect they have had on the hearts and minds of a particular oppressed people. The testing of images of Jesus in practice is firmly endorsed by Douglas. She concludes that no one symbol of Christ can encompass everything that needs to be said; rejects simple, static descriptions of Christ and argues that only a diversity of symbols and icons can reflect the diversity and complexity of human experience.[38] Christ is not only found in the lives of poor, black women, but wherever (black) women and men are struggling to bring the community to wholeness. In other words, Christ is not exclusively found in the lives of marginalized people, but in the life of anyone who is struggling against the sin of the world. Ultimately, the criteria by which images and symbols of Christ are judged are not so much whether they improve the lives of this group or of that group, but whether they improve the relationship of humankind with each other and with God.

Christ in the Lives of Deaf People

So what images and symbols of Christ can be found in the lives of Deaf people and how have they functioned in the struggle for liberation as Deaf people and for the wholeness of the world? These images and symbols can be found in two main surviving sources. One is sermons and poems by Deaf men and women published

---

[37]   Radford Ruether, 'Can Christology be liberated from patriarchy' in Stevens (ed.), *Reconstructing the Christ symbol*, p. 8. Radford Ruether's Jesus as *Sophia* or wisdom of God, arising from a feminist reading of biblical texts, is criticized by Herrara in the same volume as still being based on western philosophical ideas, glorifying the intellect and perpetuating a male-dominated academic system (ibid., p. 90).

[38]   Douglas, *The black Christ*, p. 108.

in *A Magazine Intended Chiefly for the Deaf and Dumb* and its successors between 1873 and 1884 and in the *British Deaf Monthly* of 1901/1902. Despite the fact that the sermons and poems are in English for publication they do give an insight into how educated Deaf men of a certain class from the pre-Milan days experienced Jesus Christ in their lives. These sermons can be contrasted with those by hearing chaplains in the same publication to see how the Jesus that was presented to Deaf people by the hearing chaplains compares with the Jesus preached by Deaf missioners themselves. The second source of images and symbols of Jesus to be considered are sermons and stories by Deaf chaplains and readers from the last ten years or so. These will focus on the passage from Mark 7:31–7, the story of the healing of the deaf man. These images and symbols will be assessed according to whether or not they resonate with the experience of Deaf people as liberated from hearing norms and whether they challenge and are transformative of the individual lives of Deaf people and Deaf culture.

A sermon by Samuel W. North, a well-known Deaf missioner of west London, begins 'Christ, our omniscient and all seeing Saviour'.[39] This beginning highlights one characteristic of the nineteenth-century Deaf sermons surveyed, that Christ was often referred to using specifically visual language as one who was actually looking at us. This seemingly small point is vital if we are to find a Christ to whom we can relate as Deaf people and with whom we can communicate. In the Deaf world, communication begins with seeing and being seen. Saul Magson, a Deaf preacher from Manchester, understands Jesus Christ as saying to us 'look unto Me, and be ye saved'.[40] Like North, he does seem to focus on using specifically visual terms for communication with Jesus Christ, which can be understood to mean that Jesus was preached in culturally appropriate terms. In other words, so much communication in the Deaf world starts with '*LOOK-AT-ME*' or '*SEE-ME OK?*' that it seems the Deaf preachers perceived Jesus as beginning his teaching in the same way. Jesus is understood as not only wanting people to hear him, but also to see him and in response he not only listens to people but also looks over them. Jesus, according to the nineteenth-century Deaf preachers, wanted to be in communication with Deaf people in a way Deaf people could access.

Not only did Jesus want to be in communication with Deaf people, he could communicate with them. None of the Deaf writers surveyed understand Jesus as signing, but they do seem to feel they have inward, perfect communication with Jesus in a way that transcends speech and sign. For example, a poem by O. D. in 1875 begins

Jesus, I cannot hear
My earthly teacher's voice;

---

[39]   Samuel W. North, 'Sermon' in *A Magazine Intended Chiefly for the Deaf and Dumb*, 1.2 (February 1873): 25–7.

[40]   Saul Magson, 'Sermon' in *A Magazine Intended Chiefly for the Deaf and Dumb*, 1.11 (November 1873): 173–4.

> But thou dost whisper in mine ear,
> And make my heart rejoice.[41]

Not only can O. D. 'hear' Jesus, he/she can communicate their response to him:

> For though my lips are dumb,
> And cannot speak to Thee,
> It is with loving thoughts I come,
> And Thou my heart dost see.[42]

Another Deaf person, Mary Davies writes a poem about 'hearing' Jesus:

> You say that you are 'sorry'
> For me, who cannot hear
> […]
> And if my life is shadowed
> With sorrow, sin and pain,
> I hear the voice of Jesus,
> So cannot live in vain;
> […]
> The peaceful voice of Jesus
> Speaks hope and life to me,
> So dear earth's sweetest voices
> Could never, never be.[43]

Not only does Mary Davies understand herself as being in perfect communication with Jesus, she sees this communication as rendering her lack of hearing as being of no importance. She shrugs her shoulders at those who pity her for her inability to hear and says, basically, that she can communicate with Christ and that means more than being able to hear all the voices in the world put together.

These two poems can be contrasted to one by A. S., who, by the fact that he/she refers to 'deaf ones' in the third person, I understand to be hearing:

> Till Christ shall come, and with His Word
> The missing sense restore
> That they within the Heavenly Home
> In every bliss may share,
> And sweeter from the silence here
> Shall sound the music there.[44]

---

[41]   O. D., 'For a Deaf and Dumb Christian' in *A Magazine Intended Chiefly for the Deaf and Dumb*, III.26 (February 1875): 26.

[42]   Ibid.

[43]   Mary Davies, 'The Voice of Jesus' in *The British Deaf Monthly*, XI.124 (February 1902): 364.

[44]   A. S., 'The Music of Hope' in *The British Deaf Monthly*, XI.121 (November 1901): 302.

This is a more oppressive view of Jesus in that communication with Christ does not seem to be available to Deaf people until their 'missing sense' is restored in heaven. How they might get to heaven without being able to communicate with Jesus in the first place is a mystery in this poem, but the Revd George Downing, a hearing chaplain, preaching on the healing of the deaf man in Mark, provides a clue. Deaf and dumb people are brought before Jesus by kind hearing people and then, still passively, are touched by him and, if they keep coming to church, will therefore be saved and go to heaven 'where the first words you will hear, will be the words of love, and welcome, from that same Jesus who so loves the deaf and dumb'.[45] The contrast between these views of Deaf people as passive objects of salvation and the previous two perceptions of Deaf people as actively participating subjects suggests that there were two views of Jesus, a hearing view and a Deaf view, running parallel at the end of the nineteenth century. The hearing view saw and spoke of Deaf people as being unable to communicate with Jesus, as being divided from Jesus by a barrier that could only be breached with the constant intervention of and interpretation by hearing people. By contrast, the Deaf people believed they had direct communication with Jesus; once they had learnt about Jesus, presumably from either Deaf or hearing preachers, they could understand him and be understood.

While most Deaf people today would not choose to speak of 'hearing the voice of Jesus' and would reject any intimation that even Jesus could whisper in their ear and be heard, in their nineteenth-century context these two poems are a hint that Deaf people understood Jesus as not only being able to communicate with them, but also as the person who guaranteed their equality with all hearing people. This equality is expressed in the sermons in several ways. Samuel North, for example, proclaims that being deaf and dumb makes no difference to the ability to have 'the kingdom of God within'[46] and that we can come 'just as we are'[47] to God in Christ's name. Saul Magson speaks of faith as being 'a free gift of God' with its availability not depending on hearing, but on loving God and obeying God's will.[48] Edward Rowland (the ordained Deaf missioner from South Wales) more specifically states that deaf people are the equal of hearing people in that they 'are not shut out from the Gospel tidings' but, like hearing people, 'know about God, Heaven and Hell, and redeeming love'.[49] This equality with hearing people is because of Jesus Christ. As James Muir, a Deaf preacher from Maybole in Scotland puts it, 'the benefits of Christ's death are not confined to one favoured

---

[45] Revd Geo. A. W. Downing, 'Sermon' in *A Magazine Intended Chiefly for the Deaf and Dumb*, IV.47 (November 1876): 161–3.

[46] North, 'Sermon'.

[47] Samuel W. North, 'An Easter Sermon' in *A Magazine Intended Chiefly for the Deaf and Dumb*, I.5 (May 1873): 74–5.

[48] Magson, 'Sermon'.

[49] Edward Rowland, 'Sermon for the New Year' in *A Magazine Intended Chiefly for the Deaf and Dumb*, III.26 (February 1875): 17–19.

nation or people … He died for all; He is offered to all; He is the saviour of all that believe'.[50] North agrees that by the death of Christ all people become God's 'children by adoption'.[51] Finally, in contrast to the assertion by the Revd George Downing that Jesus has special pity and mercy on the deaf and dumb,[52] the Deaf preacher and missioner from Birmingham, William Griffiths, thunders that there is no special mercy for the deaf and dumb; like everyone they have to repent and turn to Christ.[53] His sermon has a typical nineteenth-century evangelical emphasis on pitiful, sinful, fallen humanity, but to him, deaf people are neither especially pitiful nor particularly sinful; all people, deaf and hearing, are in the same boat. In fact, it may be argued that many Deaf preachers preached a higher standard of behaviour to their Deaf congregations than they expected from hearing people. For example Burns and some of his contemporaries were also strong temperance men, and involvement in some missions was dependent on taking the pledge.[54] However, Dimmock argues that the link between the temperance movement and the missions was more of a fundraising tactic than part of Deaf culture[55] so more research into the motivations of these Deaf missioners is required to decide one way or the other.

This emphasis on the universal availability of Christ may seem obvious and not worth commenting on, but in a world where Deaf people were constantly being told that they were no more than objects of Christ's pity and mercy and vehicles for his demonstration of the healing power of God and his own credentials as the Son of God it is truly remarkable. Before God, through Christ, all people, Deaf and hearing, were equal and that was all that mattered. The patronising view of the world was not important because at the end time everyone would be judged, not on whether they could hear or speak, but on how faithfully they had followed the way of Jesus. This faith in the availability of Christ for all seems to have given Deaf people the dignity and the strength to assert their rights. Like 'Jesus the equalizer' as described by Grant, Christ communicated with Deaf people and guaranteed Deaf equality in nineteenth-century Britain.

From our twenty-first-century perspective, there are problems with this vision of Christ. Primary among these issues is the fact that the practical equality between Deaf and hearing is not to be until after death or at the end time. The kingdom of God may be a place where there are no divisions between Deaf and hearing people, but that does not necessarily mean that Deaf and hearing people had any responsibility to bring about the kingdom on this earth. Finally, a universally

---

[50]   James Muir, 'Redemption by Jesus Christ' in *The Magazine for the Deaf and Dumb*, XII.1 (January 1884): 19–20.

[51]   North, 'Easter Sermon'.

[52]   Downing, 'Sermon'.

[53]   W. A. G., 'Sermon' in *A Magazine Intended Chiefly for the Deaf and Dumb*, III.34 (October 1875): 146–9.

[54]   Lysons, *Voluntary Welfare Societies*, p. 38; Jackson and Lee (eds), *Deaf Lives*, p. 34; Dimmock, *Cruel Legacy*, p. 52.

[55]   Dimmock, *Cruel Legacy*, p. 52.

available Christ, whose ability to communicate transcends speech and sign, is neither specific enough to answer the challenge that Jesus was not Deaf, nor provide a reason why Deaf people should follow him. This vision of Christ embraces the Deaf cultural understanding of what it means to be Deaf, including its weakness, that it does not, in itself, challenge the status quo.

Jesus the equalizer seems to have survived among Deaf people, even after the Milan conference effect had resulted in the Gospel being preached primarily by hearing people. Sermons and writing on religion by Deaf people seem to disappear from the records for a hundred years until the 1990s, but it is possible to argue that the conviction that equality before God through Jesus Christ meant equality with hearing people survived. For example, Ladd has traced the survival of Deaf people's sense of dignity and pride in the language,[56] a survival that can be attributed to an irrefutable sense of the dignity of a human being, the dignity of children of God. When sermons preached by Deaf people re-emerge in written records, similar themes of equality in the eyes of God, perfect communication with Christ and the universal availability of Christ to all people are still to be found.

To look at modern sermons we will focus on those preached on the text of Mark 7:31–7. This text has often been experienced as oppressive by d/Deaf people as showing a Jesus who only wants to heal them and is not interested in them in any other way. Van Cleve and Crouch, for example, argue that deafness in the New Testament is 'a means of demonstrating Jesus' ability to create miracles to accomplish things that are impossible for humans'.[57] Deaf people are reduced to objects, or, at best, sick beings in need of curing by Jesus with no sense that d/Deaf people are part of God's plan. Paddy Ladd agrees with this assessment of Jesus' view of d/Deaf people as subjects to be healed, less than human because of their difficulties in communication.[58] This text has certainly been presented to Deaf people in this way with sermons by nineteenth-century hearing chaplains such as the Revd George Downing expounding this view. In the twentieth century surviving writings by such influential people as Selwyn Oxley (hearing) in the 1930s[59] and Tom Sutcliffe (deafened as an adult) in the 1970s and 1980s[60] continue to argue that the motivation for Christian work among d/Deaf people is to follow Jesus' example and take pity on those who cannot hear.

The Revd Vera Hunt, a Deaf Church of England priest, writes in a sermon (for preaching in sign) how she feels when she sees yet another sermon on this text by hearing preachers: 'Naturally, this upsets me and leaves me feeling sad because connect the story of the healing of the deaf man with deaf people presuming that

---

[56]   Ladd, *In search of Deafhood.*
[57]   Cleve and Crouch, *A place of their own*, p. 3.
[58]   Ladd, *In search of Deafhood*, p. 28.
[59]   See for example Oxley, *Ephphatha Sunday and its meaning* (London, *c.* 1938).
[60]   Sutcliffe, *Soundless Worship.*

they, including myself, need to be "healed"'.[61] However, she goes on, in the same sermon, to attempt to engage with the text as a Deaf person and show that Jesus is not oppressive, that the usual hearing expositions of the text are missing the point. Her response is threefold. She first of all argues that Jesus was not treating the deaf man simply as a 'case to be healed' but as an individual who needed healing. The significance of this is that just because one deaf individual encountered by Jesus needed healing, that does not mean all d/Deaf people need to be healed. Secondly, she argues that Jesus communicated with the deaf man in an appropriate way, by taking him aside from the crowd, and touching him on his ears and tongue. This is similar to the way George Downing in 1876 suggests that this incident shows Jesus as the first teacher of the deaf and dumb using 'signs'.[62] Finally, Hunt, like the nineteenth-century Deaf poets discussed above, contends that d/Deaf Christians do not need to be 'healed' to hear the word of God as we have perfect communication with God in our hearts the same way as hearing people.[63]

This sermon of Hunt's illustrates how the themes of Jesus, the guarantor of equality, the welcomer of all and the perfect communicator have survived 100 years 'underground', but there are still problems with this reading of the text. For example, if we accept that Jesus communicated through 'signs' with the deaf man, it was only through primitive gestures, not through sign language as it is understood today as a true language. To people like Downing signs were simply a means to an end, a way to teach speech and lip-reading, so Jesus' gestures were 'signs' in his understanding, but this does not apply today. The gestures of Jesus were adequate to show the deaf man what he intended to do, but there is a large gulf between that level of basic communication and the level of communication required for understanding Jesus' teaching and being a disciple. Saying that Jesus 'signed' to the deaf man so we're OK is saying that we d/Deaf should accept that basic level of communication and not ask for more profound teaching in a language we can understand. This metaphor of 'Christ who signs' propagates the stereotype that d/Deaf people can only engage with simple, direct teaching and does not lead to transformation of d/Deaf people's lives. Radford Ruether argues that to be liberational and transformative, it is not enough to formulate new metaphors of Christ and God that are inclusive; they must also challenge the status quo and enable new ways of thinking.[64] This purely cultural approach to Jesus says

---

[61]   Revd Vera Hunt, 'God within deaf people – Ephphatha! Be open!!', sermon text in personal communication.

[62]   Downing, 'Sermon'.

[63]   This exposition of this passage can be compared with Hull's exploration of the healing of blind Bartimaeus (Mark 10:46–52) which argues that Jesus treated Bartimaeus with respect, as an individual and asked him what he wants instead of simply assuming that Bartimaeus wants his sight back. *In the beginning there was darkness*, p. 44.

[64]   Radford Ruether, 'Can Christology be liberated from patriarchy' in Stevens (ed.), *Reconstructing the Christ symbol*, p. 14.

that it doesn't matter if the world ignores us and limits us; we know we are different and equal, but it does not challenge the status quo.

Another way of approaching this passage is also found both in the nineteenth-century sermons discussed above and in the sermons of d/Deaf people today. This approach argues that if the deaf man wanted to be made to hear and speak, he was obviously not 'culturally' Deaf, and so this passage simply is not relevant to the lives of Deaf people today. For example, James Muir, listing some texts from the Bible to illustrate 'what Jesus is able to do' [for deaf people], does not even refer to this passage.[65] Jesus may have been able to make the deaf hear, but this simply was not perceived as relevant to Deaf people in those pre-Milan days. Similarly today, Bob Shrine, a Deaf Church of England priest in his 'Deaf awareness' sermons,[66] refers to this text only to say that it is not relevant to how Deaf people understand Jesus today; that Deaf people are complete as they are and are not incomplete hearing people, in need of healing. Shrine also refers to Jesus as guaranteeing equality because 'There is no longer Jew or Greek, there is no longer slave or free, there is no longer male and female; for all of you are one in Christ Jesus'.[67] This approach does challenge the status quo because it means that hearing people do have to face up to their own prejudices about d/Deaf people and their perceived need for healing and it continues the tradition of encouraging d/Deaf people to believe in themselves as equal to anyone as children of God and followers of Christ. However, it removes some problems in the text only to leave space for others. Primarily, it leaves the question that if we say that Christ the healer is not specifically relevant to d/Deaf people then is there any difference between d/Deaf and hearing people in who Jesus Christ is for them? All this argument does is suggest that Christ is not the oppressor, not the one who just wants to make d/Deaf people to hear again. It does not answer the question is there any particular way Deaf people can understand Christ as their liberator?

One final approach to this passage is particularly interesting because it comes from a Deaf subaltern viewpoint. Paddy Ladd defines subaltern groups as those who resist discourses and actions developed by the intellectual elite of a dominated group, or, in this case, the deaf people who 'helped' the missioner keep the others in control.[68] The subaltern viewpoint is as close as we can get to '*DEAF-*

---

[65] James Muir, 'What Jesus is Able to Do', *A Magazine intended chiefly for the Deaf and Dumb*, XII.1 (January 1884): 21.

[66] Revd Bob Shrine, 'Deaf awareness sermon', notes in Deaf Ecumenical Clergy UK minutes from the second gathering, February 2000.

[67] Galatians 3:28. This is seen as a key verse of the essential equality of all people before Christ by many minority groups. Paul Gilroy, for example, describes how Olaudah Equiano, a freed slave who became an anti-slavery campaigner, understood this verse as meaning all superficial differences were to be set aside in favour of a different relationship with Christ that offered a means to transcend human constraints. Gilroy, 'Diaspora and the Detours of Identity' in Woodward (ed.), *Identity and Difference*, p. 325.

[68] Ladd, *In search of Deafhood*, p. 7.

GRASSROOTS', the often working-class Deaf people who kept Deaf pride alive. One such Deaf subaltern, constantly challenging those who would try to put him down, confidently Deaf in his use of sign, refers to this text in passing in many of his sermons as a Church of England reader.[69] His particular view on it was that Jesus did not make the Deaf man to hear at all. The word 'Ephphatha' or 'be opened' applies not to his ears and mouth, but to his mind and heart. The miracle of Jesus was not in making this Deaf and dumb man to hear and speak, but in taking notice of this man. This subaltern identifies with the Deaf man, who must have been feeling excluded from everything that was going on, ignored by the crowd and unable to access the teaching of Jesus. In his view, the Deaf man must have given up trying, must have been feeling bad about himself, sitting by himself in a corner. But Jesus comes over to him, takes him aside and touches him on his ears and mouth as if to say 'I know you can't hear me and can't speak, but it doesn't matter, your mind and your heart can "be opened" to me if you want'. This one-to-one attention of Jesus frees the Deaf man from the crippling lack of self-esteem that was preventing him from trying to access Jesus' teaching and makes him feel loved because Jesus has considered him worthy of this attention. And perhaps, after Jesus had gone, the Deaf and dumb man 'came out of his shell' and began to 'hear and speak' or, in other words, had the confidence to demand an explanation of the people as to what was going on.

This exegesis can be criticized as not being consonant with the biblical text, but it is a brilliantly, unapologetically liberating reading of this text. Jesus as the teacher, the man of authority who takes notice of the Deaf man who is being ignored by everyone else, is the man who can help transform Deaf people's inner self, damaged by oppression. He is the man who overturns the assessment of first-century Israelite society of the Deaf man as not worthy of attention when he walks over to the Deaf man in his corner. He is the man who acknowledges his lack of ability to communicate with the Deaf man, but does not let that stop him from trying. Riet Bons-Storm, in her discussion of the interaction between Mary Magdalene and Jesus in the garden outside the tomb on the first Easter Day, has a similar understanding of Jesus from a feminist point of view. Jesus is the man who takes notice of Mary and calls her by her name and in doing so brings her 'subject quality', or her ability to be the subject of her own story rather than the object of others, to the fore.[70] The significance of being 'touched' or noticed by someone with Jesus' authority and reputation is certainly, in her understanding, a moment of inner healing of the wounds of oppression and, as with Mary Magdalene, a foundation for an active ministry in following Jesus. This modern, subaltern reading of a previously oppressive text is perhaps the first truly liberating, Deaf

---

[69] This description is from my memory of the sermon, preached by Peter Lees, first encountered in October 2001 as I was gathering material for this chapter.

[70] Riet Bons-Storm, *The Incredible Woman: listening to women's silences in pastoral care and counselling* (Nashville, 1996), p. 81.

understanding of Jesus.[71] It relates to the experience of Deaf people as it really is, as one of being ignored and excluded, and recognizes that it is not the deafness, the inability to hear, that needs to be healed, but the inner damage caused by oppression. In referring to the man as going out and 'hearing' and 'speaking', it perhaps also relates an alternative vision of the future of d/Deaf people, as visible and active in proclaiming the good news of Jesus Christ to all people, hearing and d/Deaf.

Jesus, the Deaf Liberator

One of the key features about Jesus the healer of the inner person in the previous paragraph is that he seems to recognize and acknowledge his human limitations in communicating with the deaf man. In other words, the first-century Galilean man Jesus could not sign.[72] In this particular story, it is not a problem; Jesus being the person he is it is enough for him to take notice of the d/Deaf man and show willingness (by touch) to communicate but, as I said above, touching is not enough for Jesus to teach d/Deaf people on the same level as hearing people as a general rule. It was another Deaf subaltern group who suggested, in a Bible study, a response to this difficulty. This Bible study was on the story of the healing of the Gerasarene demoniac in Mark 5:1–20. One key point about this passage as noted by D. E. Nineham is that it is one of the few occasions on which Jesus encountered Gentiles (or non-Jews).[73] Gentiles can be understood as people coming from a different culture to Jesus, so this passage gives us insight into how Jesus approached his relationship with people outside his own Jewish, hearing culture. In addition, Gentiles were despised by Jews, and so would not necessarily want to listen to someone from a culture that belittled them in this way. In this case, it is not the healing that is significant it is what happens afterwards. The people of that country of Gerasara beg Jesus to leave and go back to his own place; the man who has been healed of the demons wants to come with Jesus, but Jesus refuses and says to him 'Go home to your friends, and tell them how much the Lord has done for you, and what mercy he has shown to you'.[74] The Deaf subaltern group responded to this verse by identifying the fact Jesus recognized that as a Galilean Jew, he was limited in whom he could preach to by his culture, so Jesus called individuals, like the Gerasarene in this passage, and sent them to preach to their own people and in this way overcame his cultural limitations. In the same way, Jesus can be understood as calling d/Deaf individuals (such as the Deaf and dumb

---

[71]   This reading of the text may have existed pre-Milan and have been passed down in some form, although there is currently no evidence for either of these factors.

[72]   And as far as we know, a sign language of a sort did exist in first-century Israel, Cleve and Crouch, *A place of their own*, p. 2.

[73]   D. E. Nineham, *The Gospel of Saint Mark* (Harmondsworth, 1963), p. 151.

[74]   Mark 5:19.

man referred to above) and sending them to preach to their own people and in this way overcoming his lack of sign language.

This reading of the text and understanding of Jesus as one who recognized his own human limits and adjusted to them fits in well with Deaf Church history; the earliest Deaf preachers and missioners did seem to feel called by Jesus to spread the Gospel among their own people. Other theologians looking at Jesus from a cross-cultural point of view also suggest that Jesus recognized his own limitations, and those of his disciples, in preaching to people from a completely different culture. For example, Marina Herrara, a Hispanic woman living in the USA, briefly discusses the encounter of Jesus with the Samaritan woman (another people of a different culture, equally reviled by the Jews) at the well in John 4:4–42. Again, Jesus can be said to recognize his own, human limitations when it came to preaching the Gospel, and calls an individual from out of another culture and sends them to preach the Good News to their own people.[75] Herrara argues that this shows that Jesus was not only aware of his own cultural limitations, it also shows him being non-paternalistic in that he simply assumed that the woman at the well, or the Gerasarene man or indeed the Deaf man were capable of understanding his message and sharing it with others. At a time when women, non-Jews and Deaf people had no legal status, in part because they were considered unable to understand what was going on, this is quite remarkable.

So, the human Jesus may not have been able to sign, but he recognized his limits and called on those who could sign to spread his message to other Deaf people. What about the risen Christ we encounter in our lives today? Do we still have to find an interpreter all the time? One of the classic 'titles' of Jesus in the Gospels is as the Word (or, in Greek, the *logos*) of God. Much has been written attempting to understand what this title might mean, but it seems to be possible to summarize this as the Word of God makes known what is in the mind of the Father.[76] In other words, the idea of the Word is about God trying to communicate with his people. In the past, the English word 'Word' as a title of Jesus in John 1:1–18 has often been translated into BSL as '*PROCLAIM*' or '*WORD-FROM-MOUTH-TO-PAGE*'. The *New Testament English Version for the Deaf* suggests that it is translated as '*MESSAGE*' (which probably means the sign for *PROCLAIM*). These signs, which start from the mouth, have reinforced the impression that God communicates with us via Jesus in an oral way, and therefore the concept of Jesus as the Word of God has been experienced as something that does not relate to Deaf people, which creates and perpetuates the damaging myth that speech is superior to sign. In fact, as the Gospel begins 'In the beginning was the Word', we might view it as meaning 'in the beginning was speech'. However, if we translate *logos* or word into BSL as '*SIGN*' or use the idiomatic sign meaning 'to convey information in sign', then we are saying that Jesus Christ is the *SIGN-*

---

[75] For Herrara see Stevens (ed.), *Reconstructing the Christ Symbol*. 'Many Samaritans from that city believed in him because of the woman's testimony', John 4:39.

[76] Macquarrie, *Jesus Christ in modern thought*, p. 108.

OF GOD, the way in which God communicates with us. Glossing 'Word' as *SIGN* does not change the meaning, nor does it say that Deaf people have exclusive communication with God, but simply challenges a narrow interpretation of *logos* as meaning only the spoken and written word. In providing an alternative translation it breaks open the concept of *logos* to illuminate its meaning as God's great desire to communicate with all people, hearing, deaf, Deaf, deaf-blind, hard-of-hearing and more. Thus the challenge of translating *logos* as *SIGN* is much more than a challenge to a hearing insistence on the primacy of speech; it is also a challenge to Deaf insistence on the primacy of sign language to the exclusion of all other means of communication.[77]

Jesus, *SIGN-OF GOD* is our guarantee that God wants all people, d/Deaf and hearing, to have access to what is in God's mind for humankind in whatever way they communicate. Jesus, *SIGN-OF GOD* also demands that whoever is presenting the Good News of Jesus Christ to people must do so in a way that is clearly understood. If we present the Good News in inadequate sign language, or mumbled speech so that it goes '*STRAIGHT-PAST-EARS*' (an expressive sign to indicate lack of understanding), then we are not only failing d/Deaf and hard-of-hearing people; we are failing to implement the will of God to communicate with everyone. In our own personal communication with God in prayer, Jesus the *SIGN-OF GOD* assures us that however we pray, in sign or silently in our hearts, we will understand and be understood. Jesus, the *SIGN-OF GOD* takes the idea of perfect communication from the experience of nineteenth-century Deaf people onwards as described above and puts it on a firm theological foundation. In the end, Jesus, the *SIGN-OF GOD* can show God's own recognition of and commitment to equality of languages, particularly the equality of BSL to English if we translate 'in the beginning was the *logos*'[78] as '*BEGINNING WHAT? SIGN*'.

It is not only possible to argue that Jesus is committed to one of the pillars of the cultural model in sign language; it is also possible to show Jesus' support of another significant pillar, that of the concept of the Deaf community as being the significant social unit of identity formation for Deaf people rather than the family. The family or household[79] in both Old and New Testament times was the major unit of the social structure. C. J. H. Wright summarizes the functions of the household in Israel as being the place of inclusion, authority and spiritual continuity.[80] The household or *Bet'ab* 'was the third level of the kinship structure of Israel, and the one in which the individual Israelite felt the strongest sense of

---

[77] Recently, independently of each other, or me I have seen two Deaf clergy translating the phrase used to end readings from the Bible in worship ('This is the word of the Lord') as '*POINT-AT-BIBLE SIGN-OF LORD*', thus suggesting this concept resonates with other Deaf people too.

[78] John 1:1.

[79] The two terms are interchangeable for practical purposes.

[80] C. J. H. Wright, 'Family' in David Noel Freedman (ed.), *Anchor Bible Dictionary*, (New York, 1992) on CD-Rom.

inclusion, identity, protection, and responsibility'. So, when Jesus came along saying things like 'I have come to set a man against his father, and a daughter against her mother'[81] and 'Who is my mother and who are my brothers? And pointing to his disciples he said, "Here are my mother and my brothers"'[82] he was posing a serious challenge to the social order of the day. He was saying that to follow him was to change the focus of inclusion, identity, protection and responsibility from the family unit to the Christian community. Sometimes the two were the same, but often the household-based early churches included several people for whom natural family ties had been disrupted as a result of their response to the Gospel.[83] Above all, Jesus wanted people to feel free to follow him and put him first. If people were constrained and prevented from developing into the person they could be by family obligations and expectations then they were not truly free to follow the way of Christ.

This identification of voluntary ties rather than birth ties as being of primary significance resonates strongly with much Deaf experience. For many d/Deaf people, except for those 10 per cent born to Deaf families, the family has been experienced as a place of exclusion; a place where 'being left out' reached its sharpest focus around the family dinner table. For a sense of inclusion, identity and protection many Deaf people look to the Deaf community, and in doing so challenge a social structure that, in its own way, places the 'family unit' as high as Israelite society ever did. This identification with the community rather than the family has been used to justify much of the oppression experienced by Deaf people, to provide a reason for attempting to prevent the formation of a separate sign language. Jesus, as a person who places the obligations of family life lower than the necessity to be free to follow him, provides a valuable counter-balance to this justification. Jesus wants all his people to be free of whatever expectations and obligations are oppressing them and preventing them from developing their inner selves in relationship to him, whether this oppression is from Israelite family laws and expectations or from a modern-day family who exclude their d/Deaf member in conversation.

This freedom must, however, be understood in the light of the kingdom of God, or *GOD'S RULE* as it can be signed. History and experience seem to show that making contact with the Deaf community and becoming part of it is an essential step towards liberation and transformation for d/Deaf people in that it is often the only way for a d/Deaf person to be converted from understanding themselves in the light of the medical model to seeing themselves as a complete Deaf person under the cultural and social models. The Deaf community needs to be preserved because of the transformation it effects in the lives of d/Deaf people. However, it must be recognized that in Christian terms a strong and functioning Deaf community is not an aim in itself, but a means to an end. Jesus preaches about *GOD'S RULE* as

---

[81] Matthew 10:35; cf. Luke 12:53.
[82] Matthew 12:48–9; cf. Mark 3:33–4, Luke 8:21.
[83] Wright, 'Family' in Freedman (ed.), *Anchor Bible Dictionary*, on CD-Rom.

being far more encompassing than a world full of separate communities where people can be free to follow him. Jesus' vision of *GOD'S RULE* sees the overturning of the whole unequal social order, the eradication of all evil, including that which causes oppression of minority groups, and the embracing of all differences as no longer being of social significance. This vision does not mean that all people will be able to hear, any more than it means that all people will be male, or all people will be white; but it does mean that all people will be reconciled to each other and to God. There have been debates over the years as to whether this vision is only about some unimaginable future, or whether it is something we are required to work for here and now. Carlos Bravo, a liberation theologian from Mexico, argues that *GOD'S RULE* is something we must work for here and now because the existence of injustice and oppression in the world is actually making the full realization of *GOD'S RULE* impossible and is betraying God's will for his people.[84] Jesus' commitment to *GOD'S RULE* was absolute, so absolute that in the end he was crucified and died for it. To truly do the will of God, to fulfil the vision of *GOD'S RULE* as proclaimed by Jesus in what he said and in what he did, we must all, d/Deaf and hearing, show the same commitment to removing injustice from this world.

This vision, as proclaimed by Jesus, may seem unachievable. But, as Bravo goes on to discuss, Jesus' death was not the last word; 'God was absolutely dissatisfied with the death of his Son. In the last resort death resolves nothing, only life does.'[85] So rather than murder the murderers, God raised his Son to life again. The resurrection is what gives us hope that the vision of *GOD'S RULE* is achievable, that with Jesus on our side we can achieve anything. The resurrection challenges the cultural model which states, 'all we ask is a place of our own'; to actually ask more, to participate in the bringing in of *GOD'S RULE* and believe it, is possible.

Jesus Christ, the Man for Deaf People Today

Anthony Maciocha posed a challenge '*FEW DEAF PEOPLE INTEREST COME TO THE CHURCH BECAUSE JESUS CHRIST WAS NOT DEAF*'. He answers this challenge to his own satisfaction (and conversion) by telling of the experience of seeing a Deaf funeral in sign language – '*BUT ONE DEAF PERSON DIES. NUMEROUS DEAF COMMUNITY JOIN MARCH TO FUNERAL SERVICE. SIGNED IN LAMENTATION*' – and finds a point of contact with Jesus in seeing the tale of Jesus crucifixion and death. He finishes by celebrating the life of the Deaf Community and British Sign Language: '*AFTERWARD VISITING HOUSE HAVE A PARTY (WAKE) CROWD IN ROOM WITH FULL OF*

---

[84]   Carlos Bravo, 'Jesus of Nazareth, Christ the Liberator' in Sobrino and Ellacuría (eds), *Systematic Theology*, p. 106.

[85]   Ibid., p. 121.

COMMUNICATION. BRITISH SIGN LANGUAGE CREATED BY GOD. THANKS BE TO GOD'.[86] Maciocha believes that the fact that Jesus is not Deaf is no longer a barrier to him following Jesus, that Jesus has things to say to Deaf people too. This chapter places Deaf Liberation Christology firmly in the field with other liberation Christologies, which use indigenous culture to dramatically revise western views of Jesus and which are about transforming the world of today into a more just society, where all, regardless of gender, race, disability or hearingness, are free.

---

[86]   Anthony Maciocha, 'Psalm 151 for the Deaf Community'.

Chapter 8

What is Truly Deaf Worship?

The worship of God is central to the life of his Church.
The forms of worship authorized in the Church of England express our faith and help to create our identity.[1]

Worship is the public expression of the faith of the church; it is theology in action. It serves many functions within the church and within the lives of believers. For example, worship is one of the primary means of teaching the Christian faith. Indeed, in a congregation where there are no study groups of any kind, it is the only means of teaching. But worship is far more than an opportunity to teach; it involves the gathering of the community of faith for mutual encouragement and enrichment, the expression of our deepest needs before God, the administration of the sacraments, the opportunity to publicly praise God and much more.

As the public expression of the faith and theology of the church, worship can be said to be one of the 'marks' of the liberating or otherwise nature of a church. Many people have challenged the institutionalized worship of the church as embodying and perpetuating patriarchal, androcentric, racist, colonialist and middle-class attitudes. I will add the voice of Deaf people to this chorus, arguing that worship in the Church of England – both in the mainstream and within the Deaf church itself – embodies and perpetuates the medical model of what it means to be Deaf. It does this by focusing on giving d/Deaf individuals access to hearing worship rather than using the riches of Deaf culture to create worship that focuses and celebrates Deaf community experience before God. I will then explore what worship in the cultural and social models might be like; can truly Deaf worship exist within the liturgical parameters of the Anglican church and how can we characterize it?

To do this, I first need to clarify what 'worship' means in the context of liberation theology. Robin Green argues that the fundamental task of worship is both to give worth or value to God and to receive worth or value from God. It is a two way process, initiated by God. Worship and liturgy that fail to be what Green calls 'appropriate' or 'authentic' can actually damage us, can 'strip us of our sense of worth and dignity'.[2] Proctor-Smith suggests that inauthentic worship does not only damage individuals, it can indeed be said to damage the church's relationship

---

[1]   *Common Worship: Services and Prayers for the Church of England* (London: Church House Publishing, 2000), p. ix.

[2]   Robin Green, *Only Connect* (London, 1987), p. 5.

with God.[3] On the other hand, worship, when it is authentic, can be a wonderfully transforming and liberating experience for all involved in it; the content and form of worship, the liturgy,[4] has real power over the lives of individuals.

So what is appropriate, authentic, liberating and transforming worship or liturgy? Green suggests that an important mark of such worship is that it cares for us: 'God, through, [worship and liturgy] pays loving attention to us and we in turn are able to express the whole of our human experience to God'.[5] This process involves the creating of a safe environment where people can express, honestly and fully, both the positive and the negative parts of their experience. It involves reflecting theologically on these real, lived experiences and showing where God enters into the life of an individual or of the community and exploring God's response in ways appropriate to the context.

The problem is that in many churches, the words and structure of the liturgy have mostly been based on the experience of white, hearing, able-bodied, middle-class men. The claim that some kind of universal, common liturgy can exist is part of this danger. Liturgy has to be specific; there is no way that the experience of every person of different gender, every race and age and background can be expressed in one act of worship.

Worship in the Deaf Church

So how does worship in the Deaf church match up to this understanding of worship? To address this question I will describe an experience of worship in one particular Deaf church:

> The chapel is a room to one side of the Deaf club. It is used for other things during the rest of the week, so it has a neat, foldaway sanctuary. The congregation fill the chairs, which are arranged in rows facing the altar, and sit for the whole of the service, except for sharing the peace and receiving the bread and the wine. There are no service books or hymn books, instead the text of the congregational prayers and choruses or songs appear on the screen of an overhead projector. The text of the service is the minimum required from the communion service of the ASB[6] signed throughout in SSE by the hearing priest. A Deaf reader leads the congregational prayers in SSE and a Deaf choir with a hearing conductor lead the signing of the choruses played by a pianist. There is one bible reading, usually the Gospel, signed word for word by a member of the congregation and no sermon.

---

[3]   Marjorie Procter-Smith, *In her own rite: constructing feminist liturgical tradition*, (Nashville, 1990), p. 20.
[4]   Ibid., p. 35 points out that liturgical tradition is not based on text but on repeated liturgical events and so includes non-verbal and visual aspects of the liturgy as well as verbal.
[5]   Green, *Only Connect*, p. 2.
[6]   The Alternative Service Book (of the Church of England) published in 1980; now superseded by the new Common Worship published 2000.

Some of the congregation join in the signing of the congregational prayers and songs; many sit still and simply watch. The worship really comes alive when a Deaf member of the congregation gets up to lead the intercessions. She goes through the set prayers; each ending with a response 'Lord in your mercy' 'receive our prayer'. At the end, she asks whom we would like to pray for. Hands fly as people in the congregation sign out that their sisters are ill, that their uncle died, that their friend is out of hospital. The intercessor repeats the information to the congregation and adds 'and we pray for them'. When no one has any more requests for prayer, everyone there signs the final 'Lord in your mercy' 'receive our prayer'.

During the peace and the reception of communion, everyone has the chance to get up and greet all who are there and have a chat with their neighbours. The notices include an opportunity for any birthdays to be announced and 'happy birthday' to be signed.

The service ends, the chairs are put away and the sanctuary folded, ready for next time.[7]

This pattern is repeated in some shape or form in every Deaf church service I have attended, whether led by hearing or d/Deaf clergy (with the exception of recent acts of worship that have been deliberately designed around Deaf culture). Even a non-Eucharistic, one-off 'service of thanksgiving' for the 75th anniversary of the CMDP (in its various incarnations) and the 30th anniversary of the NDCC shows certain features in common with this service, characteristics of Deaf church worship that I would argue are neither appropriate, authentic, liberating nor transformative:

1. Sitting still in rows for the whole service, except for sharing the peace and receiving communion. This may or may not be appropriate in an audio/visual culture such as hearing culture, but it does not contribute to the sense of a community gathered for worship in a visual culture.
2. The use of a liturgy that is basically hearing, English liturgy transliterated into SSE. I have discussed some of the issues raised by the use of SSE in the chapter on hermeneutics. Further to that discussion, Shrine, in a presentation to the Liturgical Commission, argues that the language of common worship is impossible to adequately translate into sign language due to a preponderance of theological 'jargon' words, passive phrases and poetical metaphors which use the full richness of English, but cannot be adequately translated into a language that has a totally different structure and way of enriching the discourse in poetic ways.[8] In fact, Shrine observes that the use of many metaphors related to speech and hearing are inappropriate, if not actually offensive to d/Deaf people.

---

[7] Author's personal diary.

[8] Bob Shrine, *Towards a BSL Liturgy: Reflections on the way ahead*, expanded from the opening presentation to the meeting of members of the Liturgical Commission, Praxis and Chaplains Among Deaf People held at Notre Dame University Centre, London, 1 February 2002.

3. A third feature found in many (but not all) acts of worship in the Deaf church is the use of signed English hymns, accompanied by music and led (or performed) by a 'signing choir'. Hymns, especially traditional ones, are especially difficult to translate into sign language; to keep up with the rhythm of the music SSE must be used. Apart from the questionable appropriateness of hymns that can only be signed and enjoyed by those who know English, the use of music means that the 'choir' are dependent on a hearing person to keep them in time.[9]

4. The fact that the liturgy is written at all creates problems for congregational participation within a Deaf context. To quote Shrine, 'we expect the congregation to read and sign or watch a signer at the same time ... If we want our congregations to sign in unison ... do we use the original text, or do we modify the text to make it easier to sign and then print out the modified version?'[10]

5. Finally, due to the way the Deaf church has been structured over the years, most of the congregation is likely to be passively observing rather than participating in the act of worship. Apart from sharing the peace and the intercessions, those d/Deaf people actively taking part are likely to be those selected and trained by the chaplain.

Thus full participation in worship in the Deaf church, and thus full opportunity to give and receive worth, is restricted to the elite deaf who are fluent in English and approved by the structures to stand up and lead. 'Interpreted' mainstream services are even less appropriate to the needs of Deaf people, as, in addition to the issues of the use of English as described above, the interpreter tends to be always a little behind the speaker and so it is impossible for Deaf people to sign their responses at the same time as the congregation is saying them. Worship in the Church of England, as it is currently experienced, is failing to teach Deaf people anything except that they are not good enough to understand what is going on and therefore it does not give worth to Deaf people.

There are two points in the service described where the liturgy is appropriate to Deaf people: these are the intercessions and the peace. I discuss their relationship to Deaf culture below, but at these points in the service, members of the congregation cease to be passive observers and start to be active subjects in the relationship between God and themselves as expressed in worship.

---

[9]   Personally, I enjoy signing hymns with hearing people in a hearing church as an addition to worship and as a way of expressing my feelings given that I can't use my voice to do so. Signing hymns is also something that non-Deaf people find enriches their worship, so I teach hearing people to sign hymns as a way of sharing my own Deaf culture with others. However, I rarely enjoy signing hymns in a Deaf context, as it so often becomes a performance for a few people rather than a way of enhancing the experience of worship for many.

[10]   Shrine, *Towards a BSL liturgy*.

The question that needs to be asked at this point is why is there such a mixture of appropriate and inappropriate liturgy to be found in the Deaf church of today? It is neither totally alien to the Deaf people who go but nor is the aim of worship, the giving and receiving of worth, fully met. To answer this question, we need to consider the historical development of worship in the Deaf church.

History of Deaf Worship

In Glasgow in 1822 and Edinburgh in 1818 we are told that John Anderson and Elizabeth Burnside held religious services in a way they [Deaf people] could understand.[11] There seems to be no further evidence about the format of these services, but we can speculate based on knowledge of services in the Presbyterian Church of Scotland. This would suggest that these services were a collection of Bible readings, and prayers and a sermon and possibly the reading of Psalms in sign language. Deaf worship in the mid-nineteenth century continued to be a mixture of non-denominational or 'unsectarian' prayers and readings (for example Cheltenham in 1847) and the 'service of the Church of England read and communicated ... by the medium of finger spelling and signs' in RADD in 1842.[12] There is no evidence to be found regarding the content and format of worship conducted by such *DEAF-CHURCH* luminaries such as Burns and Herriot. It is likely that, as evangelical nonconformists, they followed the Presbyterian tradition of extempore prayers, Bible readings and sermon. Unfortunately for posterity, this tradition of worship does not leave written records so we are not able to look at their worship and see what the pre-Milan Deaf church worship was like.

RADD dominated the provision of worship to Deaf people throughout London and in 1861 their first (hearing) chaplain, Samuel Smith, was allowed to qualify for Holy Orders at King's College and was ordained by the Bishop of London.[13] Inspired by this, a committee of seven Deaf men began, in 1860, to look into the possibility of designing and building a church specifically for the provision of worship for the deaf and dumb. The reason given for this desire was that meeting in secular rooms encouraged unseemly behaviour; meeting in a specially built and dedicated building would, on the contrary, encourage a proper reverence in divine worship. There was initially a great deal of opposition to this idea from the (all hearing) governing body of RADD. They felt that such a church would unnecessarily perpetuate the distinction between deaf and hearing and also that few deaf and dumb were of sufficient intelligence to be able to follow the service of communion and 'to those few we should hesitate to encourage the administration in the vague language of signs except under special circumstances in which no church is required'. Finally, the governing body objected that a special church

---

[11]   Lysons, *Voluntary Welfare Societies*, p. 30.
[12]   Ibid., p. 36.
[13]   Ibid., p. 41.

would involve alteration of rubrics[14] and 'the omission of many parts of the service untranslatable in signs'.[15]

The seven Deaf men on the committee answered these objections by arguing that they were, in fact, in the same position as foreigners in London who attended services in their own language and so they were entitled to a similar provision of 'special and perfectly constituted services in their own language'. In fact, they had already been in contact with the Bishop of London, who had agreed to relax as many rubricalities as he possibly could. This would not perpetuate any distinctions that were not already there by the very fact that they were Deaf. In other words, they were different from hearing people anyway, so why worry about integration. In addition, they argued that they were entitled to receive the Lord's Supper and the language of signs was sufficient to explain the meaning and import to any Deaf person. They also pointed out that ordinary services were 'lifeless and monotonous' because of their 'inappropriateness to their condition'.[16]

The decision was submitted for adjudication to the headmasters of four of the local schools for deaf and dumb. They voted three to one against, but the building fund was established anyway and St Saviours Church for the Deaf and Dumb was opened on Oxford Street in London in 1873.[17] The fact that the Deaf committee succeeded in their aim despite the considerable opposition of the governing body and the headmasters highlights the independence and determination of Deaf people in those pre-Milan days, and is a further example of the fact that Deaf Liberation Theology can be said to have effectively begun in the nineteenth century, even if it then disappeared 'underground' for 100 years.

I have reported on this debate in some detail, as it seems to me to highlight some important strands in the development of Deaf worship. The objections by the hearing people seem to come from a number of different angles: first of all, a reluctance to acknowledge that 'the language of signs' was a fit language in which to speak of or to God; God could only be addressed, properly and appropriately in English. Secondly, the aim of worship specifically for Deaf people seems to have been to prepare them for integration with the wider hearing society. The idea seems to have been that the deaf and dumb would attend services to receive the religious instruction they did not get at school, and then, when 'up to scratch', would attend their local hearing parish church. A church built specifically for the deaf and dumb would, they feared, become the 'parish church' for all the deaf and dumb in the area and they would not move on. Perhaps the objection to the changing of the rubrics and omission of parts of the service suggests that they were afraid of the

---

[14]   Rubrics are the non-verbal parts of the liturgy; for example the instructions to stand for the Gospel reading or kneel for the confession are examples of rubrics.

[15]   Lysons, *Voluntary Welfare Societies*, p. 42.

[16]   Ibid., p. 43.

[17]   Ibid. St Saviours was closed and torn down in 1923 as the lease of land was for only 60 years. Selfridges now stands on the site. St Saviours Church was then rebuilt in Shepherds Bush.

evolution of a distinctively 'Deaf' style of worship and perhaps even a church separate from the established Church of England. These particular elements can be found again and again (although often more subtly expressed) throughout the debates and discussions of the provision of worship for Deaf people.

The strong Deaf opposition to these objections raised by the governing body of RADD in 1860 also highlights arguments that are still in use today. The comparison of the situation of the deaf and dumb with foreigners living in London and the defence of the language of signs as good enough for everything shows that Deaf people were saying in 1860 that we have a different but equal language and culture, and we have every right to appropriate worship. The same argument is being used today to argue for the need of truly Deaf worship as part of the upswing of Deaf pride in our own cultural distinctiveness.

In contrast to the lack of confidence in the fitness of sign as the language of worship expressed by hearing people, Deaf people in the early twentieth century were fully convinced that their language was not only suitable for worship, but was the most appropriate language for them to use in communicating with God. In 1904, a debate arose in the Deaf edited *British Deaf Times* over issues relating to divine service for the Deaf. 'John T. Bauley', a pseudonym for someone who is assumed from the tone of his article to be hearing, argued that signs were not adequate to the task of speaking of God in any but the simplest terms. As an example, he argues that the sign for 'Almighty' conveys the meaning of 'strong man' and the sign for 'lamb of God' was totally inappropriate: 'it is not very edifying to describe the Saviour as having horns'. In fact, as he goes on to say, the titles of Christ (such as 'Jesus is the lamb of God') are too sacred to be signed in such a material way.[18] By this he appears to mean that signs referring to God and Christ should be particularly 'holy' and 'reverent' and that the everyday signs of Deaf people used to refer to God and Christ are somehow showing a lack of respect to God. This is despite the fact that the English words used to refer to God and Christ are ordinary, everyday English words used in a particular way. The Deaf editors (Joseph Hepworth and George Frankland) of the *British Deaf Times* defiantly refute this accusation on a later page of the same issue. They point out that, in sign, facial expression creates many different grades of meaning and that the sign for 'Almighty' may be that of 'strong man', but with a suitable facial expression (and no doubt body posture as well) can indeed express adequately the concept of 'power divine'.[19] Alice C. Jennings is another Deaf person who defends sign against the accusation that it is inadequate for worship. In a poem published in 1910 she argues:

---

[18]   'John T. Bauley', 'Divine Service for the Deaf' in *British Deaf Times*, 1.10 (August 1904): 228.

[19]   Ibid.: 228. See also Desloges, 'A Deaf person's observation about *An elementary course of education for the Deaf*, in Lane (ed.), *The Deaf Experience*, p. 37 where he discusses how Deaf people differentiate between the signs for 'sky' and 'God' through the non-manual features of the signs.

But dare ye tell us that we do not pray –
We who so truly 'lift up hands of prayer',
and by the speaking gesture mark the way
Our hearts desire would take to reach Him there?[20]

Having pointed out that Deaf people (unlike hearing people at that time) obey the
biblical injunction to lift up hands in prayer, she goes on to demonstrate for the
Lord's prayer how each and every sign used unlocks something of the meaning of
the prayer that is not there in spoken English alone. Unfortunately, this Deaf
confidence that sign was more than adequate to use as the language for worship did
not survive the consequences of the Milan Conference in 1880. As Shrine points
out, one of the obstacles to the creation of a BSL liturgy today is the fact that many
Deaf church members say they want their worship in SSE,[21] a claim which has
been eagerly taken up by hearing chaplains as an excuse for not attempting to
translate the liturgy into BSL.[22] However, Shrine argues that this view of Deaf
people in the congregations is based on their internalized belief that English is
superior to sign.[23] Both Shrine and I have experienced an extremely positive
response from congregations when we have led worship in BSL; often we have
been told by Deaf people that they never really understood the services (in SSE)
before, but didn't feel able to say so.

The tensions over the fitness of sign as a language for divine worship and the
need for uniformity within the missions and conformity to the Church of England
continued to be focused on the Book of Common Prayer (BCP). However, as Deaf
people lost confidence in their own culture and language as a result of the
education policies of 1890 onwards, the hearing missioners and chaplains are the
only voice to be heard in the discussion until relatively recently.

In 1931, Ernest Ayliffe, chaplain to the Deaf in Liverpool, published a Prayer
Book for the Deaf (known as the 'red book') authorized by the then Bishop of
Liverpool. This was the Book of Common Prayer arranged and shortened for the
use at divine services for the Deaf. It has the stated aim of providing Deaf people
with a form adapted to their special needs, but calculated to keep their worship in
tune with that of the wider Church of England in the interests of uniformity and so
that when they attend their parish church they can follow the BCP service.[24] This
'red book' was firmly introduced to chaplains of the Church of England missions
to the Deaf to discourage experimentation with different forms of service. It was
republished by the British Deaf and Dumb Association in 1967 and was in use in

---

[20]   Alice C. Jennings, 'A Prayer in Signs' in *British Deaf Times*, VII.78 (June 1910): 136.

[21]   Shrine, *Towards a BSL liturgy*.

[22]   Personal observation after a number of conversations with chaplains among deaf
people.

[23]   Shrine, *Towards a BSL liturgy*.

[24]   From foreword by the Bishop of Liverpool and endnote by Ernest Ayliffe.

most Deaf churches until the publication of the Alternative Service Book (ASB) in 1980.[25]

Peter Lees, who has been involved in the Deaf church for many years, remembers the 'red book' being used. He also remembers '*IT WAS HEAVY*'; by this he means that the language was difficult to convey to the congregation in any form of sign and difficult to understand. In other words, the language was inappropriate and the liturgy irrelevant to Deaf lives. Peter talks about how he and the Chaplain tried to shorten and simplify it even further so that the congregation would stand some chance of being able to understand. The coming of the ASB in 1980 did not change anything. Despite the fact the ASB used modern English as opposed to the sixteenth-century language of the prayer book, it was still inappropriate, irrelevant and inaccessible from the point of view of Deaf people.

With the publication of *Common Worship* in 2000, the reaction among many of the chaplains working with Deaf people has still been 'How can we shorten and simplify the service to make it accessible to Deaf people?' Deaf people in the twenty-first century are still to experience only a simplified and limited form of the worship of hearing people, just as they did 70 years ago with the publication of the 'red book'. The need for 'access' to worship is part of a wider liturgical renewal (including the renewal of buildings) that has been the mark of worship in the Church of England (and in other denominations) during the last 30 years. One of the stimuli for this changing liturgy has been the criticism from many people that the church preaches 'all are one' yet excludes most disabled people (along with many others) from its worship through inaccessible buildings and incomprehensible liturgy.[26] It was this liturgical renewal that has led to the installation of loops along with ramps and large-print books in many churches. At the same time, liturgy has been made more participative and more modern in its language and so more comprehensible to the congregation as a whole. Procter-Smith criticizes the liturgical movement behind this renewal for basing their criticisms and reconstruction of liturgy on historical norms and using the practices of the past (for example of the early church) as a basis for the present. She argues that this never challenges the validity of the tradition itself, and so is not valid for women who have been silenced and marginalized for so long and so are not part of the tradition being used to renew the liturgy. The results of the liturgical movement, the new service books, may therefore share the values of the feminist liturgical transformation in being more participative, less hierarchical and in more accessible language but they do not address any of the real issues of institutionalized sexism.[27] Given that Deaf people have been equally excluded from tradition, better access to the new services of the Church of England, although

---

[25]   Anecdotal evidence from discussions with Deaf people who have been members of the Deaf church for 40 or 50 years.

[26]   Webb-Mitchell, *Unexpected guests at God's banquet*, p. 101; Eiesland, *The Disabled God*, p. 20; 'Open to all', report produced by Lichfield Diocese Access Committee (1998).

[27]   Procter-Smith, *In her own rite*, p. 20.

important, does not address the real issues of Deaf people, sign language and worship.

Two reasons have been given by chaplains[28] for the continued attempt to make the official liturgy of the Church of England accessible to Deaf people rather than encouraging us to create our own. One is the need to 'be part of the wider church' – a continuation of the desire for conformity expressed above. The other has been 'we would if we could'; in other words, they have asked Bishops for their permission to write new Eucharistic prayers, more suitable for use in sign and have been refused. The structural and institutional barriers within the Church of England are still formidable.

This negative view of sign by the wider institution may be changing. The General Synod of the Church of England recognized in 2000 that BSL was a language that could be used for divine worship along with all other minority languages.[29] The Liturgical Commission listened to the concerns expressed by Deaf chaplains and some hearing chaplains among Deaf people and agreed that we probably need to create our own liturgy rather than attempt to translate the English. Is this the first step towards a truly Deaf liturgy? And how do we relate to our heritage of ambiguity towards the fitness of our own language in worship and the history of the dominance of our worship by hearing people? Is there any more to Deaf worship today than the liturgy of the Church of England transliterated into SSE? To address these questions, I will look further at the examples of the survival of a distinctive Deaf culture or *'DEAF-WAY'* within the worship of the Deaf church.

A Deaf Liturgical Tradition: Sources

So far, I have focused on the negative or inauthentic aspects of worship in the Deaf church. However, as I indicated above, Deaf people and their culture have not been totally excluded from the liturgical tradition within the Deaf church. During the second half of the nineteenth century and the first decade or so of the twentieth, Deaf people fought their own battles and sometimes their point of view prevailed. Also there are one or two elements of Deaf culture to be seen in the services of today's Deaf church, as for example, during the intercessions in the description of a Deaf church service above. This suggests that, if we look for them, there are some elements in the liturgical tradition that are from Deaf culture and so are valid and appropriate sources for the reconstruction of Deaf church worship. In other words, there is, to some extent, a Deaf liturgical tradition which needs to be identified and named and on which we can draw.

---

[28]   In conversation and in short papers presented to the Chaplains Conference.

[29]   General Synod of the Church of England, *Draft amending Canon No. 23: the language of Divine Service and other miscellaneous matters*, GS 1323 B (London, 1999).

This Deaf liturgical tradition can be said to be in two parts. One is the layout and furnishings of the Deaf church, a tradition that stretches back to the building of St Saviours in 1861. The second is more recent, arising from the emphasis on congregation participation in worship of the late twentieth-century liturgical renewal.

Building design or layout may seem an insignificant aspect of liturgical tradition, given that services do not need to take place in a specially constructed building. However, Davies argues in an article in the *New Dictionary of Christian Liturgy and Worship* that the architectural setting of Christian worship has, through the centuries, expressed much of the developments of Christian theology by the variations in layout and furnishing and structure of the church buildings. The study of worship cannot be divorced from knowledge of the buildings in which it was conducted.[30] For example, in Calvinist Geneva, the old churches were re-ordered; pulpits were moved forward to a more prominent position, and the altar (renamed the communion table) was only brought out for services that included the Lord's Supper. Another example is from the St Hilda Community, set up in 1987 to make worship more inclusive of women than was usual in churches. They have met in many different places, but no matter where they are all services take place with the congregation sitting in a circle.[31] Both of these details of layout express something fundamental about the theology of that particular group of Christians.

The *British Deaf Times* of December 1903 includes an article on St Saviours church.[32] In it, the author details the adaptations (to the standard design of churches) for the special needs of the deaf and dumb. These adaptations include a trelliswork pulpit (so the body language of the preacher was more easily visible) and lighting illuminating the hands and face of the preacher. The article also states that if they were building again, the seats would be arranged rising in tiers. These elements of the layout of the building arise from the fact that sign language is a visual language, Deaf culture is a visual culture, and so it is vital for everyone there to be able to see the speaker. This layout of the church so that all can see may also be found in many other specially built Deaf churches. For example, St Marks, Shelton (the chapel in the Deaf centre in Stoke-on-Trent constructed in 1936) has a high, raised platform on which the altar and pulpit stand. The seats are arranged rising in tiers and there is nothing obstructing the sightlines from the different areas of the pews. In other words, by comparison with other churches of a similar age, there is no narrow chancel leading up to the altar, no seating behind the pulpit, no rood screen between the nave and the chancel and as few dark shadows as

---

[30]   J. G. Davies, 'Architectural Settings' in J. G. Davies (ed.), *A New Dictionary of Liturgy and Worship* (London, 1986), p. 26.

[31]   Monica Furlong, 'Introduction' in St Hilda Community, *The New Women Included: a book of services and prayers*, 2nd edn (London, 1996), p. 25.

[32]   *British Deaf Times*, 1.1 (December 1903). No author noted; so probably either written by the editors or one of the Deaf men who wrote for this publication.

possible.[33] Birmingham Deaf Church, a multi-purpose room to one side of the Birmingham Institute for Deaf people built in 1986, is a modern illustration of the tradition of Deaf liturgical building. The notable features of this church, in addition to the clear sightlines, include a permanent screen next to the lectern on which the congregational texts and songs are projected and a lighting system which can be adjusted according to where the speaker is standing. Adapted or specially constructed buildings are not only an Anglican phenomenon. St Josephs Roman Catholic church in Manchester, which has a largely Deaf congregation, has a lectern and altar, taken down and rebuilt in 1992, which are much lower than usual so the signing can be seen by the congregation. These buildings are a visible and distinctive expression of the visual culture of Deaf people.

Another expression of the visual culture of Deaf people found in church buildings is the pictures and carvings. These are significant for two reasons. One is that many of these are by Deaf artists and woodworkers. The article on St Saviours in the *British Deaf Times* proudly details the paintings and sculptures by Deaf artists.[34] The Deaf members of the congregation who showed me around St Marks, Shelton, were obviously very proud of the carvings done by Deaf craftsmen. The pride in these objects suggests that they represent a time when Deaf craftsmen were the equals of their hearing fellows; a pride in the visible achievements of other Deaf people rather than the focus on their problems. They also can be said to represent a time when the church provided a primary source and focus for Deaf creativity denied any other outlets. This pride in their own chapel and its decorations may also represent a sense of ownership; these buildings were Deaf space. The other significance of pictures and sculptures in the Deaf liturgical tradition is the fact that they are in themselves 'visible liturgy'. Many Deaf people can trace their spiritual journey back to a particular picture or carving that hung on the wall at their school.[35] This raises an important issue: in the hearing church the presence or otherwise of pictures and carvings in the church building says something about the theology of that particular church; for example, churches at the more 'Catholic' end of the scale are more likely to have pictures and carvings

---

[33] 'From 1850–1950, revivalism (the Gothic Revival two-room church) dominated church design'. 'Architectural Setting' in J. G. Davies (ed.), *A New Dictionary of Liturgy and Worship*, p. 35.

[34] 'Our Missions Today: St Saviours', *British Deaf Times*, 1.1 (December 1903): 6.

[35] Peter McDonough, a Deaf Roman Catholic priest, for example, remembers a 'marble façade' carved with patterns and statues of saints that used to hang on the chapel wall at St Johns Catholic School for the Deaf, Boston Spa. He describes how, despite the service being accessible via overhead projector, his eyes would often rest on this carving during worship and how he would feel refreshed and rested just looking at it. He feels that this was perhaps his first real encounter with the spiritual realm (Peter McDonough, personal communication). Peter Lees, another Deaf priest, in the Church of England, remembers the pictures from the life of Jesus on the wall of The Mount School, in Stoke-on-Trent, as being his first significant encounter with Jesus, and as sparking off his interest in finding out more about who this man was (Peter Lees, personal communication).

and sculptures on display. I would argue that this is not necessarily the case in the Deaf church. In this case, the presence of pictures, carvings and sculptures arises from the cultural context rather than the theological. We must be careful not to lose sight of the importance of these two elements of building design or layout and the use of pictures and carvings in the reconstruction of the liturgy.

The second main element to the Deaf liturgical tradition is the development that has taken place in the last 20 years as a part of the process of liturgical reform that the Church of England has been going through. By this, I mean that as part of the rhetoric of congregational participation Deaf people began to be more active participants in their services as opposed to passive observers, and so elements of Deaf culture began to creep into the liturgy.

The first two elements of Deaf culture to be seen in Deaf church worship are related to specific parts of the service: the intercessions and the peace. Intercessions, as I have already mentioned, often involve a period of discussion between the intercessor and the congregation as names are put forward for prayer. Sometimes the names and details are signed from the congregation and repeated by the intercessor. Sometimes people queue up to sign to the congregation. If the person who is being prayed for is someone who has recently died, the prayer may turn into a spontaneous eulogy as the story of their life is told. This process is never one person signing, and the rest watching. Almost always, someone will interrupt and the prayer will turn into a conversation: 'I didn't know John was ill, I saw him last week'. 'No not that John, John with the red hair, he's been ill for ages.' Sometimes these stories and conversations can be experienced as a profound interaction between the members of the congregation, the people they are praying for and God. Sometimes they go way off the point and can be experienced as a waste of time, although such examples are still affirming of the sense of community, and as such are to be welcomed. Whichever way it goes, intercessions in the Deaf church take a long time and are very lively – a distinctively Deaf way of prayer that is disconcerting for the hearing visitor used to quiet 'prayerful' intercessions.

Another aspect of the Deaf service that takes a long time is the sharing of the peace. Rather than a simple shaking of hands with those nearest to you and 'the peace of the Lord be with you' it is very often seen as a chance to have a conversation about the service so far or an opportunity to greet latecomers to the service and find out how they are. Sutcliffe in *Soundless Worship* and other hearing chaplains have argued that the peace is so significant in a Deaf church service because Deaf people feel isolated from each other in worship, not being able to hear each other as hearing people can. So the peace is an opportunity to lessen the isolation. But this argument ignores the fact that Deaf people can still see each other in worship, so there is no reason why we should feel isolated. It also ignores the greeting and farewell rituals of Deaf culture. Such basic interaction between Deaf people tends to be long drawn out and rarely formalized and hurried – for example the way Deaf people hang around talking in the streets long after the Deaf club or pub has closed. Contact with other Deaf people is so precious that it cannot be rushed.[36]

Another distinctive aspect of Deaf culture at work in the church is experienced during sermons, particularly those preached by Deaf people. Storytelling and sometimes drama are often significant aspects of any such sermon. What is often not realized is that storytelling is one of the most important cultural forms of Deaf people and has been as long as they have met together.[37] Storytelling or narrative has often been represented as a way of simplifying ideas and presenting them in a more concrete way, and as such Deaf preachers may be reluctant to admit they use it. However, it is now being recognized by western society as a significant art form in its own right and an important way of communicating ideas. Another difference experienced by Deaf preachers who preach in both hearing and Deaf churches is the increased interaction with the congregation during the sermon. Rather than simply sit back and 'listen', they will join in with questions and comments made to the preacher and to each other. In hearing culture, talking during the sermon is indicative of not paying attention; in Deaf culture, it can show that they are listening to and interested in what you have to say. Sometimes the preacher may see that the topic of conversation has nothing to do with the sermon, in which case, if they are Deaf they usually tell that person to shut up and let them get on with preaching.

Other, yet more recent examples of Deaf culture in the church have come out of the increasing confidence of some Deaf people to be who they are and the ordination of Deaf priests who have taken the opportunity to deliberately introduce Deaf culture into the church. One such example occurred at the ordination of a Deaf Roman Catholic priest in 1997. For the procession at the beginning, instead of an organ voluntary or hymn, drums were played and those in the procession waved flags and banners and strips of material. This was a very visible way of expressing the joy and triumph of the occasion. Another example is from the Christmas service of a new Deaf congregation, not hidebound by tradition; they were invited to come forward at one point to lay strips of fabric (and service sheets because they ran out of fabric) on a wooden manger. Again, the use of movement and the tangible symbols was a 'prayerful' (in the Deaf sense) moment in the liturgy.

The use of Deaf culture as a source for liturgy is growing; the Deaf liturgical tradition I have identified is something that can be built on as we reconstruct the liturgy to become truly Deaf.

---

[36]   This is another example of Deaf collectivity and the fact that the Deaf community is likely to mean more than the family to Deaf people.

[37]   See for example Paddy Ladd, 'Deaf culture, finding it and nurturing it' in Carol J. Erting et al. (eds), *Deaf Way*, 2nd edn (Washington DC, 1996), p. 13.

Towards Deaf Worship: Reconstruction

Having highlighted issues that have hampered the development of Deaf worship and identified elements of a Deaf liturgical tradition, I would like to look into the question of how we might develop a truly Deaf liturgy that can help create and shape a truly transformative church.

The first issue is the importance of having Deaf people leading worship. Procter-Smith, in the context of male/female relations in the church, argues that allowing only men into the public sphere as speakers had symbolic as well as political consequences. By this, she means that the male presence – voice, body and manner – became seen as normative for the way preachers and priests should be like. When women first began to speak in church, they were not perceived to sound like or look like 'proper' preachers and priests because of this.[38] Differences in class and accent, race and age also fit into this structure. So, for example, working-class priests felt they had to lose their local accent to be accepted by their congregations and black preachers in white churches felt they needed to 'act white'. This not only affected priests and preachers, but also congregations. It set up a normative way to speak in church, and often, if people felt they couldn't do it the way their priest could, it was better to keep quiet. This has changed over the last 10 years as a far wider variety of people have been ordained or licensed into public ministry. Women, working-class, young people and black people now feel more able to 'be themselves' in church services, to use their own voice and manner rather than try to copy the voice and manner of middle-class, middle-aged, white men.

In the Deaf church, the predominance of hearing chaplains leading worship has meant that what is seen as the normative language of the preacher or priest often is sign with voice and a high proportion of English. The style is quite formal. Many Deaf readers and clergy have, in the past, felt they ought to copy this manner and style of leading worship, and congregations feel inhibited and so do not join in unless they feel confident in their English skills. More recently, the greater variety of ways of leading worship in the hearing church has filtered through into the Deaf church, especially with the ordination of Deaf clergy, confident in their own identity and ways of signing. A Deaf preacher or priest in front of a Deaf congregation will encourage each other to be more natural, more relaxed in the service, and so enhance the quality of the relationships with each other and with God.

A striking example of the symbolic importance of Deaf leaders was seen in one particular Deaf church when the hearing chaplain left and services after his departure were covered by four Deaf women: one reader, one ordinand and two priests. The previous chaplain was very sympathetic with excellent signing skills, yet many of the congregation would often sit passively, watching him throughout the service. Under the new leadership, without much in the way of explicit

---

[38]   Procter-Smith, *In her own rite*, p. 14.

encouragement, the Deaf congregation began to join in the congregational prayers, even though they were in the same, inaccessible language as before. The atmosphere of the services changed; the congregation no longer only participated in the intercessions, but in the liturgy as a whole. I would argue that the symbolic value of Deaf leadership of the services freed them to feel more able to be themselves in the liturgy and before God in that church. So Deaf leadership of worship would seem to me to be vital in the reconstruction of Deaf worship to be transformative of the lives of Deaf congregations.

The second issue raised by Procter-Smith is the issue of memory. Feminists are aware that the names and deeds of women in the past have been distorted and forgotten and so need to be reinterpreted and reclaimed.[39] This is particularly important in the Christian tradition because remembering, or anamnesis, is at the heart of Christian liturgy. The Christian faith has a firm grounding in the particularity of historical events, and liturgical celebration in particular is about connecting the experience of the people with the history of God's faithfulness, or salvation history.[40] From memory, we construct our identity, interpret the significance of experiences and live in relationship with others. The 'memory' preserved in the Christian tradition and hence in the liturgy is largely androcentric, made up of male characters and their experiences. Women are either invisible in this tradition or are there in socially acceptable roles such as that of faithful wife, pure virgin or devoted mother. This lack of collective memory or tradition of women (or any other minority group excluded from the tradition) damages or destroys the identity of a group and places the members of that group at the mercy of others.[41] Reconstructing memory to include all groups is vital, not only to those minority groups but to the health of the whole Christian community.

The memory of Deaf people has been as invisible or distorted within the tradition as any other minority group. Most published histories of Deaf people mention them as a group of passive recipients, and the only ones mentioned by name are the star pupils of particular teachers. Within the liturgical calendar of the Church or England (the list of saints, martyrs and others whom we remember particularly in church services) there are no Deaf people at all. Within the Deaf church there are two occasions in the year when Deaf people of the past have been remembered. These are the feast of St John of Beverley,[42] and 'Ephphatha' Sunday. From about 1901 until the 1970s, this occasion was an important source of funding for many missions due to the annual Ephphatha Sunday collection in churches. This referred to the twelfth Sunday after Trinity (usually in late August) when the Church of England Book of Common Prayer prescribed that the reading from the Gospel was the story of the healing of the deaf and dumb man by Jesus.

---

[39]   Procter-Smith, *In her own rite*, p. 18.

[40]   Ibid., p. 36.

[41]   Ibid., p. 40.

[42]   The issues raised by John of Beverley as patron saint of Deaf people are discussed in Chapter 4.

Clergy were encouraged to preach on the needs of deaf and dumb people in their area, and to make a collection for the work of the missions. This is first proposed by the BDDA in 1901: 'if each clergyman would hold special services once a year for the benefit of the missions to the deaf and dumb ... individual Christians would be only too happy, in gratitude for the possession of their own blessings and in loving compassion for those who are deprived of them to contribute'.[43] Collections like this, referred to as Ephphatha Sunday appeals, are in the annual reports of the Church Mission to the Deaf and Dumb in Walsall, Wednesbury and Mid-Staffordshire from 1930 to 1968 and also in the Council for the Spiritual Care of the Deaf and Dumb reports to Church Assembly[44] from 1938 to 1949.[45] Peter Lees, a member of Walsall Deaf Church for many years, remembers that it was only with the coming of the Alternative Service Book in 1980 (which did not include this particular Gospel reading) that these collections and appeals finally stopped.

These two 'memories' within the liturgy focus on what is done for Deaf people as the passive objects of teaching and healing, rather than on them as subjects in their own right. We can only speculate on the effect this had on the self-esteem and sense of identity of the Deaf people who had these stories held up to them year after year. Ephphatha Sunday is not a significant part of Deaf church life or liturgy any more; its inappropriateness has been recognized, but St John of Beverley is still commemorated in dioceses where there are, or have been, Deaf churches that bear his name.

For the reconstruction of liturgy for Deaf people, we need to search for Deaf people in history whose memory we can celebrate in the Deaf church of today: people like Matthew Robert Burns or George Healey or James Herriot or Charles Davis or Francis Maginn or Richard Pearce. Outside the context of the church, but worthy of honouring, are any of the founders of the National Union of the Deaf who are respected worldwide for their dedication to the cause of Deaf Liberation, often at great personal cost. Many Deaf people would want to include those like Dorothy Miles in any list of Deaf people to honour. Her poetry in sign language taught many Deaf people to be proud of their language for the first time. There is no shortage of people, past and present, dead and alive, Christians and atheists, whose memory needs to be perpetuated so that Deaf people can be aware of their own history and identity and be inspired and encouraged and strengthened by it so that their own lives might be transformed.

However, reconstructing memories means more than just adding Deaf people to the list of names commemorated by the church. Procter-Smith argues that we need to generate new liturgies and new hymns using the restored history and tradition so that we can reconstruct the past and shape the future. This process allows historical

---

[43] British Deaf and Dumb Association, *Official programme of the seventh biennial congress of the Deaf* (1901).

[44] Successor of Convocation and forerunner of General Synod in the Church of England.

[45] These are the only years for which I have copies of these reports. They do suggest that it was a widespread and long-lived practice.

reconstruction to become part of collective memory.[46] Then, and only then, can the liturgy of the Deaf church truly draw on the memories of its people and become true anamnesis. An important aspect of the reconstruction of memory is imagination. The process of reclaiming history to include the stories of many more people can free the imagination to see other ways of being church than the dominant colonial, racist, patriarchal structures or find other ways of seeing God rather than the dominant male imagery or develop other ways of perceiving ourselves, male and female, black and white, Deaf and hearing as free and mutually empowering.[47] This freeing of imagination can also be expressed through liturgy, with the aim of generating new models of the church, new images of God, of humanity and of the church's relationship with God and the world. This is what Procter-Smith calls the prophetic task of liturgy, 'to present to faith communities a vision of the way things can be in the future'. The 'prophetic task' understood as proclaiming alternatives to the hegemonic worldview is shared by Brueggemann, who argues that 'the task of prophetic ministry is to nurture, nourish and evoke a consciousness and perception alternative to the consciousness and perception of the dominant culture around us'.[48] He argues that this prophetic task can be practised in, with and under all acts of ministry, counselling, preaching, education, liturgy and more.[49]

This understanding of the prophetic task of the liturgy is another way of approaching the idea that the liturgy should contribute to liberation. Uzukwu in his examination of some of the new African indigenous liturgies points out the difference between inculturation and liberation in liturgies. An African liturgy may use indigenous African music, but if it does not challenge the social equilibrium of the modern African state it is maintaining the oblivion of oppression that the church in Africa has been guilty of in the past.[50] This is an issue to be aware of in creating new Deaf liturgies too. Simply creating liturgies in BSL, using Deaf cultural forms does not make them transformative. They must be prophetic; they must use imagination to proclaim an alternative to the dominant culture or they will simply be continuing to perpetuate the oppression of Deaf people in the church.

Considering ways of developing a prophetic imagination in liturgy brings us to a fourth issue in the reconstruction of the liturgy, namely language. The language we use plays a large part in constructing or constituting reality as we experience it. As a result, one of the most significant ways we can offer a prophetic, alternative vision of the world in a reconstructed liturgy is to look at the language we use. Language, as Procter-Smith sees it, is not simply words that are spoken or signed;

---

[46]   Procter-Smith, *In her own rite*, p. 48.

[47]   Ibid., p. 18.

[48]   Walter Brueggemann, *The Prophetic Imagination*, 2nd edn (Minneapolis, 2001), p. 13.

[49]   Ibid., p. 111.

[50]   Elochukwu Uzukwu, *Worship as Body Language: introduction to Christian worship, an African orientation* (Collegeville, MN, 1997), p. 32.

there are also non-verbal forms of language such as visual language and physical/body language.[51] The liturgy of the church is full of sexist, exclusive language; for example the use of Man as a generic term to refer to men and women, stereotypical pictures and sculptures of white male and female saints and the relationship of dominance and submission expressed in much of the body language of the liturgy. It may also be argued that it is full of language that is exclusive of Deaf people too. In this context I do not mean language that is too complicated to be translated into sign, but such language as the use of 'hear our prayer'[52] to suggest that God only receives prayer by listening to us, or the use of the word 'deaf' to mean people who can't hear or refuse to listen to God, who are stubborn.[53] Another exclusive use of language is the translation of the English word 'sign' (in the sense of symbol, for example 'sign of God') as '*SIGN*', which specifically refers to the signed language of Deaf people. Visual language too is often exclusive of Deaf people; a common illustration in Deaf churches is the healing of the deaf and dumb man by Jesus as narrated in Mark 9:31–7. In this he is often portrayed either in a very submissive pose before Jesus, obviously not understanding what was happening, or after he has been healed rejoicing in his newly bestowed hearing. Exclusive body language is that which establishes or maintains dominance by for example placing the speaker higher than need be for practical purposes (standing while others sit, or on platforms) or by wearing unnecessary special clothing or other symbols of office or by having 'official space', as for example a sanctuary that only the leader enters. Another form of exclusiveness is the fact that many clergy call their parishioners by their Christian names, but are themselves addressed in formal ways as 'Revd Blank' or they touch parishioners as part of religious rituals, but are not themselves touched.[54] All these issues may be identified in the Deaf church as helping to create a relationship of dominance and submission between worship leader and congregation. It is interesting that as the issues relating to body language are all visual issues, they are likely to be identical for Deaf people as for women.

Procter-Smith identifies three stages in the process of imagining alternative ways of being in language. First of all is the stage of non-sexist (or non-exclusive) language, which avoids the use of gender-specific terms or avoids using the words 'hear' or 'deaf' or 'sign' or any other sensitive words at all. This is fine as far as it goes, but can make for a very bland liturgy that avoids all specifics. It also implies that our gender or the fact that we are Deaf is a matter of complete irrelevance to God and our relationship with him or her. The second step in the process of reconstructing language is the use of inclusive language. This aims to have an equal balance in the liturgy of gender-specific terms. The equivalent in Deaf terms is probably shown in the usual 'translation' of 'hear our prayer' into '*OUR*

---

[51] Procter-Smith, *In her own rite*, p. 60.

[52] The most usual response to intercessions in the Church of England liturgy.

[53] Many places in the Bible, for example in the Psalms, Isaiah and the Gospels.

[54] Procter-Smith, *In her own rite*, p. 81.

PRAYER, RECEIVE'. Another example of inclusive language in the Deaf church is the way that the words of hymns referring to sound and music can be changed to refer to sign. For example, Vera Hunt describes how her deaf choir were asked to sign the hymns at a service which included the hymn 'O praise ye the Lord'.[55] The third verse of this is problematic for Deaf people because of its reference to praising the Lord by all things that give sound. The choir were going to not sign that verse in protest, but after more thought, decided to change the words, remain still while the hearing choir sang the verse and then sign their version while the hearing choir sang it. Thus they changed:

> O praise ye the Lord, all things that give sound;
> each jubilant chord, re-echo around;
> Loud organs, his glory forth tell in deep tone,
> and sweet harp, the story of what he hath done.[56]

to:

> O praise ye the Lord, all things without sound;
> each jubilant word re-sign all around;
> with gestures, his glory forth tell in hushed tone,
> and sweet sign, the story of what he hath done.[57]

The problem with this from the feminist point of view is that gender-specific terms are rarely equal in social terms. For example, Queen is not the equal of King, nor is Mother the equal of Father. In Deaf terms, the problem is similar; *'RECEIVE'*, for example, does not bear the equivalent implication of 'hear' in that is does not imply a conversation in which there is an active relationship between God and humankind, and changing the words of the hymn as above to make it 'Deaf inclusive' does not change the fact that the hymn is still impossible to sign in BSL and still depends on the presence of a hearing person to sign the hymn in time with the music. In other words, changing the words of responses and hymns may make them inclusive of Deaf people, but they do not challenge the power structures that make d/Deaf people unequal to hearing people in society or the church. However, inclusive language does take the differences of gender or being Deaf seriously, and imply that we are all equal before God who sees us in our uniqueness.

Finally, Procter-Smith identifies the third stage, which in her argument is the goal of reconstructing language as emancipatory language. This is language that actively aims to transform language use and challenge stereotypes; one example of emancipatory language is the reclamation as a statement of identity by many minority groups of words such as Black, Woman and Deaf, that were formerly considered derogatory terms. Emancipatory language in the liturgy implies that

---

[55] Vera Hunt, 'Worshipping the Deaf Way' in *Signs* (Spring 1999): 13.
[56] Sir H. W. Baker, 1875.
[57] Vera Hunt, 1996.

God is actively involved in the struggle of all minorities for emancipation and the ultimate emancipation of us all.

Characteristics of Deaf emancipatory language include the making of Deaf people visible by naming them individually or as a group in the liturgy as praying subjects for example rather than objects of prayer, or specifically referring to Deaf individuals in the past or to the lived experiences of Deaf people. This may include lament over the abuse of Deaf people in the past as well as a celebration of the courage and resourcefulness of those who have struggled and survived. Emancipatory language must be honest and specific. If it leaves out the negative aspects of experience, it is being neither. If it romanticizes or spiritualizes deafness (as for example the early missioners did by regarding Deaf people as untouched innocents) it is being neither. Being Deaf in a hearing world is tough.

An example of Deaf emancipatory language in a secular context can be seen in the Blue Ribbon Ceremony, created by Paddy Ladd, which is both a ceremony of remembrance of Deaf people in the past and a celebration of the survival of Deaf culture. This ceremony, named after the colour used to identify Deaf people in Nazi Germany, was first seen on a worldwide scale at the World Federation of the Deaf XIII World Congress at Brisbane in 1999.[58] During the ceremony, Deaf individuals come on stage with a candle and sign a phrase about the people they are remembering, for example, those individuals who suffered horrendous primitive 'operations' to restore their hearing in the eighteenth and nineteenth centuries. While the person is signing, pictures related to the subject are projected on to a screen at the rear of the stage. After they have signed their piece, they retire, with their candle, to stand in a semi-circle at the rear of the stage, until, at the end, there is a row of lights as the last candle, for the future of Deaf people, is lit. The whole ceremony is incredibly moving, and certainly fulfils the criteria of a vivid reconstruction of Deaf people in history in a way that recognizes and fulfils the need of Deaf people to both mourn their oppression and celebrate their survival. It also goes further than simple remembrance of Deaf people of the past in its assertion, repeated at the beginning and the end, that Deaf people are meant to be here on earth as part of the rainbow diversity of the human race and that, in sign language, we enrich the world with new ways of seeing and being. It concludes with a call to commitment to fight against oppression, for the sake of Deaf children throughout the world. Thus the Blue Ribbon Ceremony is not only emancipatory in remembering the past, it is prophetic in its claim that oppression and discrimination is not the only way for Deaf people to live.

Recently, Deaf people have begun to create their own prayers and 'BSL hymns' to be used in worship as a definite step towards Deaf emancipatory language. One of these is the 'Psalm 151 for the Deaf Community' by Anthony Maciocha,[59] and

---

[58] The full text may be found in Ladd, *Understanding Deaf Culture*, p. 469.
[59] Maciocha, 'Psalm 151'.

'Psalm 152?',[60] created by a group of Deaf people. These both refer to the difficulties of being Deaf in a hearing church and rejoice in the presence of visual culture and sign language to facilitate the worship of God by Deaf people. This picks up on another strand in traditional Deaf culture that appears to date back to pre-Milan days and has survived within the Deaf community, and this is the practice of specifically thanking God for the gift of hands, the gift of sign languages and the gift of the Deaf community itself.[61] Another example of Deaf emancipatory language is the 'Deaf creed',[62] which specifically refers to Deaf experience, both positive and negative, the identification of Deaf people with the marginalization experienced by Jesus in his crucifixion and celebrates the culture and language of the Deaf community. It is also a celebration of a Deaf sense of identity in its assertion that I am Deaf and made in the image of God. The BSL hymns are not only created in BSL by Deaf people or groups of Deaf people but are also trying to use the full riches and resources of that language to celebrate BSL as a more than adequate language in its own right, and liberate Deaf people from the perceived need for formal 'English' type sign and rhythm dictated by music. Another way of using sign language in 'hymns' has been developed by Deaf people in Uganda. They take 'hearing hymns', and translate them into sign; this works as emancipatory language because they do not attempt to fit the rhythm of the signs to the music, in fact, they do not use the music at all. Instead, the leader establishes a rhythmic movement that the rest of the congregation join in, before beginning to sign the words of the hymn, in full visual sign language, to that rhythm. Often, at the end of the hymn, the leader and the congregation would ad-lib the last line, developing its meaning. For example, in a hymn about searching for Jesus, ending *SEARCH-HERE* (left-hand side) *SEARCH-HERE* (right-hand side) *LIGHT-FROM-HEAVEN GOD*, the congregation, led by the Deaf pastor, would repeat *SEARCH-HERE* again and again while looking under pews, behind curtains and generally moving round the church.[63] This is another example of emancipatory language in a Deaf church because, although the origin of the hymn may have been written and sung to music, Deaf people had taken it and made it their own, linguistically and culturally.

---

[60]   The question mark in the title is intentional, as written by the Deaf people who put it onto paper.

[61]   See quotes from Maisie Baillie, an 80-year-old Deaf woman from Edinburgh in Ladd, *Understanding Deaf Culture*, pp. 258 and 373.

[62]   Hannah Lewis, 'A Deaf Person's Creed', created in English and BSL.

[63]   Personal communication from Christopher Stone, PhD student at the Centre for Deaf Studies at the University of Bristol, April 2003.

Deaf Worship

In this chapter I have argued for the existence of a Deaf liturgical tradition that we can use as a foundation and principles to guide us in reconstructing the liturgy of the Deaf church to make it transformative in nature and truly Deaf in form and content. It only remains to state one obvious principle. This reconstruction must be done by Deaf people themselves. No hearing person, no matter how sympathetic or experienced in sign, can do it for us. The reconstruction of the liturgy as transformative is a process, not an end product. If we, as a group, are not involved in the creation of liturgy then we will not be transformed by it and it will not contribute to the ultimate aim of the liberation of Deaf people, body, mind and soul.

Chapter 9

A Liberating-Shaped Church

It is a fascinating – if occasionally frightening – time to be involved in the Christian church in general and the Deaf church in particular. We are living in a time of change, where it feels as if old models and certainties are collapsing all around us. More and more Church of England dioceses are cutting the funding for chaplains among Deaf people, Deaf churches have to leave the Deaf club premises they have worshipped in for so long and fewer and fewer Deaf people seem to be involved in the church. At the same time, more and more Deaf people are actively involved in creating worship, reflecting on the Bible and theology and working for the full equality of Deaf people in the structures of the church. A willingness to disagree publicly with the current secretary of the CMDDP[1] from the perspective of Deaf experience demonstrates the growing confidence of some Deaf people in the church. Deaf people increasingly feel able to stand up against 'experts' and claim the validity of their point of view.[2] Deaf Liberation has reached the church, and this book documents a process that is already happening in addition to setting out a wish list for the future.

However, all this leaves us with a question: what will the church of the future look like? How will Deaf Liberation Theology work out in practice? Will the separate Deaf church continue? Will it be an 'integrated' Deaf/hearing church, or a hearing church with an interpreter? Will there continue to be funding and a place for specialist chaplains/pastors working with Deaf people? I doubt there will be just one simple answer in this post-modern world. Each place, each group of Deaf people will need to work out for itself what they can do with the resources available, a process of discerning what God wants in that place and that time. I do however think that there are certain questions that we can ask of any church from the perspective of Deaf Liberation Theology to ensure that wherever Deaf people meet to worship and learn about God it will be a place where the liberating Gospel is fully lived. The title of this chapter deliberately echoes the call for a mission-shaped church, a church that works creatively to reach out to people in its context. It is my belief that unless the church is liberating for Deaf people, it cannot fulfil its mission to reach out and touch Deaf people's lives with the good news of Jesus Christ.

---

[1]   The Committee for Ministry among Deaf and Disabled People – it was restructured and renamed when the present secretary took up his post.

[2]   See for example Phil Maddock, 'An Inclusive Church – Deaf People Too?' and Sue Dyson, 'Let us keep our Deaf Churches' in *Signs* (Autumn 2000), pp. 18 and 20.

Deaf Space

A liberating-shaped church needs first to be Deaf space. By this, I mean a place where Deaf people feel safe to be and find themselves. The hearing world can still be a hostile place for Deaf people, a place where it is hard to relax, a place where making yourself vulnerable to meet God is too great a risk. If the Christian church simply replicates the hearing world in this respect, it is failing in its call to provide a foretaste of the kingdom of God, a place where all may encounter the reality of *GOD'S-RULE*. This does not mean that we want to exclude hearing people from Deaf space; it simply means that the pace of communication needs to be such that Deaf people can be fully included, instead of feeling left out and struggling to keep up when following an interpreter. Even the best-quality interpreting always involves a time lag between the words spoken and their reception by Deaf people, and that is without the use by hearing people of references to events, books, TV programmes, hearing jokes and idioms that need further explanation to be meaningful to Deaf people. If a church is Deaf space, all are aware of this issue, extra time is given and allowed and developed so that all understand and all contribute. If a Deaf person is acting as chair or facilitator, they can dictate the pace of communication and make sure all are included. It is even better if all involved in the discussion know and use sign language, and switch their voices off.

Deaf space is also a place where the view of Deaf people is valued, and their ownership of sign language is recognized. Even in a group where the majority of people sign well, if they are hearing they can still make a Deaf minority feel marginalized by ignoring the Deaf people's views on sign language and translation issues. Often, this is not deliberate – the hearing people still learning about BSL and deaf culture simply cannot see the point the Deaf person is trying to make, but the attitude of mind is still that of hearing superiority so they dismiss the Deaf perspective and leave the Deaf person feeling squashed. In a group operating in Deaf space, hearing people will give extra weight to the view of a Deaf person in discussion about sign language and translation.

In Deaf space, ministry and leadership opportunities need to be fully available to Deaf people. Hearing and Deaf leaders need to be aware of how they can unconsciously disempower Deaf people and how 'participation' is not automatically liberating. If a church is Deaf space, Deaf people visiting the church see people like themselves up front, in a public role and can feel confident that someone will understand their problems and someone will listen to their point of view. A Deaf space church will offer nurture and training in culturally appropriate ways, not simply through interpreted English courses, but adapting and creating material that takes seriously the Deaf person's context.

The implications for the church of the concept of Deaf space are wider than the issues relating to congregations involving Deaf people. Information from the wider church about social issues, training, denominational issues and others needs to be available in sign language. This will mean that Deaf people have access to general information available to other Christians. Signed versions of information available on websites is a simple way of doing this, as demonstrated by the websites of Sign Community (formerly BDA) and the 'Imaging the Deaf Brain' project.[3]

Storytelling Space

As well as being Deaf space, a liberating-shaped church needs to be a storytelling space as well. The stories that we need to tell and to 'hear' are the stories of Deaf people and the Deaf church from history, as well as the stories from the Bible and stories of individuals today. Telling stories serves many functions in liberation: they remind people of the history of a strong and resolute people, a people who were determined to set up their own churches, their own social clubs and their own space and can inspire Deaf and hearing people today. Telling stories of the present allows space for lament, always needed by an oppressed minority to relieve feelings, but also to leads to an opportunity for renewed hope and faith for the future. Telling the Bible stories in and amongst the stories of the past and the future interweaves the lives of Deaf people with the lives of people in the Bible, helping us to see God acting in the world today as God acted in the past.

A storytelling space can be hard to preserve in congregations who do not worship in the traditional Deaf space of Deaf clubs. Moving to worship in a hearing church building has often led to the loss of the artefacts of Deaf history and culture, the woodcarvings by Deaf men, the memorials to past Deaf heroes, as well as the stories stored in the walls of the place itself. This is not to say that Deaf congregations should only meet in Deaf clubs – a changing world is making this impossible in many situations – but thought needs to be given to how to hold on to the valuable parts of the past. How to hold on to the distinctive history and identity of Deaf people in the church while letting go of the conflict and sadness that often accompany the decision to move. To this end, it is useful to look at the example of local ecumenical partnerships (LEPs) formed when one or more denominational churches closed and moved in together. At the very least such a process takes seriously the stories, the history and identity of the Deaf church instead of dismissing it or ignoring it and therefore contributes to the ideal of the church as a liberating-shaped church.

Creative Space

Finally, a liberating-shaped church is a creative space, a place where all people are encouraged to create, to reflect on faith and on God in whatever medium they can. This can be a dramatized prayer in worship, a collage created from magazine pictures to reflect on a psalm, a cairn of stones created by all the participants in a worship service, a BSL exploration of theology and many other things. The

---

3   <http://www.bda.org.uk/> and <http://www.ucl.ac.uk/HCS/deafbrain/>.

liberating significance of creative space is in the mutual trust and sense of community that allows people to create and share what they have created.

Ultimately, it is in this creative space that Deaf Liberation Theology will continue to be developed. Unless the widest possible range of Deaf people own and create it, Deaf Liberation Theology will not fulfil its liberating purpose. We are in a fascinating and frightening period in the life of the Deaf church understood as all Deaf Christians. Ultimately, however, I have hope that we will survive, flourish and continue to spread the good news of Jesus Christ and how his life, death and resurrection led to full and perfect liberation of body, mind and spirit and the bringing in of *GOD'S-RULE*.

A Deaf Person's Creed[4]

I believe in God
Who made everything in heaven and on earth
Including me.
Full Deaf and made
In the image of God.

I believe in the only Son of God,
Jesus Christ.
Who was born, lived and died for the sake of us all.
Who knew what it meant to be despised and rejected, mocked and ignored for who he was.
I believe Jesus was killed, then rose again,
And by his resurrection we have been saved from the bondage of sin and death;
From the bondage of oppression and a world that wants me to pretend to be hearing.

I believe in the Holy Spirit of God,
Who breathes life into each one of us.
Who calls us forward when we would hang back;
Who empowers us to believe in who we are
And what we can do
And who in the beauty of Sign Language speaks to the very depths of my soul.

And I believe in a church
Where I can be myself,
Where all are equal
And where this Good News of Jesus Christ is challenged, expanded and made real
In its worship and in its work.
For now and for ever.
Amen.

---

[4] © Hannah Lewis, 2000.

A Deaf Person's Creed (BSL Version)

I believe God
Created everything heaven earth both
Including me.
Full Deaf
Created face like God.

I believe God only Son,
Jesus Christ.
Jesus born, lived, died, why?
Because-us.
Jesus knew meaning looked-down-on rejected mocked ignored why? Because-
himself.
I believe Jesus crucified, buried, then rose again
Through his resurrection we saved from prison sin death;
from prison oppression world wants me pretend hearing.

I believe God Holy Spirit
that's-it breathes life each-one
When we hang back pulls forward
strengthens us believe person are
and can achieve.
Holy Spirit signs beautiful sign language
enters-into depths-inside all-of-body

I believe church
There be myself.
There all people equal
There Good News Jesus Christ
challenged, expanded, created real
Through worship and through work
Now for ever.
Amen.

Bibliography

Primary Sources

'A. S.', 'The Music of Hope', *British Deaf Monthly*, XI.121 (November 1901): 302.
British Deaf and Dumb Association, *Official programme of the seventh bienniel congress of the Deaf* (London, 1901).
——, *Proceedings of the ninth biennial congress* (London: The Fraternity Press for the Deaf, 1905).
——, *Sixth biennial report* (London: The Fraternity Press for the Deaf, 1903).
Central Advisory Committee for the Spiritual Care of the Deaf and Dumb, *Annual Report* (1926).
——, *Annual Report* (March 1931–March 1933).
——, *Report to Church Assembly*, CA 483–CA 912 (1935–49).
——, *Statistics of Work in the various Diocese of England & Wales* (January 1920).
Church Mission to the Deaf and Dumb in Walsall, Wednesbury and Mid-Staffordshire, *Annual Report*, 44–81 (1930–68).
Committee for the Spiritual Care of Deaf Mutes, *The Spiritual Care of Deaf Mutes*, Report presented to the Convocation of Canterbury, lower house, 499 (1916).
——, *The Spiritual Care of the Deaf and Dumb*, Report presented to the Convocation of York, 313 (1917).
Committee for the Spiritual Care of the Deaf and Dumb, *Church Assembly Report*, 439 (1933).
Council of Church Missioners to the Deaf and Dumb, *Papers for the guidance of Christian workers with deaf people* (1968).
Davies, Mary, 'The Voice of Jesus', *British Deaf Monthly*, XI.124 (February 1902): 364.
Downing, Revd Geo. A. W., 'Sermon', *A Magazine Intended Chiefly for the Deaf and Dumb*, IV.47 (November 1876): 161–3.
Dyson, Sue, 'Let us keep our Deaf Churches', *Signs* (Autumn 2000): 20.
——, 'A Modern Image for NDCC', *Signs* (Autumn 2001): 11.
General Synod of the Church of England, *Draft amending Canon No. 23: the language of Divine Service and other miscellaneous matters*, GS 1323B (London: Church House Publishing, 1999).
Hunt, Vera, 'Worshipping the Deaf Way', *Signs* (Spring 1999): 13.

Jennings, Alice C., 'A Prayer in Signs', *The British Deaf Times*, VII.78 (1910): 136.

Maciocha, Anthony, 'Psalm 151 for the Deaf Community', *Signs* (Spring 2000): 3.

Maddock, Phil, 'An Inclusive Church – Deaf People too?' *Signs* (Autumn 2000): 18–19.

Magson, Saul, 'Sermon', *A magazine intended chiefly for the Deaf and Dumb*, II.11 (1873): 173–4.

Muir, James, 'Redemption by Jesus Christ', *A magazine intended chiefly for the Deaf and Dumb*, XII.1 (1884): 19–20.

——, 'What Jesus is able to do', *A magazine intended chiefly for the Deaf and Dumb*, XII.1 (1884): 21.

Murray, Brian, on behalf of National Deaf Church Council, *Spiritual and Pastoral Care for the Deaf*, draft report for presenting to the Archbishop of Canterbury (*c.* 1984).

——, *... and no birds sing*, General Synod Council for the Deaf (*c.* 1978).

National Bureau for Promoting the General Welfare of the Deaf and Dumb, *The Deaf Handbook: containing information relating to statistics, and schools, and missions* (Westminster, 1913) and revised edition (1924).

North, Samuel W., 'Sermon', *A Magazine Intended Chiefly for the Deaf and Dumb*, I.2 (1873): 25–7.

——, 'An Easter Sermon', *A Magazine Intended Chiefly for the Deaf and Dumb*, I.5 (1873): 74–5.

North Staffordshire Deaf and Dumb Society, *The glass wall: a century of progress 1868–1968* (Stoke-on-Trent, 1968).

'O. D.', 'For a Deaf and Dumb Christian', *A Magazine Intended Chiefly for the Deaf and Dumb*, III.26 (1875): 26.

Oxley, Selwyn, *Work for the deaf: Operations of the Guild of St John of Beverley, for the deaf and hard of hearing* (London, 1925).

——, *A pageant entitled 'The deaf of other days': in twelve episodes* (London, 1928).

——, *Ephphatha Sunday and its meaning* (London, *c.* 1938).

Read, Donald, *Some Facts on North East Deaf Churches* (2000).

Rowland, Edward, 'Sermon for the New Year', *A magazine intended chiefly for the Deaf and Dumb*, III.26 (1875): 17–19.

Royal Association for the Deaf and Dumb, *Questionnaire to Missioners working with deaf people* (1901).

Rundle, Arnold and Paul Northam, *The Plymouth Deaf Clubs from 1897 to 1997*, (Plymouth, 1997).

Scarff, Len, *A brief history of the Bolton Deaf Church and the involvement of Church of England priests and others, in religious services to deaf people in the Bolton Deaf Society area* (2000).

Shrine, Bob, *Towards a BSL Liturgy: Reflections on the way ahead*, expanded from the opening presentation to the meeting of members of the Liturgical

Commission, Praxis and Chaplains Among Deaf People held at Notre Dame University Centre, London, 1 February 2002.

Smith, Samuel, *The Deaf and Dumb: Their deprivation and its consequences* (London: William Mackintosh, 1864).

Sutcliffe, T. H., *Soundless Worship: Spiritual care of the deaf and dumb*, report from the Central Advisory Council for the Spiritual Care of the Deaf and Dumb (*c.* 1950).

'W. A. G.' [Griffith, W. A.], 'Sermon', *A Magazine Intended Chiefly for the Deaf and Dumb*, III.34 (1875): 146–9.

Secondary Sources

Alker, Doug, *really not interested in the Deaf?* (Darwen: D. Alker, 2000).

Anderson, Digby C. (ed.), *The kindness that kills: The churches' simplistic response to complex social issues* (London: SPCK, 1984).

Anderson, Jeff, *The Lion Graphic Bible*, illustrations, Jeff Anderson, script, Mike Maddox, lettering, Steve Harrison, 1st paperback edn (Oxford: Lion, 2001).

Baker-Shenk, Charlotte, 'Breaking the Shackles: Liberation Theology and the Deaf Community', *Sojourners*, 14/3 (March 1985): 30–32.

Bell, Alexander Graham, *Memoir upon the formation of a deaf variety of the human race* (Washington DC: National Academy of Sciences, 1884).

Beresford, Peter, 'Poverty and disabled people: challenging dominant debates and policies', *Disability and Society*, 11/4 (1996): 553–67.

Bevans, Stephen B., *Models of contextual theology*, 2nd printing (Maryknoll, NY: Orbis, 1994).

Brenner, Athalya and Carole Fontaine (eds), *A feminist companion to reading the Bible: approaches, methods and strategies* (Sheffield: Sheffield Academic Press, 1997).

Chadwick, Owen, *The Victorian Church*. Part 1 (London: Adam & Charles Black, 1966).

The Church Among Deaf People: a report prepared by a working party of the Committee for Ministry Among Deaf People for the General Synod of the Church of England's Advisory Board of Ministry, Advisory Board of Ministry paper 14 (London: Church House Publishing, 1997).

Cleve, John Vickrey van and Barry A. Crouch, *A place of their own: creating the Deaf community in America* (Washington DC: Gallaudet University Press, 1989).

Corker, Marian, *Deaf and Disabled, or Deafness Disabled?* (Buckingham: Open University Press, 1998).

Daniels, Marilyn, *Benedictine roots in the development of deaf education: listening with the heart* (Westport, CT, London: Bergin & Garvey, 1997).

Dimmock, A. F., *Cruel Legacy* (Edinburgh: Scottish Workshop Publications, 1993).

Douglas, Kelly Brown, *The black Christ* (Maryknoll, NY: Orbis, 1994).

Drake, Robert, 'The exclusion of disabled people from positions of power in British voluntary organisations', *Disability and Society*, 9/4 (1994): 461–80.

——, 'Charities, authority and disabled people: a qualitative study', *Disability and Society*, 11/1 (1996): 5–23.

Eiesland, Nancy L., *The Disabled God: towards a liberatory theology of disability* (Nashville, TN: Abingdon Press, 1994).

Eijndhoven, J. van (ed.), *Religious education of the deaf: Proceedings of the International Catholic Conference on Religious Education of the deaf, Dublin, July 1971* (Rotterdam: Rotterdam University Press, 1973).

Erikson, Per, *The history of deaf people: a source book* (Orebo, Sweden: SIH Laromedel, 1993).

Farrar, Abraham, *Arnold's Education of the Deaf* (London: Simpkin, Marshall & Co., 1901).

Firth, George C., *Chosen Vessels* (Exeter: G. Firth, 1988).

Fischer, Renate and Harlan Lane (eds), *Looking Back: a reader on the history of Deaf communities and their sign languages* (Hamburg: Signum Press, 1993).

Fletcher-Campbell, Felicity, *Literacy and Special Educational Needs: a review of the literature* (London: Department for Education and Employment, Research Report RR 227, 2000).

Garrett, Mary Smith, *Possibilities of Deaf Children* (Philadelphia, 1906).

Govig, Stewart D., *Strong at the broken places: persons with disabilities and the church* (Louiseville, KY, Westminster: J. Knox Press, 1989).

Green, Robin, *Only Connect: worship and liturgy from the perspective of pastoral care* (London: Darton Longman and Todd, 1987).

Gregory, Susan and Gillian M. Hartley (eds), *Constructing Deafness*, 2nd edn (London: Open University in conjunction with Pinter, 1994).

Gutiérrez, Gustavo, *A theology of liberation: history, politics and salvation*, rev. edn with new introduction, trans. Inda Caridad (London: SCM Press, 1988).

Higgins, Paul C., *Outsiders in a hearing world: a sociology of deafness* (Beverly Hills, London: Sage Publications, 1980).

The Holy Bible: English Version for the Deaf (Grand Rapids, MI: Baker Book House, 1978).

Horne, Simon Timothy, *Injury and Blessing: a challenge to current readings of biblical discourses concerning impairment* (PhD thesis, University of Birmingham, 1999).

Hull, John M., *In the beginning there was darkness: a blind person's conversation with the Bible* (London: SCM Press, 2001).

International Ecumenical Working Group Conference, *The Place of Deaf people in the Church: the Canterbury 1994 conference papers* (Northampton: Visible Communications for the International Ecumenical Working Group, 1996).

Jackson, Peter W., *Britain's Deaf Heritage* (Edinburgh: Pentland Press, 1990).

—— and Raymond Lee (eds), *Deaf Lives: Deaf people in history* (Feltham: British Deaf History Society Publications, 2001).

Kyle, J. G. and B. Woll, *Sign Language: the study of deaf people and their language* (Cambridge: Cambridge University Press, 1985).

Ladd, Paddy, *In search of Deafhood: towards an understanding of British Deaf culture* (PhD thesis, Bristol University, 1998).

——, *Understanding Deaf Culture: In search of Deafhood* (Clevedon: Multilingual Matters, 2003).

Lane, Harlan, *When the mind hears: a history of the deaf* (London: Penguin Books, 1988).

——, *The mask of benevolence: disabling the deaf community*, 1st Vintage Books edn (New York: Vintage Books, 1993).

—— (ed.), *The deaf experience: classics in language and education*, trans. Philip Franklin (London, Cambridge, MA: Harvard University Press, 1984).

Lee, Raymond (ed.), *Writings from deaf liberation: a selection of NUD papers 1976–1986* (Feltham: National Union of the Deaf, 1992).

Lee, Raymond and John A. Hay, *Bermondsey 1792* (Feltham: National Union of the Deaf, 1993).

Lysons, Clifford Kenneth, *Voluntary Welfare Societies for Adult Deaf Persons in England, 1840–1963* (MA thesis, Liverpool University, 1965).

McDonough, Peter, 'Presenting the Word of God in Sign Language', in McDonough, Peter (ed.), *Ephphata: Proceedings from the International Catholic Deaf Religious Conference 1996* (Monmouth: A. & K. Publications, 1998), pp. 55–80.

——, *Signs of God: Lectionary for deaf people* (Chawton: Redemptorist Publications, 2002).

McLoughlin, M. G., *A history of the education of the deaf in England* (Gosport: Ashford Colour Press, 1987).

MacNutt, Francis, *Healing*, rev. edn (London: Hodder & Stoughton, 1989).

Macquarrie, John, *Jesus Christ in modern thought* (London: SCM Press, 1990).

MacRobert, Iain, *The black roots and white racism of early Pentecostalism in the USA* (Basingstoke: Macmillan Press, 1988).

Maddocks, Morris, *The Christian healing ministry*, new edn (London: SPCK, 1990).

Madsen, Willard J., 'You Have to be Deaf to Understand', in Taylor, George and Bishop, Juliet, *Being deaf: the experience of deafness* (London: Open University in conjunction with Pinter, 1991).

Miles, Dorothy, *British Sign Language: a beginner's guide* (London: BBC Books, 1988).

Monteith, W. Graham, *Disability: faith and acceptance* (Edinburgh: St Andrew Press, 1987).

Müller-Fahrenholz, Geiko (ed.), *Partners in Life: the handicapped and the church* (Geneva: World Council of Churches, Faith and Order paper No. 89, 1979).

Oliver, Michael, *Understanding Disability: from theory to practice* (London: Macmillan, 1996).

Pailin, David A., *A gentle touch: from a theology of handicap to a theology of human being* (London: SPCK, 1992).

Pattison, Stephen, *Alive and kicking: towards a practical theology of illness and healing* (London: SCM Press, 1989).

Pinn, Anthony B., *Why Lord? Suffering and Evil in Black Theology* (New York: Continuum, 1995).

Pokorny, Daniel (ed.), *My Eyes are My Ears: a collection of papers*, International Ecumenical Seminar on Pastoral Care of the Deaf, 1971 (New York: MSS Information Corporation, 1974).

—— (ed.), *The Word in Signs and Wonders: a collection of papers delivered at the second International Training Seminar on Christian Ministry Among the Deaf, Washington, DC, 1975* (New York: Arno Press/MSS Information Corporation, 1977).

Procter-Smith, Marjorie, *In her own rite: constructing feminist liturgical tradition* (Nashville, TN: Abingdon Press, 1990).

Rée, Jonathan, *I see a voice, a philosophical history of language, deafness and the senses* (London: Harper Collins, 1999).

St Hilda Community, *The New Women Included: a book of services and prayers*, 2nd edn (London: SPCK, 1996).

Sanford, John A., *Health and Wholeness* (New York: Paulist Press, 1977).

Segovia, Fernando F., *Decolonising biblical studies: a view from the margins* (Maryknoll, NY: Orbis Books, 2000).

Shapely, P., 'Charity, status and leadership', *Journal of Social History*, 32/1 (1998): 157–79.

Shrine, Robert G., *The language and culture of Deaf people: some implications for the Church* (MA dissertation, Open University and St Johns College, Nottingham, 1997).

——, *The Church's mission among deaf people: reflections on principles and practice* (Diploma of the Committee for Ministry Among Deaf People, 2000).

Sleight, William, *A Voice from the Dumb* (London: Hamilton, Adams & Co., 1848).

Sobrino, Jon and Ignacio Ellacuría (eds), *Systematic Theology: perspectives from Liberation Theology* (London: SCM Press, 1996).

Stevens, Maryanne (ed.), *Reconstructing the Christ symbol: essays in feminist Christology* (New York: Paulist Press, 1993).

Stokoe, William, *Sign Language Structure* (Studies in Linguistics Occasional Papers 8, 1960).

Sugirtharajah, R. S. (ed.), *Voices from the Margin: Interpreting the Bible in the Third World*, new edn (London: SPCK/Maryknoll, NY: Orbis, 1995).

Sutcliffe, T. H., *The Challenge of Deafness* (Taunton, 1990).

Taylor, Michael, *Not angels but agencies: the ecumenical response to poverty – a primer* (Geneva: WCC Publications/London: SCM Press, 1995).

Uzukwu, Elochukwu E., *Worship as body language: introduction to Christian worship, an African orientation* (Collegeville, MN: The Liturgical Press (OSB), 1997).

Webb-Mitchell, Brett, *Unexpected guests at God's banquet: welcoming people with disabilities into the Church* (New York: Crossroad, 1994).

West, Gerald O., *Biblical hermeneutics of liberation: modes of reading the Bible in the South African context*, rev. edn (Maryknoll, NY: Orbis, 1995).

White, Sarah and Romy Tiongco, *Doing theology and develoment: meeting the challenge of poverty* (Edinburgh: St Andrew Press, 1997).

Wink, Walter, *Engaging the powers: discernment and resistance in a world of domination* (Minneapolis: Fortress Press, 1992).

Wolffe, John (ed.), *Evangelical faith and public zeal: evangelicals and society in Britain, 1780–1980* (London: SPCK, 1995).

Woodroofe, Kathleen, *From charity to social work in England and the United States* (London: Routledge & Kegan Paul, 1961).

Young, Pamela Dickey, *Feminist theology/Christian theology: in search of method* (Minneapolis: Fortress Press, 1990).

Index